Climax
The History of Colorado's Climax Molybdenum Mine

Stephen M. Voynick

Mountain Press Publishing Company
Missoula, Montana 1996

Publication of this book has been made possible by a grant from the Cyprus Climax Metals Company. A portion of the proceeds from the sale of this book will benefit the National Mining Hall of Fame & Museum, Leadville, Colorado.

All photographs and illustrations courtesy of the Climax Molybdenum Company unless otherwise noted.

Library of Congress Cataloging-in-Publication Data
Voynick, Stephen M.
    Climax : the history of Colorado's Climax Molybdenum Mine / Stephen M. Voynick.
      p. cm.
    Includes bibliographical references and index.
    ISBN 0-87842-354-0 (pbk.)
    1. Climax Mine (Colo.)–History. 2. Molybdenum mines and mining–Colorado–Leadville Region–History.   I. Title.
TN490.M7V68 1996
338.7'622347646'0978846–dc20   96-21331
                                          CIP

MOUNTAIN PRESS PUBLISHING COMPANY
P. O. Box 2399 · Missoula, MT 59806

For the men and women whose dedication,
determination, and effort helped build the Climax Mine.

Contents

*Bartlett is a mountain of ore . . . awaiting
the day when man, armed with the power
of science—should reach forth and take it.*

—Carbonate Chronicle
*Leadville, Colorado
April 15, 1918*

*I heard the freight train whistle
And it's time to say good-bye
Forever to Dear Old Climax
That hellhole near the sky.*

—anonymous Climax miner,
mid-1930s

*AMAX lost that grand old history it had,
mainly because molybdenum crashed. Like
many companies, it gets its grandeur from
some ore body, then there's a crash. . . .*

—The Denver Post
November 7, 1993

Preface

Thirteen miles north of Leadville, Colorado, State Highway 91 crosses the Continental Divide at 11,318-foot-high Fremont Pass. Travelers remember Fremont Pass not because of the Divide, the elevation, or the timberline pines that give way to alpine meadows and to craggy peaks above. They remember it because of Bartlett Mountain, a mountain unique for what nature and man have done to it. Bartlett Mountain is always a compelling sight, but never more than when the late afternoon sun casts a warm, reddish light across its most prominent feature—the Climax Glory Hole, a gaping, half-mile-wide, thousand-foot-deep crater created by nearly three-quarters of a century of underground mining.

A sprawling industrial complex of plant, office, and warehouse buildings, power lines, railroad tracks, roads, pipelines, and conveyors lies at the foot of Bartlett Mountain. Atop the Continental Divide, there is no adjacent urban or industrial clutter to temper the striking contrast between nature and industry. Yet that contrast seems somehow fitting, for Bartlett Mountain is no ordinary mountain, and the Climax Mine is no ordinary mine. Together, they inspired a grand adventure in mining, metallurgy, and American enterprise.

In 1989, the Climax Molydenum Company commissioned me to research and write the history of the Climax Mine. Along with free access to company files, records, and publications, I received a single set of instructions: "Write the story as you see it."

With that in mind, I have tried to be as objective as possible. All lengthy, complex challenges, whether corporate or personal, have their ups and downs, successes and failures, and triumphs and tragedies, and the Climax story is no different. I included all as I found them, and became intrigued as a remarkable story slowly took form.

Prospectors, puzzled by veinlets of a gray-blue mineral, staked the first claims on Bartlett Mountain more than a century ago. Decades passed before mineralogists finally identified that mineral as molybdenite, but even that revelation created no excitement, for molybdenum was a laboratory curiosity, a metal with neither use nor value.

But during World War I, after metallurgists learned that molybdenum substantially enhanced the toughness and durability of steel, men rushed to Bartlett Mountain to fight for the right to mine molybdenite. When the molybdenum market collapsed with the Armistice, production abruptly ceased, leaving the Climax Molybdenum Company with a mountain of molybdenum that wasn't worth mining. But following an unprecedented five-year research, development, and promotional effort, Climax created a market and reopened the mine in 1924.

Mining at Bartlett Mountain was never easy. From the beginning, it was a battle against isolation, elevation, the elements, human limitations, the vagaries of national and international politics and economics, and the cold, hard rock itself. Miners of the 1930s cursed Climax as "that hellhole near the sky," but the molybdenum metal that poured from Bartlett Mountain generated enormous profits that astounded Wall Street financiers and elated Climax stockholders. In the 1940s, the federal government designated Climax as the nation's highest-priority mine; protected by extraordinary military security measures and pushed to the limits of men and machines, the Climax Mine supplied virtually all the molybdenum that toughened the steel for the armor and weaponry that carried the Allies to victory in World War II.

Climax grew into the world's largest underground mine in the 1950s with its own community—the highest town in North America and, as many former residents still insist, the best company town ever built. As advancing technology made possible ever higher tonnages in the 1960s, mining men from around the world journeyed to Climax to study the recognized model of mining innovation and efficiency. Climax reached its historic peak in the 1970s as the "Giant on the Hill," when cumulative ore production was measured in the hundreds of millions of tons and dollar production values soared into the billions.

But the giant fell in the 1980s in a devastating succession of layoffs and cutbacks, victim of a complex scenario of market upheaval, increasing regulation, foreign competition, internal corporate demands, and, perhaps, in the end, its own size. Today, with enormous ore reserves still waiting within Bartlett Mountain, the Climax Mine is working to become competitive in a new economic order.

Until now, the remarkable history of the Climax Mine has never been formally compiled; instead, it was passed on as a loose collection of detached events and personal reminiscences, along with more than a few embellished legends. Yet the history survived, its corporate side documented in voluminous company records, correspondence, and technical reports. Its human side survived in the memories of the men and women who played a part in the Climax story.

The Climax story is not simply one of mine development and production. It is a much broader story, one woven inextricably with those of a mountain, a metal, and the many individuals whose collective efforts helped make the name Climax synonymous with the word *molybdenum*.

STEPHEN M. VOYNICK
Leadville, Colorado
January 1996

1

A Most Unusual Mineral

Eventually this mineral will become much better known commercially, most people will then be able to spell it correctly, and those of us who are more familiar with it will not, on account of uncertain supply and treatment problems, be compelled to occasionally allude to it as molybedamnite.

—Engineering & Mining Journal, *April 1915*

In August 1879, a solitary prospector named Charles Senter searched for gold high on the west-facing slope of Bartlett Mountain in central Colorado's Mosquito Range. Others had sought gold there before him and found bits and flakes of the yellow metal in the lower creeks and gulches that drained the mountain. Since the early 1860s, prospectors had also unsuccessfully searched Bartlett's steep slopes and rocky cliffs for the lode source of the placer gold.

High on Bartlett Mountain, Charles Senter had no more luck than his predecessors, but apparently had a greater innate curiosity. Although he found no gold, he became interested in a yellow-stained outcrop at an elevation of 12,000 feet on the mountain's barren western face. Climbing the steep talus slopes to investigate the outcrop, Senter noted that the bright yellow color came from a powdery, sulfurlike, surface encrustation.

Senter hammered some of the yellow-crusted rock apart to reveal a light gray, finely crystalline matrix laced with thin, dark veinlets. Ranging from gray-blue to nearly black, the veinlets had a slightly greasy feel. Probably graphite, the prospector surmised, or perhaps an unusual form of lead. Much more interesting were the tiny, glit-

Charles J. Senter, Civil War veteran, Indian fighter, mule skinner, prospector, and discoverer of the Bartlett Mountain molybdenite deposit. Photograph taken about 1920.

tering bits of pyrite, the common disulfide of iron. While worthless in itself, pyrite often indicated the presence of more valuable metals, such as gold and silver.

Suspecting—or, more accurately, hoping—that the strange rock contained gold, Senter soon returned to the high outcrop carrying wooden claim markers fashioned from timberline spruce. On August 17, 1879, Charles Senter paced off and staked three lode claims, which he named the Gold Reef Numbers One, Two, and Three. At that point, Senter had already gained a niche in history: He was the first prospector to stake claims on Bartlett Mountain specifically for the light gray rock with the gray-blue streaks.

Senter doubtlessly believed that his Gold Reef claims had little, if any, value, for fourteen years passed before he recorded them at the Summit County Courthouse across the Mosquito Range in Breckenridge. But the long delay caused no problems, for no other prospectors were interested in Bartlett Mountain.

Charles J. Senter typified many of the men who searched the central Colorado Rockies for mineral wealth in 1879. Born in 1846, Senter was a veteran of both the Civil War and the Plains Indian wars.

After mustering out of the U.S. Army in Denver, he took a job as a mule skinner, driving a freight wagon over 13,018-foot-high Mosquito Pass to join the frenzied rush to Leadville.

In 1879, Leadville had captured the imagination of the country. Two years earlier, prospectors had drilled and blasted small shafts into a huge, shallow deposit of easily smelted sulfide ores containing hundreds and even thousands of troy ounces of silver per ton. Development was rapid: 400 underground mines soon poured out $10 million in silver and lead each year, and in just eighteen months, Leadville became the biggest metropolis between St. Louis and San Francisco.

Leadville was, at once, the best and worst of the western mining frontier: Opera houses and grand hotels stood just blocks away from cribs, flophouses, and dismal slums; culture and wealth collided face-to-face with violence, sickness, and poverty. Leadville drew from every level of American and even foreign society; its population of 30,000 placed honest, hardworking miners, teamsters, and tradesmen shoulder-to-shoulder with a legion of con men, prostitutes, and criminals.

After big silver strikes in the 1870s, Leadville grew into one of the West's biggest mining camps and would later be profoundly impacted by molybdenum mining at Bartlett Mountain. Photograph taken in 1904.

A rare photograph of Bartlett Mountain (left) and Ceresco Ridge as they appeared in the early 1880s.

At an elevation of 10,150 feet, Leadville was the highest city on the continent. Thin air and an unforgiving alpine climate demanded that laborers and miners be in top physical condition, for those in poor health literally risked their lives. The seasons dictated activity. Construction, hauling, and prospecting proceeded at a breakneck pace during the short summers, but mining continued year-round, even during the long, bitter winters, when men struggled to keep the roads open and the firewood piled high. Leadville was remote and isolated; the most direct route to the "outside" was a treacherous wagon road over Mosquito Pass to Fairplay. Nevertheless, the flow of silver was so vital to Colorado's developing economy that Leadville was very nearly named the state capital.

Charles Senter had arrived in Leadville at the peak of the silver boom in summer 1879, but remained in the chaotic city only a few weeks. Seeking independence and solitude, rather than excitement and wealth, he followed the Arkansas River north to its headwaters, then crossed over Arkansas Pass to prospect for placer gold.

4

Senter prospected at McNulty Gulch in the shadow of Bartlett Mountain. Although miners had worked the little gulch during the Pikes Peak gold rush years two decades earlier, Senter still panned enough color to encourage him to stay. He built a small cabin three miles north of the pass at the head of Tenmile Canyon, set up his sluices, and settled into a quiet life as a placer miner and prospector. When August signaled the approaching end of the brief alpine summer, he climbed high onto the shoulder of Bartlett Mountain to the yellow outcrop, discovered the strange rock with the gray-blue streaks, and staked his three lode claims.

Civilization seemed to follow Senter. In 1879, prospectors discovered lead-silver ores in Tenmile Canyon, giving birth to the camps of Robinson, Recen, and Kokomo, along with dozens of mines, several mills, and a smelter. As wagon traffic between Leadville and the Tenmile camps increased over Arkansas Pass, the rough road was improved. A stage line using light wagons in summer and sleighs in winter established the first scheduled transportation service over the pass. By the end of 1879, Arkansas Pass was better known as Fremont Pass, after Colonel John C. Fremont, the U.S. Army explorer who traveled the region in 1845.

Mountain transportation took a bigger step forward in July 1880, when the Denver & Rio Grande Railroad, building up the Arkansas River from Pueblo, laid rails into Leadville. Eyeing additional business from the Tenmile camps, the Denver & Rio Grande (D&RG) continued building north along the Arkansas River toward Fremont Pass, reaching the summit just before the heavy snows of late November. D&RG crews called the summit site "Climax" in recognition of Colorado's first narrow-gauge railroad crossing of the Continental Divide. Rushed and haphazard construction enabled the first regular train from Leadville bound for the Tenmile camps to steam past the water tower atop Fremont Pass in February 1881. Intent on preventing any rival railroad from building north up the Tenmile Valley and over Fremont Pass into Leadville, the D&RG quickly extended its line north past Kokomo all the way to Frisco and Dillon, occupying the best right-of-way in the narrow canyons.

But that didn't discourage the upstart Denver, South Park & Pacific Railway (DSP&P), which built north from South Park through Breckenridge to reach Frisco in 1883. The following spring, determined to win its share of the booming Leadville business, the

5

DSP&P, familiarly known as the "South Park," boldly laid rail south up the Tenmile Valley on the only remaining right-of-way left—a daring route along rushing creeks and narrow ledges, beneath steep cliffs, and across jumbled talus slopes. By August 1884, the South Park had brazenly pushed its "High Line" through Kokomo to Fremont Pass, ascending more than 2,000 vertical feet in a grueling, 22-mile-long climb. Atop the pass, South Park crews quickly built a siding, water tower, and two small bunkhouses, formally naming their lofty station "Climax." Fremont Pass, crossed four years earlier by only a rough wagon road, now hosted two competing narrow-gauge railroads, which, at the summit, paralleled each other just 100 yards apart.

The South Park continued building down the Arkansas River, reaching Leadville in September 1884. Construction was well worth the effort, for the South Park's High Line immediately became the preferred rail route from Leadville to Denver. The trip to Denver on the 200-mile-long South Park route took fifteen hours, five hours and 50 miles less than D&RG's circuitous Denver route via Pueblo.

The D&RG soon admitted defeat and abandoned its Leadville-Dillon line, conceding Climax and the Tenmile Canyon to its rival. Although the railroad battle was over, the battle with the elements was just beginning. Travel on the South Park's High Line was truly an adventure. The steepest grades on both sides of Fremont pass reached 8 percent, requiring helper locomotives on all trains of more than three cars. Winter avalanches often blocked the line for days, and on several occasions actually swept entire trains off the rails. In spring, rushing torrents of snowmelt water frequently washed away the rail bed.

By 1890, Fremont Pass had its first permanent residents, German settler John Buffehr and his wife. Two miles north of the pass summit, the Buffehrs dammed a section of upper Tenmile Creek to form a small lake and erected a cabin, lean-to barn, and icehouse. In what may have been the nation's highest serious agricultural endeavor, they tended a few cattle, sheep, and chickens, and harvested a summer hay crop. They even grew a few turnips and cabbages, the only vegetables hardy enough to mature in the abbreviated alpine growing season of less than forty frost-free days. The Buffehrs made their living selling milk, eggs, bread, vegetables, and meat to the lower Tenmile camps and to the South Park's passengers, who twice daily spent a half hour at Climax, gazing up at the weathered, yellow face of Bartlett Mountain while the locomotives took on water.

Although Leadville and the Tenmile camps boomed through the 1880s, there was little interest in Fremont Pass, Climax, or Bartlett Mountain. Only the haunting wail of the whistles from the little narrow-gauge locomotives straining mightily on the steep Fremont Pass grades marked the succession of short, wonderful summers and long, bitter winters. South Park railroad timetables listed Climax as a regular station, but passengers referred to it as "the station where nobody gets on and nobody gets off." South Park supervisors often threatened lazy or inept employees with permanent winter assignment at Climax.

Interest in Bartlett Mountain picked up in 1890 when several Denver-based prospectors, Edward G. Heckendorf and the Webber brothers, John and Sam, collected samples of the yellow-stained outcrop rock. When assay reports indicated the dark veinlets in the gray rock were a form of galena, or lead sulfide, a mineral often associated with silver, the trio staked claims near Charles Senter's Gold Reef group.

But the assays were incorrect, and the true identity of the Bartlett Mountain rock remained a mystery. Senter, meanwhile, forwarded his own samples to mineralogists at the Colorado School of Mines in Golden for qualitative analysis. This time the report indicated "antimony and graphite, with some sulfur," in grades that were "commercially worthless." The assayer commented that the sample was "a most unusual mineral."

In 1893, when the federally supported silver market collapsed with repeal of the Sherman Silver Purchase Act, Leadville, the Tenmile camps, and most other western silver camps plunged from boom to bust. That same year, Charles Senter finally recorded his Gold Reef claims at the Summit County Courthouse in Breckenridge. His motivation was twofold: First, of course, was the arrival of Heckendorf and the Webber brothers; second, an eastern chemist had suggested that Senter's samples contained neither graphite nor lead, but a sulfide of the rare metal molybdenum.

The principal mineral form of molybdenum is a disulfide called molybdenite. Discovered in antiquity, molybdenite was long confused with graphite and galena because of its dark color and greasy feel. The ancient Greeks called lead *molybdos*, generally using that term and *molybdaena* to define all similar minerals. Medieval alchemists furthered the confusion. Even Agricola (Georg Bauer), whose *de re Metallica* was the most enlightened mineralogical work of the mid-1500s, referred to both lead and galena as molybdenum.

By the mid-1700s, chemists had finally differentiated graphite and molybdenite from lead. In 1778, the Swedish scientist Carl Wilhelm Scheele showed how nitric acid could convert molybdenite—but not graphite—to an acidic white powder he named molybdic acid. Scheele then produced the same compound by roasting molybdenite in oxygen to drive off a gas he recognized as sulfur dioxide, correctly concluding that molybdenite was the sulfide form of a previously unknown metallic element he named molybdenum.

Peter Jacob Hjelm, another Swedish researcher, isolated the metal four years later. Hjelm heated a mixture of molybdic acid and carbon in an oxygen-free atmosphere to produce carbon dioxide and a heavy, dark powder of nearly pure molybdenum. Molybdenum proved exceedingly difficult to work with. Preparation of its metallic form was difficult, and fusing the powder into a mass suitable for metallurgical study was impossible because of its extraordinarily high melting point. Furthermore, molybdenum seemed rare in nature; the only known significant source was a high-grade, vein-type molybdenite deposit at Knaben, in southern Norway.

Scientific and industrial study of molybdenum began in earnest in 1890, when German chemists succeeded in preparing metallic molybdenum by reducing calcium molybdate with carbon, then leaching the product with acid. In 1894, metallurgists at Schneider & Co., the French military works, found that small amounts of molybdenum added to steel, while not increasing hardness, seemed to enhance toughness.

In 1898, another Frenchman, Henri Moisson, used an electric furnace to obtain the purest molybdenum yet isolated. The 99.98 percent pure metal greatly aided chemists in establishing molybdenum's chemical and physical properties. Molybdenum, a silver-gray metal, was assigned an atomic number of 42. It was about as heavy as lead, but much less common. Molybdenum's two most notable properties were a melting point of 4,730 degrees Fahrenheit, about 2,000 degrees higher than most steels, and an interesting and potentially valuable ability to toughen steel.

American metallurgists first attempted to employ molybdenum in high-speed tool steel in 1898. Unfortunately, failure to determine critical heat-treating ranges produced alloys that performed erratically, branding molybdenum with an undeserved poor metallurgical reputation that deterred further development.

In 1895, Colorado School of Mines Professor Rudolph George positively identified the Bartlett Mountain samples as molybdenite. Qualitative assays became standard, but quantitative assays remained a big problem. The only reasonably reliable analytical procedure required dissolving the finely ground sample in three reagents, followed by precipitation, filtration, evaporation, and, finally, firing in arsenic-free hydrogen before weighing. The complex procedure tended to compound any errors present, and the exact steps varied widely among individual chemists. Quantitative assays of the same Bartlett Mountain samples, which actually contained about 1.0 percent molybdenite, ranged wildly from 0.5 to 5.0 percent. Cost was another consideration. At a time when accurate gold assays cost only fifty cents, molybdenum assays, however unreliable, cost the princely sum of $5.00 each—nearly twice the pay a Leadville miner received for a long underground shift.

Nevertheless, the *Engineering & Mining Journal*, a popular trade publication widely read by both mining professionals and field-trained prospectors, began carrying news about molybdenum. Realizing now that molybdenum did have some value and its occurrences were not that uncommon, prospectors were eager to learn more. The *E&MJ* printed this query on October 13, 1900:

> Is there not something mysterious about the rare metal molybdenum and its ores? I am anxious to know what metallic molybdenum can be sold for and to whom.

The editor replied:

> There is nothing mysterious about molybdenum or its uses. It is used in certain special steels. The demand for the metal is small, and the business of recovering it from ores is in a few hands. The parties treating the metal can get all they need without trouble. . . . In most ores, it would hardly pay to save the molybdenite, unless it can be treated by a simple process of concentration.

The handful of molybdenite buyers demanded ores containing not less than 50 percent molybdenite. Therefore, only high-grade deposits with at least inch-thick veins had any real value, for the ore had to be laboriously hand-cobbed to the required concentration. At the going price of $50.00 per ton of concentrate, one pound of contained metallic molybdenum was worth about ten cents. Bartlett Mountain molybdenite, which occurred in tiny veinlets and very low grades, would never have commercial value until metallurgists and engineers developed an efficient, inexpensive method of concentration.

In the latter half of the nineteenth century, mining's greatest technological advances were the introduction of mechanical rock drills and modern dynamites, which speeded the basic process of breaking rock. Frontier metal mining had boomed on ores rich enough to be hand-cobbed, gravitationally separated, or direct-smelted. But most bonanza ores were exhausted by 1900, and metal mining's future rested squarely on its ability to mass mine large deposits of low-grade ores and to concentrate them economically. The best hope for the latter was a new concept called flotation separation.

Flotation separation depended on the tendency of oil-covered mineral particles, particularly metal sulfides, to adhere to air bubbles. In operation, mill workers mixed a finely ground ore slurry with an oily reagent, then vigorously agitated and aerated the mixture in tanks. The mineral particles adhered to the rising air bubbles and floated as an oily froth, while particles of nonmineralized rock, or gangue, fell to the bottom. The first practical flotation system, patented in 1904, was used commercially in Australia and Great Britain. The following year the Utah Copper Company tested it successfully on low-grade ores at Bingham Canyon, Utah.

When development of the flotation separation process was just beginning in 1900, another individual became involved with Bartlett Mountain in absentia. He was Hugh Leal, a redheaded banker from Greenwood, Nebraska. Nearing retirement and looking for some mining properties to "play with," he asked a personal friend, a Colorado forest ranger, to keep his eyes open for any promising gold prospects. The ranger forwarded samples from the Bartlett Mountain outcrop; Leal apparently liked their looks and asked his friend to stake five lode claims in his name. Hugh Leal's Mountain Maid

Numbers One and Two, the New Discovery Numbers One and Two, and the Mountain Chief claims were located at an elevation of 12,300 feet and parallel to Charles Senter's Gold Reef group. A nephew, Eric Leal, performed the required annual assessment work, and Hugh Leal patented the claims in his own name in 1905.

That year George Collins, a Denver mining engineer, offered the first professional evaluation of the Bartlett Mountain molybdenite occurrence. In a private report, Collins recommended acquiring and holding large tracts on the mountain. Considering the poor demand and low prices for molybdenum, as well as the inability to concentrate low-grade molybdenite, Collins's opinion was well ahead of its time.

Nevertheless, it may have lured A. M. Gillespey, a Denver speculator, to Bartlett Mountain. Gillespey seemed to know exactly what he wanted to do. He located a single claim, the Denver Number Two, between the Leal and Senter groups. It was the first Bartlett Mountain claim knowingly staked for molybdenite. Senter, Leal, and Gillespey had now claimed the entire yellow-stained outcrop on the western face of Bartlett Mountain.

Bartlett Mountain remained quiet for the next few years, and the biggest news at the Climax Station on Fremont Pass was that the Colorado & Southern Railroad had assumed ownership and operation of the now-defunct Denver, South Park & Pacific's Leadville-Denver route.

But the molybdenum market was slowly coming to life. Heightening European militarism renewed industrial interest in the tough, but untested, new molybdenum steels. By 1910, the price of molybdenum was nudging $1.00 per pound.

The following year, A. M. Gillespey patented his Denver Number Two claim. Meanwhile, Ed Heckendorf and the Webber brothers, who had let their claims lapse years earlier, returned to find the entire outcrop staked. Searching for new prospects, they discovered molybdenite 1,500 feet lower along the Arkansas River near the southern end of Chalk Mountain. Grubstaked by a new backer from Denver, Dr. John Harris, Heckendorf and the Webbers drove short exploratory tunnels, but encountered only nonmineralized rock. They had discovered nothing more than molybdenite boulders that ancient glaciers had scoured loose from Bartlett Mountain. Charles Senter experienced similar disappointment after prospecting and driving short tunnels at the northern end of Chalk Mountain.

11

Hugh Leal, heading west from Nebraska to a California retirement, also arrived to personally inspect his claims for the first time. Leal, determined to find gold, was prepared to drive a tunnel through Bartlett Mountain if that's what it took to find it. With his nephew Eric and two Leadville miners, Hugh Leal began work on his tunnel. When work halted in late September 1911, he had advanced the seven-foot-high, five-foot-wide Leal Tunnel 200 feet. The dump below the tiny portal contained nothing but molybdenite.

The rising molybdenum prices also attracted the interest of Colorado Springs mining men, a group of whom formed the Colorado Molybdenum Company. They staked a number of lode claims, seemingly at random, and were mostly interested in gathering molybdenite from the Leal Tunnel dump and the nearby talus slopes. Using a mule-drawn wagon, they hauled tons of rock down a murderously steep path that descended 1,000 vertical feet in just one mile.

By the end of August, they had stockpiled tons of rock at the Climax siding of the Colorado & Southern Railroad. On September 18, 1911, Leadville's *Carbonate Chronicle* printed the first account of mining at Bartlett Mountain:

MOLYBDENUM ORE SHIPPED FROM CLIMAX

The manager of the Colorado Molybdenum Company yesterday stated that his company has a carload ready to be shipped from its property at Climax and that within the next sixty days from ten to twelve thousand tons of the ore will be sent to the plant in Denver for concentration. He says they have a body of molybdenite in their mines at Climax large enough to supply the world for the next three years. This, according to the manager, is a conservative estimate as the body appears to be almost inexhaustible. . . .

The manager of the Molybdenum Company's mines, at Climax, states that as the supply of the metal increases, the demand for the metal will also increase, as new uses will be found for the metal when scarcity is no longer a problem. He says that the great problem in connection with the mining of molybdenum is the expense entailed in the process of concentration.

The discovery of a cheap method of concentration is what is needed to stimulate the mining of molybdenum into one of the greatest industries of this state.

Both the manager's and the writer's comments about molybdenum supply stimulating demand, as well as the vital need for an economical concentration method, were insightful. But the Colorado Molybdenum Company was a bit ahead of its time. The company did ship molybdenite to a custom mill near Denver, but was never heard from again. The company's obituary appeared in the *Engineering & Mining Journal* annual report in January 1912:

> No commercial production of molybdenum is known to have been made in the United States in 1911, according to the U.S. Geological Survey. About 60 tons of rock carrying molybdenite are said to have been mined in the Ten Mile District, Summit County, Colorado, and shipped to Denver for concentration, but the material was too poor to pay for treatment.

The Colorado Molybdenum Company's failure to concentrate molybdenite with the flotation separation process dampened molybdenum interest in the United States. But molybdenum continued to show great promise in Europe, where German armament manufacturers bought all they could get. At Knaben, Norway, peasants hammered apart the rich vein outcrops, hand-cobbed the molybdenite to a 75 percent concentration, then traded it for butter on a pound-for-pound basis.

Of significance, however, was a successful flotation separation test conducted with low-grade Knaben molybdenite at a mill in Kvina, Norway. Even with the mill feed, or "heads," containing a mere 1.0 percent molybdenite, the mill achieved 80 percent grades in both recovery and concentration. By late 1912, the Kvina mill was processing 35 tons of ore per day at a cost of only $1.00 per ton and selling the concentrate to Germany at a handsome profit.

The widely publicized Kvina mill tests failed to spark serious molybdenum interest at Bartlett Mountain, where hopeful molybdenite miners had two big concerns: One was the limited demand for molybdenum; the other was a newly discovered, small, but much richer molybdenite deposit at Red Mountain, forty miles northeast of Climax. The Red Mountain molybdenite deposit, which graded as high as 2.0 percent, was controlled by the Primos Chemical Company of Pittsburgh, Pennsylvania.

In 1913, mining men agreed that if the United States were to ever become a significant producer of molybdenum, the ore would certainly come from Red Mountain, not from the low-grade deposit at Bartlett Mountain. Nevertheless, Ed Heckendorf and Charles Senter continued to try to generate interest in Bartlett Mountain molybdenite. Heckendorf personally canvassed eastern steel mills without success. Senter took things a step further, writing directly to Germany's Krupp armament works. Krupp replied that it did indeed employ molybdenum in certain alloys, but limited consumption hardly justified opening another source of supply.

Bartlett Mountain had considerably more people wanting to mine molybdenite than those who wished to buy it, but that didn't discourage another arrival, Otis Archie King. A recent college graduate, King had worked at an Iowa bank, where his determination and rapid learning ability caught the attention of a director, Wilson H. Pingrey. Even though King knew nothing of mining, Pingrey ordered him to Colorado to oversee his previously mismanaged mining interests at Kokomo.

King arrived in the Tenmile District in 1912 to manage the Pingrey Mines & Ore Reduction Company. As King later recounted, he met an old prospector with "long, gray hair and kindly blue eyes" to whom he took an immediate liking. The prospector was Charles J. Senter, then sixty-six years old and anxious to do something—anything—with the Gold Reef claims he had staked thirty-three summers earlier. He quickly interested King, who, after a cursory visit to the claims, invested $40,000 of Wilson Pingrey's money in an option, payable at $500 up front and $50 per month.

As World War I raged in Europe in 1914, German, British, French, and Russian armament manufacturers competed to buy all available molybdenum. Norwegian peasants enjoyed boom times, and now traded a pound of hand-cobbed molybdenite for three pounds of butter.

Meanwhile, on the battlefields, Germany unveiled an arsenal of unexpectedly superior weaponry. British analysis of captured German weapons revealed, as expected, that the best gun barrels and armor plates were fashioned from advanced molybdenum steel alloys.

Britain moved immediately to cut off the German supply of Norwegian molybdenum. But Norway, with no particular wartime allegiance, continued to sell to the highest bidder, leaving Britain with no alternative but to outbid the Germans. By December 1914, molybdenum prices had reached $5.00 per pound. The soaring prices finally triggered the first commercial molybdenum mining in the United States. It began not at Bartlett Mountain, but at Red Mountain, under direction of the Primos Chemical Company.

Otis Archie King and his wife, Marietta, during their first visit to Colorado in 1905.

But activity also picked up at Bartlett Mountain. Charles Senter and his old friend John Buffehr became partners in ten new claims. Ed Heckendorf kept busy picking up options. Even Hugh Leal, with his tunnel now into 800 feet of nothing but light gray rock with gray-blue streaks, abandoned his dreams of gold and began thinking of molybdenum. Otis Archie King, meanwhile, had leased the old Leadville District Mill in nearby Leadville to experiment with flotation separation of base metal ores. Eyeing the record price of molybdenum, King knew it was time to run some Bartlett Mountain molybdenite through his flotation circuits.

Metal-market analysts warned that the record molybdenum prices reflected only the frenzied European bidding war, not true market supply and demand. Nevertheless, even though European arms producers had already amassed substantial stockpiles, molybdenum speculation in the United States continued unabated. In April 1915, the conservative *Engineering & Mining Journal* issued a word of caution:

> Our attention recently fell upon the prospectus of a promoter who promised to make all of his suckers wealthy out of the dividends to be

A 1943 map of the Tenmile Mining District shows the jumble of confused claims that once covered Bartlett Mountain, Fremont Pass, and Ceresco Ridge.

derived from a molybdenum mine. The production of molybdenum is a nice little business, but it is not big enough to make one man rich, much less a bunch of stockholders. Molybdenite ore realizes prices that appear to the uninformed to be fabulous, but the total transactions amount to only a few tons. . . . Eventually this mineral will become much better known commercially, most people will then be able to spell it correctly, and those of us who are more familiar with it will not, on account of uncertain supply and treatment problems, be compelled to occasionally allude to it as molybedamnite.

Otis Archie King, however, was not discouraged. In May 1915, he enlisted some Colorado Springs backers, leased the Senter-Buffehr claims, hired twenty men, and began mining a fifty-foot-wide open cut high on Bartlett Mountain. Burros packed the ore down in 100-pound canvas sacks; in August, King's crew loaded 900 tons aboard Colorado & Southern wooden gondola cars for shipment to the Leadville District Mill.

On September 12, King and his mill superintendent, George Backus, started the flotation separation circuit. The first concentrates graded a disappointing 22 percent. But switching flotation agents to a Georgia pine oil quickly improved concentrate grades to 70 percent. Although the overall recovery rate was a modest 50 percent, King and Backus milled 648 tons of ore, recovering 5,820 pounds of 72 percent molybdenite concentrate.

Although King's test was a great success, the molybdenum market failed to cooperate. Molybdenum had topped $6.00 per pound in July—then crashed. King still managed to sell his concentrate to the Pennsylvania-based York Metal Alloy Company for $1.75 per pound of contained molybdenum, leaving him a total profit of $1,606, or about $2.50 clear profit per ton of ore. Considering the hand drilling, burro haulage, railroad shipping costs, and inefficiency of experimental milling, the profit was remarkable.

But a letter bearing bad news accompanied King's check. King's shipment of molybdenite concentrate, by far the largest the York Metal Alloy Company had ever received, was enough to satisfy projected world demand for the next two years.

Bad news or not, it didn't take an engineer or an accountant to project what mechanized mining and on-site milling might accomplish at Bartlett Mountain. The Leal Tunnel had revealed the enormity of the deposit, and King had demonstrated a cheap and efficient milling process.

17

But would molybdenum demand ever warrant mining? Knowing he faced a big decision, King agonized over that question. In fall 1915, King held options on the original Senter claims, a lease on the new Senter-Buffehr claims, and recently acquired options on the five Leal claims, thus controlling the best ground on Bartlett Mountain. But the molybdenum market was dead, and he couldn't afford to hold all the idle properties indefinitely. Accordingly, he dropped his options on the Leal claims. Just days later, Ed Heckendorf picked them up.

Otis Archie King's decision would prove a big mistake. With Ed Heckendorf controlling the Leal claims, the stage was set for the battle of Bartlett Mountain.

2
The Mountain of Molybdenum

The mineralized rock, which filled the mountain, was a light gray, finely crystalline, highly silicified granite shot through with an intricate and endless maze of veinlets containing a bluish quartz.

Bartlett Mountain was created not by a single geological event, nor by any simple sequence of geological events, but by a lengthy and complex process of building, faulting, mineralization, alteration, and erosion. Even the basement rock atop which the mountain rests, the 1.8-billion-year-old Idaho Springs Formation, consists of schists and gneisses that were later intruded by Silver Plume granite. During Paleozoic time some 500 million years ago, the submerged basement rock slowly became covered by a mile-thick layer of ocean sediments, which formed strata of sandstones, limestones, and conglomerates. Heat and pressure eventually metamorphosed the sediments into quartzites, dolomites, and grits.

During these ancient times of rock formation, the continents existed in a cluster, each on its own tectonic plate. The Earth's crust is composed of a dozen such large, rigid plates floating atop a mass of magma. Each plate is about sixty miles thick and bordered by midocean ridges and deep ocean trenches. Magma wells up from the depths at the midocean ridges to solidify into new sections of crust. At the trenches, the edges of tectonic plates are drawn under those of adjacent plates, forced downward, and remelted into magma. This continuous circulation of crustal and magmatic material imparts a slow but powerful motion to the plates. Although that motion may amount to only a few inches per year, when measured against hundreds of millions of years of geologic time, travel distances become global in scope and explain the present relative positions of the continents.

In Paleozoic time, Colorado was generally located near the center of the North American plate, which extended from the Arctic Ocean in the north to the Caribbean Sea, and from the East Pacific Rise to the Mid-Atlantic Ridge. In the east, the plate formed a stable continental shield, or craton, while the south and west became less stable basin-and-range areas. Colorado was located between these two sections, atop a relatively narrow north-south belt that had been structurally weakened by repetitive faulting and folding.

Some 300 million years ago, Colorado emerged from receding seas as a highland, subject to slow erosion of the thick, accumulated Paleozoic sediments. The Mid-Atlantic Ridge then began spreading, forming the Atlantic Ocean and sending the North American plate on a slow westerly drift. As the plate drew away from Europe and Africa, tectonic stresses buckled its weakened central belt upward, creating the Ancestral Rocky Mountains. The Ancestral Rockies were relatively short-lived; within 50 million years, erosion had reduced them to coarse gravels that built the floors of broad valleys.

Sixty-five million years ago, as dinosaurs neared extinction at the end of the Cretaceous period, the North American plate had drifted westward 1,500 miles to collide with the Pacific plate, generating enormous new stresses and another mountain-building episode. Again, the weakened central belt buckled, lifting great blocks of both Precambrian basement rock and Paleozoic sediments upward to form the New Rocky Mountains, the Rockies we know today. Although hardly recognizable, the basic central ranges of modern Colorado—the Front, Park, and Sawatch ranges—had been created.

As the North American plate slid farther over the edge of the Pacific plate, continuing stresses caused a massive regional upheaval, lifting the southwestern United States, including Colorado, to its present elevation. Severe crustal fracturing and faulting associated with both the mountain building and the uplift permitted magma to surge upward.

20

In southwestern Colorado, lava extruding onto the surface built the San Juan Mountains and other associated massive volcanic formations. Volcanism was less frequent in central Colorado, where magma surged into subsurface crustal fissures and faults, fracturing the surrounding country rock and solidifying into porphyritic intrusions as sills, batholiths, and massive stocks. Hydrothermal events sometimes followed the magmatic intrusions, injecting superheated solutions into the fracture zones. The solutions physically and chemically altered the country rock, sometimes depositing minerals in bodies of widely varying composition, concentration, and configuration. Mineralization occurred frequently in a 150-mile-long, 30-mile-wide arc stretching diagonally across Colorado from present-day Boulder to the San Juan Mountains. This heavily mineralized belt—now known as the Colorado Mineral Belt—contained a wealth of precious, base, and alloying metal deposits.

The Park Range, one of Colorado's most impressive mountain systems, transected the Mineral Belt as a north-south succession of high peaks with three subranges: the Gore Range in the north; the Tenmile Range; and, in the south, the Mosquito Range. Originally, most Park Range mountains were faulted anticlines rising as symmetrical folds. But stresses overcame the limited crustal flexibility and created faults—long breaks in the rock with relative displacement of opposing crustal blocks. The faults dramatically altered the western slopes of the mountains in the Tenmile and Mosquito Ranges.

Rising near the conjunction of the Tenmile and Mosquito Ranges, Bartlett Mountain was a fine example of a faulted anticline. Originally, the mountain was much more massive and perhaps a mile higher than it is today. Bartlett Mountain ascended gradually on the east, crested in a peak and high, jagged ridges, then dropped steeply in the west along the thirty-mile-long Mosquito Fault.

Magma had intermittently intruded the area near Bartlett Mountain, forming intrusive mazes of granitic sheets and sills. But in mid-Tertiary time, perhaps thirty million years ago, a major magmatic intrusion made Bartlett Mountain mineralogically unique. A column of wet silici-alkalic magma thrust upward through the Precambrian basement rock into the heart of the mountain, forming a large intrusive stockwork. Composite in structure, this porphyritic stock was emplaced by four separate irruptions, or columnar movements of magma, which thoroughly fractured the surrounding country rock.

21

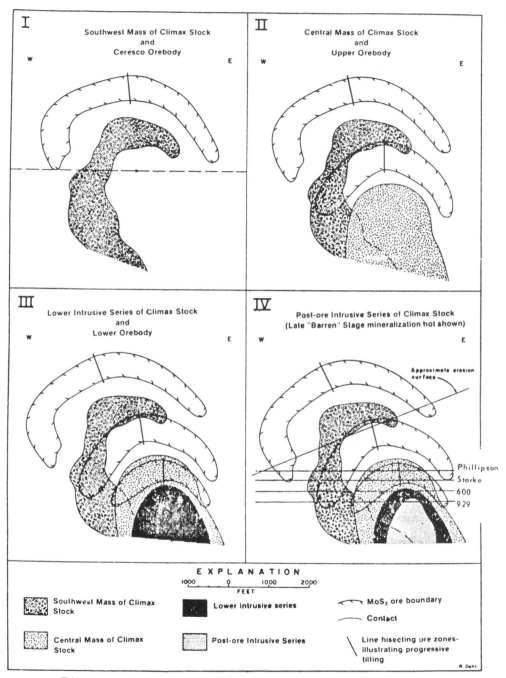

Diagrammatic sections showing the sequence of multiple intrusions and mineralizations, and relative positions of ore bodies within Bartlett Mountain.

The four massive irruptions, involving perhaps thirty square miles of magma, were powerful enough to dome the mountain and rotate it slightly to the west. The first and most powerful irruption penetrated to within a few thousand feet of the surface, very nearly becoming a volcanic rather than an intrusive event. The resulting stockwork was columnar in configuration, between 1,000 and 4,000 feet wide, and many miles deep, eventually connecting with a master magmatic reservoir.

A hydrothermal event followed each irruption, injecting superheated quartz-rich solutions into the adjacent fracture zones. The solutions accompanying the final irruption contained no mineralization, but the first three carried substantial quantities of certain metals, notably molybdenum, iron, tungsten, and tin. The solutions first silicified the country rock, then, as temperatures and pressures decreased, deposited their contained molybdenum and iron as sulfides, and the tin and tungsten as oxides.

The first and most powerful irruption created what geologists now know as the Southwest Mass of the Climax Stock; above it, hydrothermal solutions formed the Ceresco Orebody in the shape of a 4,000-foot-wide inverted bowl. The second irruption created the Central Mass and the smaller Upper Orebody. Even before this phase of mineralization was complete, a period of intensive silicification replaced the metals with quartz, leaving a barren core within the Upper Orebody. The third and smallest mineralizing event, called the lower intrusive series, formed the Lower Orebody.

The final result was a complex, composite, mineralized body much different from the small, rich, vein- and replacement-type deposits typical of the Colorado Mineral Belt. Although low in metal concentration, it was enormous in size and could be compared in shape to the top half of a hollowed cantaloupe three-quarters of a mile wide and a half-mile deep.

The mineralized rock, which filled the mountain, was a light gray, finely crystalline, highly silicified granite shot though with an intricate and endless maze of veinlets containing a bluish quartz. Molybdenum was present as the disulfide molybdenite, a dark mineral intimately associated with the quartz and imparting to the veinlets a gray-blue to near-black color. The dark quartz veinlets laced virtually the entire mass of mineralized host rock. Disseminated uniformly throughout the deposit were countless small, glittering crystals of brass-colored pyrite.

A typical piece of Climax molybdenite ore is a gray, silicified granite laced with blue-gray molybdenite veinlets and bits of pyrite.
–Stephen M. Voynick

After the mineralization of Bartlett Mountain, the Mosquito Fault became active, displacing its west and east blocks by as much as 9,000 vertical feet. The displacement brought the Paleozoic sediments on the west into contact with the altered, mineralized rock of Bartlett Mountain. The displacement sheared off much of the western face of the mountain, taking with it a substantial part of the Ceresco Orebody and leaving a high, steep fault scarp vulnerable to accelerated erosion.

Over eons, the cumulative effects of water, wind, and ice slowly and steadily reduced and reshaped Bartlett Mountain. Severe erosion of the scarp face modified the steep cliffs and cut a high canyon that divided the mountain into two parts: the summit on the north; and the slightly lower, rocky ridge to the south that would one day be called Ceresco Ridge. Erosion removed most of the Ceresco Orebody, leaving only two remnants, one in Bartlett Mountain, the other in Ceresco Ridge.

Surface erosion also established basic drainage patterns. The headwaters of the ancestral Tenmile Creek came together in the high alpine canyon that divided Bartlett Mountain from Ceresco Ridge; the headwaters of the ancestral Arkansas River flowed from the much broader alpine amphitheater south of Ceresco Ridge.

The final sculpting of Bartlett Mountain occurred in very recent geologic time, when global cooling spawned the Pleistocene Ice Ages. Although the great northern continental ice sheets did not reach

Colorado, regional alpine glaciation swept the higher elevations. Over many centuries, accumulating deep snowfall compressed perpetual high snowfields into heavy glacial ice masses. Glaciers emanated from the headwaters of both Tenmile Creek and the Arkansas River, carving out the high canyons into open, horseshoe-shaped alpine cirques. At their peak, the glaciers may have extended twenty miles down their respective drainages. Slow, powerful glacial movement scraped some areas to barren bedrock, while covering others under deep moraines of glacial debris.

The Tenmile glacier also scoured the face of Bartlett Mountain, exposing some of the sulfide mineralization in the remnant Ceresco Orebody. Atmosphere and water converted the surface and near-surface pyrite into rust-colored iron oxide; the exposed molybdenum disulfide slowly altered into molybdite, a bright yellow oxide somewhat resembling elemental sulfur, which imparted a distinctive yellow coloration to the outcrop.

That yellowish outcrop was the visual clue to the internal mineralization of Bartlett Mountain, yet it hardly hinted at the awesome overall size of the deposit. Even though faulting, erosion, and glaciation had removed much of the original deposit, the remaining portion amounted to more than two billion tons of mineralized rock. Contained within that mineralized rock were an astounding six billion pounds—three million tons—of elemental molybdenum, making Bartlett Mountain the largest molybdenum deposit in the world.

When moderating temperatures ended the Pleistocene Ice Ages some 10,000 years ago, Bartlett Mountain and its environs were recognizable. The summit stood 13,336 feet above sea level and was separated from Ceresco Ridge to the south by a horseshoe-shaped cirque. The mountain's imposing western face, still quite steep and marked by the yellowish outcrop, loomed high above the talus slopes, alpine meadows, the broad saddle of a partially forested mountain pass, and, farther to the west, the rounded bulk of 12,037-foot-high Chalk Mountain.

Chalk Mountain and Ceresco Ridge, as well as the 11,318-foot-high pass between them, sat squarely atop the Continental Divide. The waters of Tenmile Creek flowed north through Tenmile Canyon into the Blue River, then into the Colorado River and on to the Pacific. South of the pass, the Arkansas River headwaters flowed south, eventually leaving the mountains to cross the Great Plains and join the distant Mississippi River before emptying into the Gulf of Mexico.

Although a mix of conifers grew atop the pass, only a few stunted spruces dotted the lush alpine meadows that sprawled above the 11,500-foot-high timberline. Above the meadows was an arcticlike tundra and, finally, the barren rock of the highest cliffs, ridges, and peaks.

Spring arrived in May as a brief seasonal transition. From June through August, the alpine summer was pleasantly cool; wildflowers blanketed the green alpine meadows in a profusion of color, beaver dammed the Arkansas and Tenmile drainages right to timberline, deer and elk grazed in the higher meadows, and marmot and pika thrived in the jumbled talus slopes. Autumn, like spring, was glorious, but brief. By late September, the fiery yellow and gold aspen leaves that broke the dark monotony of the timberline forests had faded and fallen.

Climatologically, winter dominated Bartlett Mountain and the pass below. Snow fell during all months of the year, and the cumulative snowfall from October to May often exceeded 300 inches. Bitter winds howled down from the peaks and ridges, driving the snow into drifts twenty and even thirty feet deep. Avalanches periodically thundered down the steeper slopes, temperatures plunged well below zero, and the Arkansas and Tenmile headwaters lay locked in ice and mantles of snow.

Humans first climbed the pass to look upward at the bold, stained face of Bartlett Mountain perhaps 8,000 years ago. More recently, when the Utes were the summer hunters of the high mountains, a primitive trail traversed the pass, connecting the Tenmile and Arkansas drainages and the hunting grounds beyond.

Before any European had even seen the pass, it became a prominent point in the political and territorial division of North America. The Arkansas River was the first local feature to receive an English name; both its headwaters and the nearby pass, which straddled a vague "Great Divide," were formal boundary points for New France and New Spain, then for the republics of Mexico and Texas, and finally for the United States. French adventurers may have reached the pass by 1800, and American trappers by 1820, but left no record. For a few more decades, Bartlett Mountain and its environs would belong only to the nomadic Ute hunters.

26

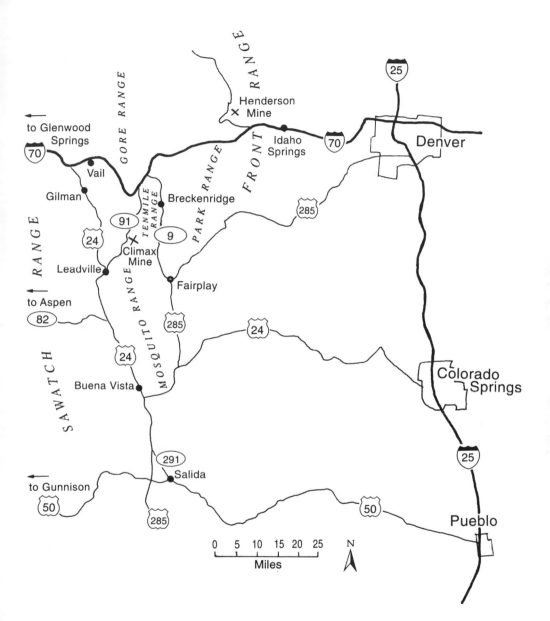

In 1858 and 1859, the nation's second western gold rush lured tens of thousands of "fifty-niners" to Colorado. Following a trail of placer gold, they founded a string of mountain boomtowns with names like Central City, Idaho Springs, Georgetown, Fairplay, Breckenridge, and Oro City. By 1860, prospectors had followed the Arkansas River to its headwaters, crossed the nearby pass, which they named Arkansas, and struck gold in Tenmile Canyon. And in the shadow of Bartlett Mountain, they found gold in McNulty Gulch.

Seeking the possible lode source of the McNulty Gulch gold, they climbed high onto the mountain that rose immediately to the east and were drawn to a yellowish outcrop on the steep western face. Breaking open outcrop samples, they found the light gray rock laced with tiny gray-blue veinlets and glittering with specks of brassy pyrite. But the rock contained no gold, and they descended the mountain to return to their sluices in Tenmile Canyon.

For five summers, miners sluiced both the Arkansas and Tenmile gravels. Through use, the ancient Ute trail that crossed Arkansas Pass became a rough wagon road. But the gold rush soon ran its course, and the miners departed to pursue their dreams elsewhere. Most of the nearby peaks, ridges, creeks, and gulches now bore English names, but the reasons why they had been named, or for whom, would often be forgotten. The overgrown, rutted wagon road still crossed Arkansas Pass, and a trail of cut tree stumps, rotting sluices, and collapsed cabins followed the Arkansas River and Tenmile Creek far downstream.

More than a decade later, miners struck a huge lead-silver deposit thirteen miles down the Arkansas River near the old gold camp of Oro City. Thousands flocked to the new city of Leadville. And, finally, on August 17, 1879, near the end of the alpine summer, a lone prospector named Charles Senter climbed to the yellow-stained outcrop on Bartlett Mountain to stake three claims.

In 1879, there was little activity in the area around Bartlett Mountain. The headwaters of the Arkansas River and Tenmile Creek were dotted with the rotting cabins of departed placer miners.

3

The Battle for
Bartlett Mountain
1916–1919

---

*Goddamn you, King, get off our property before I
fill you full of lead!*
    *—Jack White, first superintendent
    of the Climax Mine, to Otis Archie King,
    summer 1917*

By August 1916, the European war had raged for two years; with no end in sight, concern grew that the conflict would eventually involve the United States. The molybdenum stockpiles of 1915 were depleted, and armament manufacturers again bought all they could get, driving molybdenum prices back up to $2.00 per pound. Ed Heckendorf, holding the Leal claim options, remained determined to find a buyer for molybdenite. He hired Pelimon Alonzo Balcom, a smooth-talking Denver soap salesman, armed him with claim and option records, maps, tunnel diagrams, and assay reports, then sent him east for another try at the steel companies.

In October, Balcom returned empty-handed. Keeping his one remaining appointment on the eighth floor of the Foster Building in downtown Denver, he found himself seated across a desk from The American Metal Company's manager of western operations, a forty-year-old, five-foot-five-inch German immigrant named Max Schott.

The American Metal Company had evolved from an eighteenth-century family business in the German feudal states. In the 1860s, the owners reorganized and incorporated the profitable business as Metallgesellschaft. Opportunity for international expansion arose

31

when Metallgesellschaft patriarch Phillip Abraham Cohen married off a daughter to Raphael Moses of London. After Moses officially changed his name to Merton, a son, Henry Ralph Merton, founded the London-based Henry R. Merton & Company, a firm closely associated with Metallgesellschaft. Later, a second son, Wilhelm Merton, filled a Metallgesellschaft director's seat at the company's Frankfurt headquarters.

As a major buyer of ores and metals, Metallgesellschaft emerged as a leader of a powerful German metals cartel. To move into the supply end of world markets and strengthen its influence on world metal prices, Metallgesellschaft directly extended its interests to Great Britain. Further international expansion along Metallgesellschaft's traditional family lines came when Wilhelm Merton's daughter married into Frankfurt's wealthy Ladenburg family. The newly married Ladenburgs moved immediately to New York City, where the husband founded the investment banking firm of Ladenburg, Thalmann & Co.

Metallgesellschaft found American mineral resources increasingly attractive, for the chaotic frontier precious-metal rushes were history and mining was rapidly becoming an organized industry with access to large deposits of industrial metals. In 1886, with the ready help of Ladenburg, Thalmann & Co., Wilhelm Merton and Jacob Langeloth, a Metallgesellschaft associate, founded The American Metal Company, Ltd. Incorporated on June 17, 1887, The American Metal Company was capitalized at $200,000 and firmly controlled by Metallgesellschaft, which held 49 percent of the shares. The remainder of the stock was distributed among just forty shareholders, with most held by Henry R. Merton & Co. associates and The American Metal Company directors, including Jacob Langeloth.

The certificate of incorporation reflected typical German conservatism, and specifically excluded direct mining activities in favor of such less risky businesses as treating and trading metals and ores. That approach enabled The American Metal Company to survive unscathed both the 1889 world copper-market crash and the 1893 American silver-market crash, events that devastated many foreign and American mining companies.

The "Metal Company," as it was known to insiders, steadily expanded its interests to include American precious and base metals, Mexican copper, and Canadian nickel. The directors organized

A stock certificate of The American Metal Company issued in 1887. The people and expertise of The American Metal Company were largely responsible for the success of the Climax Molybdenum Company in its earliest years.

all new ventures that entailed any significant risk as syndicates, seeking investment capital from "suitable" partners, usually directors, existing Metal Company shareholders, or family members, thus maintaining close control while minimizing company liability.

In October 1916, The American Metal Company headquarters occupied the twenty-eighth floor of a thirty-two-story building at 61 Broadway in New York City. Jacob Langeloth was chairman of the board, and his longtime associate Bernard Hochschild was president. Their manager of western operations, Max Schott, was at that time seated in his Denver office, listening to a soap salesman expound on the potential of a molybdenite deposit in Bartlett Mountain, located somewhere near an isolated railroad water stop called Climax.

Max Schott did not share in the Metal Company's background of wealth, tradition, and family ties. Born in Germany in 1876, he emigrated to the United States at age seventeen, taking a job as an office boy at The American Metal Company's New York headquarters. He improved his halting English at night school, where he also learned Spanish and French and became familiar with business law. He got his break in 1906, when the Metal Company appointed him as assistant manager of its St. Louis office. Distinguishing himself, he quickly moved up to a management position at the company's smelting works in Monterrey, Mexico. In spring 1916, the Metal Company again promoted Schott, this time to manager of western operations at its new Denver office.

From his initial discussion with Pelimon Alonzo Balcom, Max Schott sensed possible potential in both molybdenum and the Bartlett Mountain molybdenite deposit. He immediately ordered two Metal Company men, geologist Marden Hayward and engineer Harry Brown, to Climax for a preliminary inspection. When their report confirmed the property was as Balcom had described it, Schott boarded a Colorado & Southern train in early November for a personal visit to Climax.

Deep snow already covered Fremont Pass and Bartlett Mountain when Max Schott and Ed Heckendorf snowshoed up to the portal of the Leal Tunnel. The Leal Tunnel, now 900 feet long and showing nothing but solid molybdenite all the way, sold Max Schott on the potential of Bartlett Mountain.

November 1916. Max Schott's (second from left) inspection team prepares for a snowshoe trek from Ed Heckendorf's cabin on Fremont Pass to the Leal Tunnel.

Schott knew that winning the interest, much less the support, of the Metal Company's directors and its new president, Carl Loeb, wouldn't be easy. In New York, Schott presented a detailed report, recommending an immediate exploration program. As he expected, the directors balked. They lectured Schott that molybdenum was outside the company's realm of metals experience; furthermore, they never assumed the considerable risks inherent to mining ventures. Schott tactfully reminded everyone that the molybdenum market was firming, a prolonged European war was likely, and the company couldn't afford not to look at the Climax deposit. Max Schott left New York with what he had come for: authorization to take a short-term option on the five Leal claims from the Heckendorf-Webber-Harris group.

With the first option payment of $12,500 due in January 1917, Schott moved quickly. He shipped five tons of molybdenite from the Leal Tunnel dump to J. M. McClave, a Salt Lake City metallurgist.

November 1916. Hugh Leal (left), Max Schott (center), and Marden Hayward snowshoe up to inspect the Leal Tunnel.

Using a modified flotation separation process, McClave reported recovery and concentration grades of 60 percent—high enough to convince Schott to make the first payment.

Still unconvinced, the Metal Company directors refused to come up with further direct funding, but indicated that a syndicate might possibly provide funding, provided the Metal Company's risk was limited to 10 percent. Only when Schott demonstrated personal confidence in the venture by putting up some of his own money did he elicit the tentative participation of the Loeb Family, Metal Company Chairman Bernard Hochschild, and Dr. Otto Sussman, a consulting engineer.

In January 1917, as the United States drifted ever closer to active involvement in the European war, American steel companies conducted their first serious studies of molybdenum steels. Their purchases helped drive the price of molybdenum to $3.00 per pound. Ed Heckendorf, thinking this might be his last chance to sell the Leal claims, wasn't about to wait for Max Schott and a final decision by The American Metal Company directors. He sent his soap salesman to Butte, Montana, where Pelimon Alonzo Balcom found strong interest in Bartlett Mountain molybdenite from the Butte & Superior Copper Company.

On the January day the first option payment was due, Ed Heckendorf sat in Max Schott's Denver office, waiting impatiently for a telephone message of approval from New York. Less than one mile away in the Brown Palace Hotel, Hugh Leal waited with a vice president and an attorney of the Butte & Superior Copper Company. Finally, Schott received the awaited telephone call from New York: the Metal Company directors had formed a syndicate and would provide funding for the first payment. With a sigh of relief, Schott wrote out the check to Heckendorf. Had approval not been granted, Heckendorf was prepared to telephone Hugh Leal at the Brown Palace Hotel, who would have taken immediate receipt of a similar check from the Butte & Superior Copper Company for the option on his five Bartlett Mountain claims.

With the second $12,500 payment due in February, Schott worked quickly to secure accurate assays. Although January was the worst possible time, he hired Eric Leal to drive exploratory crosscut drifts in the Leal Tunnel. Leal recruited some Leadville miners, bunking them in the long-abandoned, thirty-five-year-old Denver & Rio Grande Railroad station shack. Each day before dawn, they snowshoed through the bitter cold and deep drifts up to the Leal Tunnel, packing their supplies on burros. Keeping the workings as small as possible to save time, money, and effort, the miners drove three crosscuts off the main tunnel. Drilling with obsolete hammers and hand steels, they completed six 100-foot-long drifts in just six weeks. Max Schott, meanwhile, knowing the Butte & Superior Copper Company was waiting to pick up the option, persuaded the syndicate to come up with the second monthly payment.

The news from the Leal Tunnel was both good and bad. The crosscuts had encountered nothing but molybdenite. But, even though the mineralization appeared uniform to the eye, the assays were worthless, for grades of identical samples varied wildly from 0.1 percent to 3 percent.

With the final payment of $25,000 due in August, Schott knew the syndicate would never authorize payment on the basis of such erratic assay reports. He ordered Eric Leal's miners to extend the crosscuts as rapidly as possible, sacking every tenth shovelful of muck,

1917. Hand drilling in the Leal Tunnel.

or broken rock, until they had 1,200 pounds to ship to Salt Lake City. J. M. McClave immediately ran three separate batches, one from each crosscut, through his flotation separation circuit. Recovery and concentration grades of 60 percent, the same for all three crosscut batches, indicated a uniform molybdenite grade of about 1 percent.

As J. M. McClave worked with the molybdenite samples, the United States formally entered the war against Germany and the Central Powers. American industry mobilized, creating record demand for molybdenum steels for the emergency manufacture of everything from gun barrels and armor plate for the mass-produced Renault "baby" tanks to high-stress components for NC-4 Liberty aircraft engines. For the first time, American steel manufacturers began considering molybdenum not only for its own steel-enhancing qualities, but as a substitute for foreign supplies of tungsten and manganese. In a seller's market, molybdenum prices soared to $4.00 per pound.

Max Schott was elated when he read McClave's test reports, for they indicated that the Bartlett Mountain molybdenite body was as uniform as it was large. He found more good news when he calculated projected mining and milling costs. With molybdenum selling for $4.00 per pound, his total production costs would be about $2.00 per pound.

In late April 1917, Schott petitioned the syndicate for development capital. When the syndicate approved his request, things were never the same again at Fremont Pass. Almost overnight, crews erected a dozen big, white army tents alongside the Climax station house. The first compressor, along with a steam engine and mechanical rock drills, arrived in May. In just five weeks, Schott's "machine miners" drilled and blasted out another 1,000 feet of exploratory drifts—more than Hugh Leal's hand steel miners had managed in five years. And they had drilled through nothing but molybdenite.

The syndicate then summoned Schott to New York to personally justify the rapidly mounting development expenses. Schott would recall that meeting years later. The directors were "sitting around on their handkerchiefs" while Schott argued for all-out, immediate development of a mine and mill. One director looked him squarely in the eye and snapped, "All right, Schott, if you think Climax is that good, how much will you pay me right now for my shares?"

"Ten dollars a share," Schott fired back instantly.

"Schott, you're crazy," the director replied. But after a long pause during which Schott never dropped his eyes, the director added softly, "But I'd probably be crazier to take it."

When Max Schott left New York with the syndicate's authorization for mine development, he headed directly to Pittsburgh to meet with Dr. George W. Sargent, president of the Electric Reduction Company and the foremost practical alloy steel man in the United States. That meeting cleared the last big hurdle that stood in the way of making mining at Bartlett Mountain a reality. Schott secured a contract to sell every pound of molybdenite concentrate the mine could produce to the Electric Reduction Company at market price on delivery.

The final payment of $25,000, made in August 1917, secured the $100,000 option-purchase agreement, and the Climax Syndicate took title to the twenty-five acres covered by the five patented Leal claims. The directors formalized organization of the Climax Syndicate, assigning 65 percent of the stock to individual partners; 25 percent to the Heckendorf-Webber-Harris group, which still had to settle with Hugh Leal; and 10 percent to The American Metal Company, Ltd.

September 1917. Top management of the Climax Mine (from left to right): Harry L. Brown, Dennis F. Haley, Ira Renick, John H. "Jack" White. The woman and two children are unidentified.

The directors allocated the entire $250,000 raised from sale of stock for mine and mill development.

Meanwhile, Max Schott assembled the first management team of the Climax Mine. For his general superintendent, Schott brought in John H. "Jack" White, a tough ramrod from Tonopah, Nevada. Dennis F. Haley and Harry L. Brown, two veteran Metal Company men, filled the top engineering positions. Schott then named James R. Welsh as the first mine superintendent, Ira Renick as mill superintendent, John Horgan as construction superintendent, and a young surveyor, Arthur Storke, as construction foreman. For a mill site, Schott purchased or took options on the Nichols, Tenmile, and Harris placer properties, which covered the flattest half square mile of land atop Fremont Pass.

The booming wartime molybdenum prices assured that the Climax Syndicate was not alone at Bartlett Mountain. In early 1917, speculators, most of whom could neither spell nor pronounce the word molybdenum, had staked more than fifty claims. Although speculation was rampant, only two interests other than the Climax Syndicate seriously intended to mine and mill molybdenite ore. They were A. M. Gillespey, owner of the patented Denver Number Two, and Otis Archie King, representing the Pingrey Mines & Ore Reduction Company.

Competitive development began on Gillespey's single claim, the Denver Number Two. The Waltemyer brothers of Denver found backers from the wealthy Longyear family of Minneapolis, owners of the Longyear Engineering Company. They leased the claim and organized as the Molybdenum Products Company. Among the Molybdenum Products Company's most urgent priorities was securing land for a mill site.

The only remaining suitable ground nearby was the half-square-mile Buffehr Ranch, located north of the summit of the pass. John Buffehr and Charles Senter, still joint claim owners, had been close friends for nearly thirty years. Senter remained absolutely loyal to Otis Archie King, who had already approached Buffehr about using the ranch as his own mill site. But King had only talked. An attorney representing the Mineral Land & Finance Company, the land subsidiary of the Molybdenum Products Company, had visited Buffehr with

1917. The Lower Camp of the Molybdenum Products Company under construction.

check in hand to lease the ranch. When Buffehr took the check, the Molybdenum Products Company had its mill site. And John Buffehr and Charles Senter came to an abrupt, bitter parting of the ways.

Otis Archie King lagged behind in the development race, still trying to prove his claims and secure investment capital. His open cut on the original Senter claims, high on the outcrop overlooking the horseshoe-shaped cirque, showed molybdenite all the way. King also controlled much of Ceresco Ridge, where he had found more molybdenite. He hired an old prospector, Eric Bear, to drive a narrow exploratory tunnel straight into the ridge. When the Bear Tunnel encountered nothing but molybdenite over its entire 350-foot length, geologists realized that the Bartlett Mountain outcrop deposit and the Ceresco Ridge deposit had once been part of the same huge body.

In spring 1917, the crews of all three competing companies lived in camps of clustered shacks and tents. King described his camp in *Gray Gold*, a book he wrote many years later.

> We immediately began the shipment of lumber, stoves, dynamite, drills, steel, snowshoes, skis, powder, fuse, caps, etc. We erected first a cook shanty and dining room, built of two-by-fours and shiplap, capable of taking care of thirty-five men.
>
> A large range was installed in the kitchen and a large round-bellied stove in the dining room. Around this building in a half-circle, were erected ten or twelve bunkhouses. The floors were made of shiplap, and three boards of the same material were placed on edge as side-walls, with a two-by-four erected in the center of each, with another connecting them as a ridge pole. Over this was stretched a tarpaulin. Out of the same material bunks were built on each side, and they were then ready to accommodate four men each. They were thoroughly air-conditioned; in fact, they had more fresh air than anything else, as they were not supplied with stoves. Usually our socks, boots and clothing would be frozen stiff by morning, and it would be necessary to thaw them out in the dining room before we could get into them.

Even with little capital, King had certain advantages. He controlled the original Senter claims, which extended high into the cirque and afforded valuable priority water rights for future milling operations. He also had his eye on the Ella N. property, the last of the level ground that remained on Fremont Pass. The forty-acre Ella N. placer tract included a section of Tenmile Creek and was located strategically between the mine and mill sites of the Climax Syndicate and the Molybdenum Products Company.

Column-mounted machine drills arrived at Climax in May 1917, greatly speeding exploration in the Leal Tunnel.

King saw the Ella N. listed for tax sale at Breckenridge, but Ed Heckendorf had seen it first, purchased the title for $500, and begun "advertising out" the heirs. But King reached the heirs first; tracking down two in Denver and two more in Chicago, he bought out their full interests. But upon his return, he quickly learned that his competition wasn't wasting time with legalities. Both the Climax Syndicate and the Molybdenum Products Company were busy surveying routes for aerial tramways—directly across King's Ella N. property.

In mid-August 1917, Leadville's *Carbonate Chronicle* reported Fremont Pass bustling with activity:

> A white city, springing up almost overnight, within less than an hour's ride by train from Leadville, is among the most interesting features that mark mining development in this section. The scene of the latest activity is Climax, the Colorado & Southern station perched on the very summit of Fremont Pass, where a sign near the track informs the visitor that he is 11,303 feet above sea level. A month ago, Climax

and Buffehr's Spur showed few signs of life or activity. Today, upwards of 300 men are engaged in mining and construction work on mills and boarding houses, surface plants, and other operations. . . .

The work is being undertaken by two companies, the American Metal company, and the Molybdenum Products corporation, the former with headquarters at Climax and the latter at Buffehr's Spur. . . .

The objective of all this activity is the practical development of the immense molybdenite deposits that have been lying fallow in the mountains surrounding Climax, and which can now be treated on a commercial basis and large scale.

It was not until the American Metal company came into the field, however, that the actualities of development began to materialize. The company, which is one of the largest in the United States, with its mines, mills, smelters, and refineries, has sent its engineers and experts into the field and their reports and preliminary tests being favorable, lost no time in getting actual construction underway.

Present efforts are directed to getting the main buildings under cover, and this is what Superintendent John H. White is bending every energy to accomplish. The foundations for the first part of the mill are practically completed, and the largest part of the outside work should be completed by November 1st, and this part of the plant should be running by December 1st. . . . This present plan of the company is to deliver ore from the mine by means of an aerial tramway about a mile long.

The actual extent of the deposit is not known except as it has been exposed by the enormous slides and small tunnels opened on the American Metal company's holdings and those of the Molybdenum

August 1917. Construction underway at the Climax Lower Camp. An "X" marks the site of the Leal Tunnel. The Colorado & Southern station is in the foreground.

Products company further up toward the head of the great amphitheater. It is one of the possibilities, however, that the whole mountain carries a material that can be treated successfully and in that case mining will essentially be prosecuted on a scale similar to that at Bingham, Utah, where low grade copper ore forms the body of the whole mountain.

The permanency of the work planned by the company is indicated by the fact that two large boarding houses are being erected, one near the mine, the other near the mill. These houses will be sufficient to accommodate a large force of men, and it is planned to have them as modern and comfortable as possible. Shower baths will be supplied for the men, and in order that the long winter nights will not be tedious, card rooms and reading rooms will be provided.

Climax is now one of the busiest stations along the line of the C&S. Twenty-five tents dot the ground in the vicinity of the station, and the company has turned the old Rio Grande section house into an eating house where the men are provided with excellent meals. There are now 215 men employed in construction and other work, and this force will be increased to 250 within the next month. . . .

The other enterprise launched for the purpose of developing a group of claims on Bartlett Mountain, the Molybdenum Products company, has established its headquarters at Buffehr's Spur. The company is now laying the foundation for a mill with a capacity of 500 tons per day, the ore to be treated by a process controlled by the company. A large boarding house is in construction and preparations are being rushed [so] as to get under cover by the time the snow flies. The ore will be brot down from the mine a distance of 7,320 feet by aerial tram, crushed and treated with some form of flotation. . . .

Already surveying parties are in the field, and it is understood that the Pingrey Mines company is planning to prosecute some kind of development work. . . .

By late summer, dozens of ax- and saw-wielding woodsmen, after firewood, mine timbers, and construction lumber, had reduced the pine and spruce forests on Fremont Pass to fields of stumps. As the big timber tram towers marched boldly up Bartlett Mountain toward the mines, Public Service Company crews erected power poles up the Tenmile Valley, stringing cable to carry high-voltage power to Climax. Fifty C&S hands assigned permanently to Climax, but forced to "room" in wooden boxcars, worked twelve hours per day laying ties and spiking down narrow-gauge rail on new freight sidings at Climax and Buffehr's Spur. Crews worked from sunrise to sunset grading rough streets between foundations that would soon become offices, mill buildings, warehouses, and living facilities, while oth-

Summer 1917. Dennis Haley's young daughter fishing for trout in the small lake originally located atop Fremont Pass. The old DSP&P station house and Chalk Mountain appear in the background.

ers improved the mule trail connecting the Lower Camp at the mill with the Upper Camp near the mine into the roughest of wagon roads.

As the three-way development race crowded Fremont Pass, friction between competing crews was inevitable. Fighting and equipment theft were commonplace, and with the Summit County sheriff headquartered in Breckenridge, forty miles away over bad roads, matters of "legality" usually favored the side with the most muscle. When weapons of choice shifted from fists to knives and pickaxes, even old Charles Senter began wearing a gun "for the first time since the Indian wars." King later wrote, "the mountain air was filled with tobacco juice and profanity."

Virtually all the Bartlett Mountain claims were disputed, and miners often slept on their claims to ensure being there first in the morning. King recalled working on some disputed Senter-Buffehr claims when a horseman on a white stallion rode up from below. The rider reined to a halt in front of King, pointed a rifle squarely at his chest, and muttered through clenched teeth, "Goddamn you, King, get off our property before I fill you full of lead!" Otis Archie

46

King had just made the acquaintance of his neighbor, Jack White, the first superintendent of the Climax Mine.

In Leadville, Breckenridge, and Denver, newspaper reports about the Climax Mine never noted the existence of the Climax Syndicate, but referred often to the syndicate's prominent minority partner, The American Metal Company. The name was rarely used correctly, appearing as "the American Company," "the Metals Company," or even "the American Molybdenum Company." The correct name, however, would soon become far better known, for The American Metal Company, Ltd., was becoming the focus of national news.

After the United States declared war on the Central Powers in April 1917, the Trading with the Enemy Act authorized seizure of all enemy-owned property. President Woodrow Wilson appointed former congressman A. Mitchell Palmer as alien property custodian. In effect, Palmer headed a vast, quasi-governmental trust company that functioned both as an investigative agency and as a court of equity. As alien property custodian, Palmer was empowered to seize

September 1917. An eight-horse team hauls the first primary crusher to the Upper Camp.

any and all enemy-owned property, materials, and securities in the United States, then dispose of them in a manner that furthered the national wartime interests. Most properties and securities were initially exchanged for war bonds, the primary source of war funding.

In October 1917, Palmer ordered all enemy-owned property and interests to be fully declared and registered within three months. The flood of declarations that poured into his office represented alien property worth hundreds of millions of dollars, and included a Connecticut chocolate factory, a Chicago brewery, Florida lumber mills, and even the investments of Countess Szechenyi—the former Gloria Vanderbilt—which alone amounted to $9 million.

Palmer had two special targets: southern cotton production, and metal mining and milling in both the United States and Mexico. The war presented a fine opportunity to destroy, once and for all, that powerful and troublesome German metals cartel led by Metallgesellschaft. In the Western Hemisphere, Metallgesellschaft's strength rested in three companies: Beer, Sondheimer & Co., Inc.; L. Vogelstein & Co.; and The American Metal Company, Ltd.

The American Metal Company was by far the most American-ized; its directors were all American citizens, and Metallgesellschaft currently controlled only 47 percent of the stock. The Metal Company filed its required declaration in December. On December 16, 1917, *The New York Times* reported the company was in full compliance with the alien property regulations:

SEQUESTERED METAL COMPANY STOCK

A matter of interest to the metal trade lies in the sequestration with the Government Alien Property Custodian of the minority stock of the American Metal Company. The action has followed mechanically the Federal decision to hold enemy property during the war. The stock in question is owned largely by the Metallbank and the Metallurgische Gesellschaft of Frankfurt, Germany, but the control both of the company's stock and management is in this country. Rumors heard of late that the concern would be managed by the government have no foundation, as far as can be learned, and the business will be conducted as it has since the war began. . . .

Palmer sequestered the German-owned 47 percent of The American Metal Company stock, returning an equal value of Liberty War Bonds. Alien property custodian agents investigated the directors, approved each, and permitted them to continue managing the now officially "Americanized" company.

The two other companies of the Metallgesellschaft triumvirate were not as cooperative. Beer, Sondheimer & Co. and L. Vogelstein & Co. both delayed compliance until Palmer charged them with attempting to "camouflage" German ownership. Palmer finally seized their German-owned shares in March 1918 and replaced five German directors with American citizens.

The alien property actions never affected Climax Syndicate operations; nor, contrary to rumor, was the federal government concerned about disposal of the future molybdenite concentrate. Every pound would be shipped by rail to the Electric Reduction Company in Pittsburgh. After conversion to alloy-ready forms, the government would direct allocation to U.S. steel companies and other Allied armament producers, based upon war production requirements.

As The American Metal Company filed its alien property declaration in New York, the three companies competing for control of Bartlett Mountain were busy filing lawsuits, for the wave of theft, threats, and violence had escalated to blatant claim jumping. The five Leal claims and the Denver Number Two were the only patented lode claims on Bartlett Mountain. The unpatented claims, which now numbered about 150, were a hopelessly confused jumble of unsurveyed or poorly surveyed, superimposed, or already adversed claims that represented a bonanza for local lawyers.

Most claim jumpers simply tore down posts and markers, or "shinplastered" them with new notifications pasted atop the originals. The claim jumpers respected nothing; they even shinplastered all three of Charles Senter's thirty-eight-year-old Gold Reef claims, the first claims ever staked on the upper part of Bartlett Mountain and recognized by surveyors as uncontested reference points. Plaintiffs filed a lengthy succession of lawsuits in the Summit County Court at Breckenridge. The *Summit County Journal* carried weekly reports of court proceedings, such as this item, which appeared on October 10, 1917:

SENTER WINS OUT OVER LEAL AND ASSOCIATES
Is by Verdict of Jury Given Possession of
Valuable Claims He Located Years Ago

The suit of Charles J. Senter vs. Ed. H. Leal went to the jury . . . and the verdict was in favor of the plaintiff.

The suit involved some hair-trigger rulings on matters of mining law on the part of the court. Chief among them was one by which the defendant was barred under his pleadings from introducing testimony calculated to prove that Senter, during the years following location of his mining claims involved, had failed to perform the assessment work required by law. . . . Thus the case was narrowed down to the question of whether or not Mr. Senter's location and record of the Gold Reef and the Gold Reef No. 2 and 3 lodes were valid ones in the first place. . . the case will go to the Supreme Court.

The lawsuits contested water rights, water diversion, fulfillment of assessment requirements, purported trespassing, and, most often, the legal right of claim owners or part owners to enter into complicated lease and option agreements. This item appeared in the *Summit County Journal* on December 15, 1917:

> . . . the most interesting case to be called was that of Chas. J. Senter and the Pingrey Mines Company vs. John Buffehr and the Mineral Lands and Finance Company, defendants. It was a case to determine which company held the legal right to a bond and lease on some molybdenite claims at Climax. After considerable testimony and some very brilliant addresses by the attorneys, the case was decided in favor of the plaintiffs, who were given possession of the disputed property.

Otis Archie King did well in court, winning each of the dozen cases he was involved in. But the endless legal battles drained his time, energy, and, most of all, money. King needed substantial backing quickly, and in mid-December it seemed he had found it when a group of unusually distinguished prospective investors arrived at Leadville on a special Colorado Midland Railroad train, then rode the Colorado & Southern narrow-gauge to Climax. They included some of the most prominent mining and railroad men in the country: A. E. Carlton, president of the Colorado Midland; Spencer Penrose, the Cripple Creek gold-mining magnate; C. M. McNeill, who was turning Utah's Bingham Canyon copper deposit into a huge open pit mine; and H. H. Hopkins, head of Dominion Molybdenite of Canada, that nation's largest molybdenum producer. On December 22, 1917, the *Carbonate Chronicle* described the train as "The One Hundred Million Dollar Special," in reference to what its passengers were purportedly worth.

DISTINGUISHED PARTY OF FINANCIERS
MADE INSPECTION OF MOLYBDENUM FIELDS—
PRESIDENT OF CANADIAN COMPANY INTERESTED

". . . The properties at Climax look good," Carlton said. "We tramped all over the mountains out there and it appeared that ore was everywhere. We did not have time to make a careful inspection, but, judging from the places we visited with Mr. King, there were wonderful deposits in control of the Pingrey Company."

This was one of the most distinguished parties of mining men and financiers which has visited Leadville in many months. The fact that the members of it made their visit here with the special aim of inspecting the molybdenum properties recently opened up in the Climax district, indicates the importance now being attached to this field of mining.

As King worked desperately to raise capital, Climax took on the look of a rough community. A one-room schoolhouse opened in January 1918. The first teacher, Eva Miller, of Kokomo, instructed children from all three competing camps. The four-story, 250-ton-per-day Climax mill, by far the biggest structure on Fremont Pass, was nearly completed. With more than 300 men working on Fremont Pass, tiny Williams' Store, just across the Colorado & Southern tracks from the Climax General Office Building, added an extra room to handle its booming business.

Climax now had an official United States Post Office, with May King, of Kokomo, as the first postmistress. The Climax Post Office was actually one of five post offices along a five-mile-section of the Colorado & Southern. The United States Post Office Department justified the unusual number by citing the "rugged terrain and deep snow that makes it impossible to get mail between the various big companies working in the district." The string of post offices began at Wortman, a mile and a half south of Fremont Pass, and included Climax at the summit, then Buffehr's Spur and Frawley, and ended with Kokomo farther north in the Tenmile Valley.

Although a schoolroom and post offices lent a peaceful community facade to Fremont Pass, relations between the competing camps grew uglier than ever. Fistfights occurred daily, and armed guards patrolled the supply yards. When some of Jack White's men met Otis Archie King on a narrow trail near the mines, they promptly pitched him bodily down the steep slope. Fortunately, he landed in a deep snowdrift, unhurt—but fed up. King immediately recruited the services of a notorious Leadville hired gun, then returned to the claim he had literally been thrown off, encountering some of John Buffehr's men working an open cut. In *Gray Gold*, King recalled the words of his "hired hand" as he calmly leveled two Colt .45s at the workers: "Boys, I think it's a disgrace to work; I intend to work here myself, but I don't want anybody lookin' on, so get th' hell outa here and be damn quick about it."

The violence soon tapered off, not because of King's hired gun, but because the men in the three camps learned what it was like to work through the winter atop Fremont Pass. With the Leadville-Climax road blocked by snow since mid-December, the camps relied entirely on continuing operation of the Colorado & Southern Railroad for vital supplies of food and coal. But in mid-January 1918, a three-day succession of blizzards dropped four feet of snow; howling winds piled it into ten-foot-high drifts that blocked the railroad for four days. Food and fuel supplies had become critically low before three smoke-belching locomotives from Leadville finally forced a steam-powered rotary snowplow through to Climax, an event reported by the Leadville *Herald Democrat.*

BUCKED ITS WAY THROUGH DRIFTS
C&S TRAIN REACHES HERE IN AFTERNOON AFTER BEING ON
ITS WAY SINCE WEDNESDAY—RECORD BREAKING BLIZZARD
. . . Mining work in the new molybdenum camps at Climax and Buffehr's Spur came practically to a standstill this week, the workmen being unable to work in the face of the blizzard. It is largely to accommodate the men of these camps, and take them their provisions, that the C&S is making a determined effort to run its passenger train every day.

Four days of continuous heavy snow followed by flurries, exceptionally high winds, and biting zero temperatures have made railroading on this narrow gauge mountain system decidedly difficult this week. The blizzard was still raging on Fremont Pass yesterday . . . blistering winds prevented teamsters from seeing a foot ahead of them.

As blizzards howled atop Fremont Pass, the Climax Syndicate formally incorporated as the Climax Molybdenum Company, with headquarters in a single room on The American Metal Company floor of 61 Broadway in New York. Since the new corporation shared common directors, officers, shareholders, and management with The American Metal Company, it was often assumed to be a Metal Company subsidiary. Actually, the Climax Molybdenum Company was a fully independent company with 10 percent of its stock held by The American Metal Company.

During the six months preceding the railroad blockage of January 1918, Climax general superintendent Jack White had taken receipt of 800 Colorado & Southern railcar loads of equipment and construction materials. With the mine and mill ready, White impatiently awaited arrival of the final parts needed to make the aerial tramway operational. Continuing railroad snow blockages in South Park delayed the arrival of the parts until February 16. Finally, on February 23, 1918, the mine, mill, and aerial tramway began coordinated operations. The *Summit County Journal* reported the start-up:

AMERICAN METALS COMPANY MOLYBDENUM MILL
AT CLIMAX NOW IN OPERATION—THE BIGGEST ENTERPRISE
IN SUMMIT COUNTY NOW BUSY TURNING OUT
CONCENTRATE FOR THE U.S. GOVERNMENT

The first 250-ton unit of the big mill of the Climax Molybdenum Company, a subsidiary of the American Metal Company, commenced operations this week, and is now running in good order and molybdenum concentrates are being made for the first time on a large scale in Summit County. . . .

Mr. White stated that the entire output of the mill is to go to the United States government for the manufacture of molybdenum steel which is rapidly becoming essential in the production of war materials and munitions. The company is making every effort to maintain a maximum capacity of their mill, in order that this source of their molybdenum may be available for the government and the allied nations. . . .

. . . Near the mill a new bunkhouse equipped with steam heat, hot and cold water, baths and modern plumbing has been erected to provide living and sleeping quarters for sixty men. A number of cottages will be put up to accommodate married men in the employ of the company who will want to spend months at the property. A large four-room office building has been completed as a main office and sleeping quarters for the office staff. A commissary building has been added and is now stocked with a large supply of commodities which the company employees and other people at Climax may purchase. A new laboratory is being completed.

. . . Around the little narrow gauge box that formerly marked the siding at Climax, and was a joke to all the passengers as to being a dreary and dismal place, an extensive and very modern cluster of buildings have sprung up, giving the appearance of a bustling mining camp. . . . It is in reality situated at the top of the world. Located at the climax of the Continental Divide, what promises to be a very important part of Summit County has grown up overnight.

With all these operations on Bartlett Mountain, we may look forward to the day when one of the largest cities between Denver and Salt Lake will be located in Summit County. Bartlett Mountain is today the scene of the greatest mining activity ever known in Summit County, and the huge old mountain presents a very inspiring sight at night all lighted up with electric lights from the large mills to the very crest of the peaks.

Although the Leal Tunnel was never designed for production, it provided quick, cheap access to the ore body. Mine superintendent

53

James Welsh widened the narrow tunnel, graded the floor for ties and thirty-pound rail, and prepared for "glory hole" mining just 200 feet from the portal. Mine crews drove short drifts parallel to and just 40 feet from the surface contours, drove raises upward to the surface, then blasted out the pillars between them. The collapsed ore fell into the lower drifts, ready for handmucking into one-ton ore cars.

Meanwhile, deeper in the mountain, miners drove a series of parallel haulage drifts, each 50 feet apart and 860 feet long, that ran diagonally across all five Leal claims. Then they drove stope raises 30 feet apart, widened them into cone-shaped pockets, and fitted each with steel grizzly bars and chutes. Finally, the miners further widened the pockets until they connected into long stopes ready for shrinkage stope and chute-and-grizzly mining. A 40-foot-thick pillar left between each stope provided space to drive raises to accommodate manway ladders and service lines for the drills. Ore mined in the stopes fell by gravity through the grizzlies and into the chutes for gate-controlled loading into ore cars. Mules hauled the loaded ore cars to the portal.

A 700-foot-long "Little Tram," slinging two half-ton-capacity ore buckets, conveyed the ore from the Leal Tunnel portal to the Upper Camp 250 feet below, where a crusher reduced it to minus three inches. A 400-ton-capacity holding bin stored the crushed ore, then chuted it into the buckets of the "Big Tram," a 4,730-foot-long, jig-back, Leschen aerial tramway, which suspended thirty-eight half-ton-capacity buckets from heavy 1.25-inch cable. The Big Tram conveyed the ore down a vertical descent of 600 feet to the mill at the Lower Camp. When winter snowdrifts blocked the camp road, the Big Tram was the only connection with the Upper Camp. State mine inspectors turned their backs when miners used the Big Tram's swaying buckets to transport mail, food, dynamite, blasting caps—and themselves—to the Upper Camp.

Mill hands ran the ore through a secondary crusher, ground it in a six-by-six-foot Allis Chalmers ball mill, then routed it through a Dorr classifier that separated the fines by overflow and sent the coarser sands back to a regrind mill. Then they piped the fines into nine air-mechanical flotation tanks, mixed them with a flotation reagent, and agitated the slurry with impellers while releasing compressed air from the bottom of the tanks. Most of the oiled molybdenite particles floated as a gray froth for overflow recovery.

March 1918. Engineers and surveyors prepare to assist in development of the Big Tunnel. Marvin Kleff, surveyor, on left; Jack White, general superintendent, on right.

Since the ore contained three times as much pyrite as molybdenite, it was critical to determine the best type of flotation agent, pH level, and degree of both mechanical and pneumatic agitation needed to float off the maximum amount of molybdenite, while still dropping the pyrite. By mid-March, engineers coaxed both the recovery and concentration grades above 70 percent. On the infrequent days when all went well, the Climax mill recovered, dried, filtered, and packed about two tons of molybdenite concentrate.

Mine superintendent James Welsh already had miners at work developing a second, bigger haulage tunnel. At an elevation of 11,935 feet, 210 feet below the Leal Tunnel, the "Big Tunnel" portal was conveniently located right at the Upper Camp. Welsh planned two raises: One would be an ore pass, permitting Leal Tunnel ore to drop into the Big Tunnel and be hauled directly to the crusher, thus eliminating need for the Little Tram; the other would be an internal, two-compartment shaft for men and material, which would eliminate

Spring 1918. Development of the Big Tunnel, a double-tracked haulage tunnel.

use of the steep, exposed, icy trail that Leal Tunnel miners climbed before and after each shift.

Development of the Big Tunnel was routine, except for one thing that surprised geologists—the Big Tunnel did not pass through any molybdenite ore. That concerned no one, for the Big Tunnel was to serve only as a haulage tunnel for the Leal Level ore, of which there was plenty.

The Climax Mine shipped its first concentrate on April 2, 1918. The twenty-five tons of 70 percent molybdenite concentrate, containing 21,000 pounds of metallic molybdenum, filled two special Colorado & Southern railcars. At the market price, now $5.00 per pound, the shipment was valued at $100,000. Four armed Pinkerton guards accompanied the two cars all the way to Pittsburgh. Leadville's *Herald Democrat* reported the historic shipment in banner headlines.

MOUNTAIN OF METAL HERE THAT WILL WIN THE WAR!
MOLYBDENUM DEPOSITS OF BARTLETT MOUNTAIN
LARGEST IN WORLD

56

Not to be outdone, especially since the Climax Mine was part of Summit County, the *Summit County Journal* headline read:

TREASURE VAULT NOW REVEALED!
ONE OF COLORADO'S GREATEST MINING ESTABLISHMENTS
NOW FIRMLY ESTABLISHED AT CLIMAX—
FIRST SHIPMENT VALUED AT $100,000

General superintendent Jack White didn't witness the first ship- ment, having already left for a badly needed vacation in Nevada. White had put in sixteen-hour days battling avalanches, bitter winter weather, a high labor turnover, and experimental mill problems, yet managed to turn 800 rail freight loads of material into a producing mine and mill in the remarkably short time of seven months. In the process, White had elicited both fear and respect from his men. Otis Archie King described him as "hard as nails," and White himself often said that he was paid "to make mines, not friends." In recog- nition of Jack White's effort, Max Schott formally renamed the Big Tunnel in his honor—the White Tunnel.

1918. Leal Level ore being loaded into ore cars on the White Level.

From the beginning, Climax was unlike other mines in Summit and Lake counties, which relied upon a single nearby community for food, services, transportation, supplies, ore treatment, and housing. Climax was independent and largely self-sufficient; the Colorado & Southern hauled supplies in and hauled concentrate out, and Climax had its own school, store, and mill, and was even building its own housing. Summit County, of course, collected substantial property taxes, but gained few additional benefits. But as combined camp employment neared 400 and the monthly payrolls topped $15,000, both Summit and Lake counties became interested in where most of those payroll dollars would be spent.

Climax was located forty miles from Breckenridge and thirteen miles from Leadville on the Leadville-Breckenridge road, a poorly graded and essentially unmaintained dirt track that avalanches, snow-drifts, and washouts blocked for about six months of the year. The payroll dollars would obviously fall to whichever county improved and maintained its section of the road. If one county improved its road, the other would be economically compelled to do the same. Accordingly, the commissioners of Summit and Lake counties met jointly in October 1917 and agreed to improve their respective road sections. The first step was to jointly resurvey the county line to accurately determine each county's road improvement respon-sibilities.

The Lake-Summit county boundary had been established in 1881 as a line running due west from a point with a somewhat confusing statutory description. The point in question was located on the "Great Snowy Range," an outdated term for the Continental Divide, and was further defined as "the northwest corner of Park County." The vague statutory description actually suited two different points, and thus made possible two different county lines. One line bisected Buffehr's Lake, one mile north of the Fremont Pass summit; the other crossed well south of the pass. Long aware of the statutory discrepancy, the county fathers had once suggested a "compromise line" crossing the summit of Fremont Pass.

But with nothing of apparent value at Fremont Pass, no one really cared in 1881 or in the decades that followed where the county line was. Besides, if Park County considered its "northwest corner" to be 13,771-foot-high McNamee Peak, the highest point on the eastern end of Ceresco Ridge, that was good enough for Summit and Lake

58

counties. A line extended west from that point placed most of Ceresco Ridge and all of Bartlett Mountain and Fremont Pass clearly in Summit County, and the matter was forgotten for thirty-six years.

The joint resurvey, conducted in October 1917, actually adjusted the line one-eighth of a mile farther south. That was fine with the Lake County commissioners, for the boundary adjustment made Summit County responsible for improving both Fremont Pass grades, the steepest and most expensive sections to build and maintain along the entire Leadville-Breckenridge road. Lake County might spend as little as $4,000 on road improvement, and still have the closest city to lure most of the Climax payroll dollars. And as one Lake County commissioner emphasized, since Summit County collected the Climax property taxes, it was only right that it foot most of the road improvement expense.

Residents of both counties considered the resurvey a mere technicality that warranted little interest, with one exception—Otis Archie King. King studied the resurvey closely, realizing that a new county line might give him a huge advantage in his legal battles for possession of claims on Bartlett Mountain and Ceresco Ridge. King had to move quickly, for when the six-month period to publicly question or contest the resurvey expired in spring 1918, the new county line would become legal forevermore.

On the morning of March 16, 1918, King and Charles Senter stood first in line when the Lake County Courthouse opened for business. Before the Lake County Clerk's office closed that day, they re-recorded every claim they had on Ceresco Ridge and Bartlett Mountain, twenty-two in all, including Senter's original Gold Reef claims.

King had just enough time to make his next appointment, a meeting of the Lake County commissioners. In front of a large crowd, King delivered a compelling speech explaining how the resurvey represented an extraordinary property tax opportunity for Lake County. In fact, King went on, jabbing a finger in the air for emphasis, Lake County might suffer a "serious injustice" should the present county line stand. Furthermore, the commissioners were morally and legally bound to act immediately and decisively for the good of Lake County.

Knowing he had his audience spellbound, King then launched into an exposé of the illegal wheelings and dealings of certain companies at Fremont Pass, concluding with an interesting "fact" that concerned him greatly: One of the companies working at Fremont Pass had ties to the enemy—Germany.

King's speech had its desired effect, as shown in the headline article of the *Herald Democrat* on March 18:

BOUNDARY LINE IN DOUBT BETWEEN SUMMIT AND LAKE
SURVEY MADE LAST SUMMER TO ESTABLISH LINE
NOT CONSIDERED SATISFACTORY, AND SUIT MAY BE BROT TO
SECURE JUDICIAL DETERMINATION OF QUESTION—
WHERE ARE THE MOLYBDENUM DEPOSITS LOCATED?
COUNTY BOARD TO TAKE ACTION AT ONCE

Lake County is decidedly the loser by the new survey if it is allowed to stand, for a large part of the new molybdenum field now being opened in the Climax district would be ascribed to Summit County, in which the mining properties of that region would then pay taxes. . . .

There has been some gossip to the effect that competition between the molybdenum properties in the Climax district is leading one company to dispute the boundary question in an effort to hinder the operations of the other.

Efforts on the part of various individuals to inject molybdenum company disputes into the Lake-Summit boundary question, now raised to high heat by the disclosures of the past week, brought warm protest last night from citizens who see in the subject only one point of interest for the majority of Lake County residents. That point is this: Lake County is entitled to their hearing in court on any changes in the boundary, regardless of all claims entered by interested companies.

. . . claims located by the two companies were by location, necessitating filing of location certificates in the counties in which the properties lie. Priority of filing governs in location cases.

If one company should have filed in Lake County and the boundary had been changed, so that its location would fall in Summit County, or vice versa, the boundary question becomes of paramount interest to the companies involved. . . .

All sorts of allegations, including "German propaganda," and other matters alleged to be camouflage by citizens, were thrown into the controversy. . . .

Thousands of dollars of taxes for Lake County are involved in the question, providing the molybdenum companies become steady producers, as it is now predicted. It has been estimated that there is enough molybdenum on Bartlett Mountain to produce 1,000 tons of ore per day for 25 years.

Mr. King alleged that shin plastering of claims occurred on the Gold Reef, on which the Pingrey company did assessment work. . . . In the following November after the American company, he alleged, had filed on part of the same ground by locating the Harris claim, J. H. White, superintendent of the company, ordered him and a Colo-

One of the certificates for Charles Senter's Gold Reef claims filed in Lake County in March 1918, as part of Otis Archie King's attempt to "jump" his competition by relocating the claims in the anticipated new county of record.

rado Springs man off the property at the point of a gun. . . . He said that the dispute between the two concerns is "somewhat bitter". . . .

Mr. King declared the American company is largely owned—to about forty percent—in Frankfort, Germany, and that a chart in the January issue of Mining and Scientific Journal shows the connection between it and its operations in the Climax district. He also showed a clipping in which it was alleged that A. Mitchell Palmer, custodian of alien property for the government, had taken over the German-owned shares of the company in this country. . . .

The morning after that issue hit the Leadville streets, another line waited for the Lake County Courthouse to open. In it were Hugh Leal, Ed Heckendorf, John Harris, Dennis Haley, and Harry Brown, the latter two representing the Climax Molybdenum Company, along with nine other prospectors and speculators. Within the next four days, the Lake County Clerk dutifully re-recorded 149 additional lode claims on Ceresco Ridge and Bartlett Mountain. But King had jumped everyone: If the county line was to be moved north, King had gained filing priority in the new county of record.

Meanwhile, Lake County citizens and commissioners hotly debated whether or not to file a lawsuit to "claim" Climax. Proponents spoke of gaining both property taxes and the prestige of adding Climax mineral production figures to Lake County's already impressive totals. Opponents pointed to Lake County's poor record in previous intercounty lawsuits and to the estimated legal cost of $5,000, adding that the county didn't have that kind of money to "throw away to lawyers" over some metal most people still couldn't pronounce.

With time running out, the Lake County commissioners decided to proceed with a lawsuit in state court to move the county line one and one-eighth miles north. The commissioners emphasized that this "friendly" suit was not intended to offend the "wonderful folks" in Summit County. On March 23, 1918, the *Summit County Journal* reported that the wonderful folks of that county were indeed offended:

LAKE-SUMMIT BOUNDARY IN COURTS
COUNTY COMMISSIONERS OF LAKE COUNTY
HAVE FILED SUIT AGAINST SUMMIT COUNTY

Last Monday night the Lake County Board of Commissioners decided to start suit against Summit County over the boundary line established by joint survey last summer. This survey was made because of the fact that the definite boundary between Lake and Summit Counties had never been staked out, although the law seemed plain in the matter. The survey was supposed to be friendly . . . Summit gained a strip of territory about an eighth of a mile wide and a couple of miles long. When we say gained, we only meant that Summit County came into its rightful ownership, as the taxes from this strip, like every possible tax such as sheep taxes, etc., have been grabbed by Lake County up to the present time, because the People of Summit County were peace loving, and did not stir anything up even when it was her own right. This time however things have changed and the People of Summit will fight to gain its own rights, and a few cheap lawyers and surveyors who have been looking for a haul out of this, but stirring it up against the wishes of the majority of residents of Lake County, will look at two cents when this case is finished, and they will have succeeded in fleecing the taxpayers out of fees, that no one else in the district would have given them interest on, for a lifetime of service.

. . . the main dispute is not over the boundary line. It is a fight between the companies at Climax, and the taxpayers are going to be the goat to settle the bills. Mr. McNeill [Lake County surveyor] also says that German propaganda has been brought into the matter.

. . . Summit County is going as a unit and will fight to the finish.

By April 1918, when the "County Line War" was just beginning, the United States had been at war in Europe for one year. To fund the war effort, the federal government pushed the sale of Liberty War Bonds harder than ever, assigning every county in the nation a sales quota based on population. Fulfilling war-bond quotas became a matter of civic and patriotic pride.

Summit County, which still included Climax until the courts said otherwise, had a bond quota of $24,600. Concerned about the growing "German connection" rumors, Max Schott and Jack White thought it might be wise to use the bond drive to make a clear patriotic statement. In other words, Climax Mine employees were going to buy more war bonds than any outfit in Summit County. White made the rounds of the mine and mill, covering all shifts, taking each man aside and expressing his deep concern for "our boys" fighting on the battlefields of Europe. Looking each man squarely in the eye, White explained how it would be "a real good idea" if that man were to

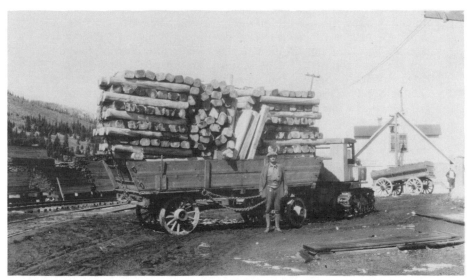

1918. A tractor-towed wagon load of timbers bound for the White Tunnel.

personally support the war-bond drive. And doing so would be no trouble at all, for White had thoughtfully arranged a convenient direct payroll-deduction plan.

When the ladies of the Summit County Liberty Bond Committee visited Climax on April 18, their splendid reception earned a front-page article in the *Summit County Journal:*

CLIMAX CAMP MAKES GOOD IN LOAN DRIVE
PUTS COUNTY FAR OVER QUOTA

On the visit the ladies found the subject already well agitated and the field well prepared by different officials, superintendents and foremen, for a whirlwind campaign. Bright and early the ladies were taken to the mine, 12,017 feet in altitude, taken through by Mr. Welsh to every place where a man was stationed at work, then back to the lunch room at 11:30, and the result was subscriptions amounting to $2,500 that were written 300 feet in the mine. At noon, the party returned to the boarding house, met about 100 men at their dinner, and explained the payments, necessities and advantages of purchasing, meeting with a liberal response, and enjoying an especially good dinner. Later in the afternoon they journeyed to the mill where Mr. G. O. Anderson [mill foreman] had already secured a number of promises for them, and who very kindly showed them the mill and explained the process to them, taking them over to the bunk house, where there were more prospective buyers, then back to the office for a very excellent supper at the lower boarding house. The results of the trip to this particular plant show $6,500 in subscriptions. . . . The ladies are extremely enthusiastic in their praise of the camp, the officials and the employees, the wonders of the plant, the patriotism of everyone, and the excellent work done by both committeemen, Mr. [Harry] Brown and Mr. Bart King [mine foreman]. They claim they couldn't have had any more comfort in the city of New York and are positive they couldn't have enjoyed themselves half as much in the metropolis as they did selling bonds at the top of the world.

Mr. Bart King very kindly took the ladies over to the adjoining camp of the Pingrey Mines Company where Mr. Backus, the superintendent, had assembled about ten of the employees, from which number they secured subscriptions from seven employees amounting to $200. . . . They also journeyed a mile and a half down the C&S track to Buffehrs where the Molybdenum Products company is located but were unable to do any business.

As Jack White knew it would be, the war-bond drive was an overwhelming success. The Climax Mine subscribed for $15,500, which, together with the $6,500 from its employees, accounted for 87 percent of the entire Summit County war-bond quota. At the

Climax station, Jack White graciously thanked the ladies for visiting and expressed profound disappointment that the other camps hadn't cooperated quite as enthusiastically. As his men doubtlessly commented when their general superintendent was out of earshot, Jack White might not make many friends, but he sure could make mines and war-bond quotas.

The ladies of the Summit County Liberty Bond Committee had been the first women to enter the Climax underground, and not all of the Climax miners liked it. Wary of the old miners' superstition that women in the underground brought bad luck, two Climax miners quit.

Meanwhile, the Molybdenum Products Company began production, mining ore on its single claim, the Denver Number Two, from a 600-foot-long tunnel with short crosscuts and 12-foot-wide stopes. A 7,430-foot-long Leschen aerial tramway, the longest ever built in the United States, conveyed ore down to the mill at Buffehr's Spur. The Molybdenum Products Company milled ore by a "company-controlled, secret process," which every miner in the district knew was a four-cell flotation system using an alkaline, pine-oil flotation reagent

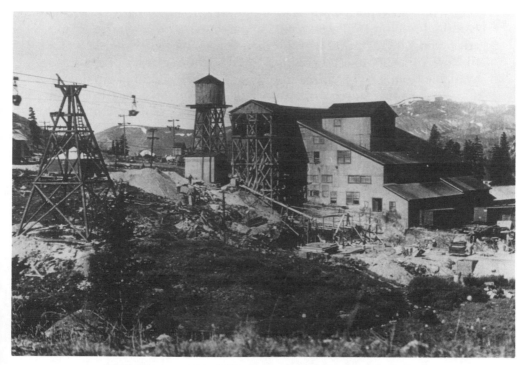

1918. The completed Climax mill and tramway terminal.

designed to produce concentrates grading as high as 95 percent. But mill operation was a different story. A month of mill tests in April produced only two tons of concentrate of very poor grade.

Things went much better at the Climax mill, where overall recovery reached 75 percent and concentrate grades neared 80 percent. Climax made its second shipment of fifty tons on April 30, 1918, then began a regular shipping schedule of three twenty-five-ton lots each month.

Newspapers widely publicized the value of the second Climax shipment as "over $200,000," a very substantial sum in 1918 dollars. Hopeful prospectors considered molybdenum a bona fide "bonanza" metal, and as the snows left the high country, they scoured the Colorado Rockies for new deposits. Throughout the summer, they made "strikes" almost weekly; although all were trace occurrences or small deposits, local newspapers heralded many as "the next Bartlett Mountain."

In June 1918, Otis Archie King nervously awaited the decision that would determine his success or failure. His prospective investors who had visited Climax in December 1917, aboard the "One Hundred Million Dollar Special," had formed a loose syndicate and advanced King $70,000 to continue his legal battles. Now they met in New York City to study the best molybdenum-market projections available from government and industry before making a final decision. But things started off badly, for the War Minerals Board in Washington refused to even speculate on the future of molybdenum.

Meanwhile, A. E. Carlton met personally with Henry Ford in Detroit to ascertain his interest in molybdenum steels. When Carlton returned to New York, he brought bad news: Ford, doubting molybdenum's future, would use high-grade carbon steels for his high-stress automotive components. Ford believed that molybdenum's place in American industry was still twenty years down the line. Carlton, for his part, didn't have twenty years to wait. He pulled out, and the pending deal with Otis Archie King collapsed.

Heartsick, King returned to Denver, where he unexpectedly found a last glimmer of hope. The E. J. Longyear Engineering Company, which backed the Molybdenum Products Company, wished to immediately discuss a possible merger of interests on Bartlett Mountain.

1918. The first Climax packing plant packed and shipped molybdenite concentrate in numbered canvas sacks.

As Otis Archie King headed for Minneapolis for what he knew was his last shot, Jack White orchestrated another flag-waving display of patriotism to bury any remaining "German connection" rumors—a special Fourth of July celebration. Just as the Climax general superintendent had hoped, the *Carbonate Chronicle* reported the celebration on its front page.

BIG HOLIDAY AT CLIMAX
OVER 500 PEOPLE ENJOY HOSPITALITY OF
MOLYBDENUM COMPANY—$800 WORTH OF WAR SAVINGS
STAMPS DISTRIBUTED AS PRIZES—BARBEQUE AND SPORT!

Yesterday was a red letter day for Climax. The annals of the greater Climax to come will record the day with a just pride, for the busy little mining town had made a name for itself that will live forever in the minds of the 500 or more men, women and children who enjoyed its Fourth of July hospitality. . . .

The celebration was novel in two important respects. It comprised a program of events that would speak well for any city in Colorado; and everything was free.

White openly invited everyone in Leadville and the Tenmile camps, even arranging for a special Colorado & Southern passenger train to depart Leadville at 9:00 A.M. When 300 hundred people

67

jammed onto the three coach cars, the railroad added another. But when the crowded four-coach train finally departed, 100 disappointed people were left at the Leadville station.

At Climax, crews bedecked the station and general office building with red, white, and blue bunting and dozens of fluttering American flags. Jack White, dressed, as always, in his knee-high, laced leather boots, personally greeted the arriving guests. The crowd moved first to the "athletic field," an almost-level clearing dotted with spruce stumps just east of the mill, to participate in baseball games, tug-o'-war and broad jump contests, and horse and foot races. Spectator events included competition between the mine and mill first-aid teams and mine-drilling contests, the latter drawing the biggest crowds.

With the elevation of the drilling rock precisely surveyed to 11,356 feet, Jack White declared the drilling contest the highest ever staged. To allow for the thin alpine air, the double-jacking time limit was reduced from fifteen to ten minutes. The four competing teams finished within one-half inch of each other. The winning team drilled twenty inches with the hammer and steels, a very respectable performance considering the abbreviated time limit and the thin air.

Jack White, standing tall next to an American flag, delivered a few words about "our boys" in Europe, then awarded Liberty War Savings Stamps to the contest winners. The crowd then moved to the barbecue pit, where Climax boardinghouse cooks waited with "a couple of hindquarters of veal, two mutton carcasses, and wieners enough to fill a fruit basket."

The Fourth of July was a great success at Climax, but it had not gone well for Otis Archie King. After discussing the situation at Bartlett Mountain with executives of the E. J. Longyear Engineering Company, King and the Longyear executives reached an inevitable conclusion: Merging King's Bartlett Mountain interests with those of the Molybdenum Products Company was pointless. While a merger would combine large ore reserves with an operating mill, they had no contract to sell the concentrates. Max Schott, King's arch-rival, held the only molybdenum contract existing in the United States. King had two unenviable choices: continue fighting the endless string of lawsuits, or go to Max Schott and salvage what was left.

King chose the latter. On October 3, 1918, he and Max Schott signed an agreement ending the battle for Bartlett Mountain. All lawsuits were dropped. King received a check for $200,000 and took uncontested control of all Ceresco Ridge claims, which, without a mill site or water, had little immediate value. The Climax Molybdenum Company took control of all the King-Senter claims on Bartlett Mountain, including the vital Ella N. property and its associated water rights.

The Molybdenum Products Company withdrew just weeks later. Its ore reserves were limited to a single claim, the Denver Number Two. In six months the company had produced only thirty-two tons of molybdenite concentrate with a commercially unacceptable grade of 65 percent. In mid-October, even before sales terms were finalized, the Climax Molybdenum Company took over the Denver Number Two, the long Leschen aerial tram, and the mill at Buffehr's Spur.

The withdrawals of King and the Molybdenum Products Company from Bartlett Mountain, while perhaps inevitable, were certainly accelerated by the rapidly declining fortunes of the molybdenum market. Russia had been a major foreign buyer of molybdenum, but, torn by the Bolshevik Revolution, it had signed a separate peace and withdrawn from the European war. Furthermore, the end of hostilities for the remaining participants was clearly in sight.

The snow was already deep at Fremont Pass when the Armistice of November 11, 1918, ended World War I, leaving metal analysts to

1918. The upper camps of the Climax Molybdenum Company (left) and the Molybdenum Products Company (center). Looking north toward Bartlett Mountain from Ceresco Ridge.

debate the future of the molybdenum market. Some believed that peacetime applications of molybdenum steels would actually stimulate the market; most predicted complete collapse.

At Climax, Jack White had little time to worry about molybdenum prices. He had completed his summer construction projects, but now faced a new problem—the worldwide influenza pandemic that was already wreaking havoc in nearby Leadville. Leadville's death toll soared to 223 by Christmas. Doctors feared that if influenza were to sweep through Climax, the added extremes of elevation and climate could be disastrous. White converted the mill clubhouse, a large reading and card room, into an emergency twenty-bed hospital, then cancelled school classes and turned the recently expanded two-room schoolhouse into a women's isolation ward. The one in four who showed early symptoms of influenza were confined to bed or quarters for four mandatory days of treatment. White's precautions proved remarkably effective: Although the disease ravaged many lower mountain towns, Climax reported not a single case of fully developed influenza.

During 1918, the Climax Mine produced 800 tons of molybdenite concentrate worth $1.8 million. It was already the largest mine in Colorado and, in January 1919, one of the few still operating. But the national postwar economic depression worsened daily. When base metal prices crashed after the Armistice, Leadville and most other western metal-mining districts quickly went from boom to bust.

Climax continued to fill its contract with the Electric Reduction Company, even though molybdenum prices had fallen back to $1.00 per pound. When European steel producers began dumping big stockpiles of molybdenum on the market, rumors flew that Climax couldn't continue operating much longer. In March 1919, the Electric Reduction Company, citing depressed market conditions, abruptly cancelled the remainder of its Climax contract. On March 29, the *Summit County Journal* announced the inevitable news:

CLIMAX SHUTS DOWN MINES ON THURSDAY
MOLYBDENUM MILL TO CLOSE MONDAY;
COSTS GIVEN BY OFFICIALS AS REASON

. . . "Lack of Demand for molybdenum" is given by officials at the Climax offices as the reason for the shut-down. It was stated Friday that the mine would not be "shut down tight" but "only temporarily" as it was stated that a demand for the metal was looked for at future times when the commercial value becomes more largely known. . . .

It was announced Friday the 65 to 70 men would be laid off from the force at the mine and 18 from the mill. . . .

In Leadville, where Climax payroll dollars had considerable economic impact, the *Herald Democrat* also ran a front-page story:

> . . . The immediate effect of closing the mine is not so serious as what extended idleness at the Climax workings will mean to the life of the community during the spring and summer. It was expected the molybdenum mine would be a big producer this year before the halt of hostilities in Europe knocked the bottom out of the market for molybdenum products. With the property closed for what employees say will be an indefinite period, development activities are at an end for the present and what Climax will offer in the way of employment and buying during the summer months becomes entirely uncertain. . . .
>
> It is reported here that the company intends to maintain its organization at Climax so far as the office staff and superintendents are concerned, so that activities may be resumed at any time with a minimum of delay. About six employees will be retained to keep the property in condition . . .

John H. "Jack" White resigned when the mine closed, returning to Nevada "to find another mine to develop." Max Schott appointed Robert C. Merriam as general superintendent. With no mine or mill production to tend to, Merriam spent much of his time dampening a wave of Climax-related rumors. A few Leadville residents believed that the Climax shutdown had somehow been tied to the seizure of the enemy-owned shares of The American Metal Company, which were just then being advertised for federal auction in New York City. It seemed unlikely that the big, new Climax mill would remain closed very long. Some guessed it would reopen when scientists figured out "those German alloys"; others predicted the federal government would "come in and open 'er up."

Climax shipped its last sixty tons of stockpiled molybdenum concentrate to the Electric Reduction Company in May. The shipment spurred more rumors, this time of imminent reopening. More than 100 out-of-work Leadville miners rushed "up the hill" to Fremont Pass, only to be disappointed. Two weeks later, Robert Merriam laid off his supervisors and office staff, retaining only six men as caretakers.

Ironically, although molybdenum mining at Fremont Pass had ceased, the "County Line War" it had precipitated was just coming to court. Summit County's attorneys contended that the 1861 Territorial Legislature had properly intended that the disputed line run due west from McNamee Peak; attorneys for Lake County insisted that the only point satisfying the Territorial Legislature's true intent lay farther north along the Continental Divide. Lake County surveyors identified and labeled that point on maps as "Point C." The trial opened in Leadville on September 22, 1919, with all attention focused on four specially prepared charts depicting various geographical and legal interpretations of what the Territorial Legislature had meant by "the northwest corner of Park County."

One by one, the court called expert witnesses for testimony and cross-examination. Among the more influential, and certainly entertaining, was J. M. Kleff, a Leadville surveyor who often "moonlighted" for Climax. Kleff cautioned the court not to consider any territorial precedent, for in his expert opinion the contested strip of territory had always been a "no-man's-land" that fell in neither county, a view that brought guffaws from the crowd and objections from the Summit County attorneys.

When court was adjourned, bailiffs displayed the four charts in the Lake County Courthouse lobby for the benefit of the betting public, who, amid thick cigar smoke and pointing fingers, placed wagers on the outcome of the trial. Some, of course, still criticized the folly of "throwing away five thousand good dollars on a circus over a closed-down mine."

Two weeks later, as the trial neared a conclusion, Lake County Attorney John Ewing offered what many thought was the decisive testimony. Asked to explain exactly what a "corner" was, Ewing replied, "That depends whether you mean a corner of territory or a corner of wheat," then waited for the laughter to subside before beginning his argument. Ewing believed that only one way existed for the court to properly determine what was meant by the term "northwest corner of Park County." The court must first establish the northwest quadrant of Park County by projecting and intersecting Park County's true north-south and east-west lines. Then, Ewing continued, the court must extend a northeast-southwest tangent across the northwest quadrant. The farthest point along the geographic boundary touched by the tangent would therefore represent the most northerly and westerly point in Park County. And that point, which Ewing dramatically indicated on a map, was "Point C"—exactly as the Territorial Legislature of 1861 had always intended.

On October 6, 1919, the *Carbonate Chronicle* headlined the court's decision:

COURT FINDS FOR LAKE COUNTY
NORTHWEST CORNER OF PARK COUNTY
EXACTLY WHERE STATUTORY DESCRIPTION INDICATED,
JUDGE HERSEY SAYS IN HIS DECISION

Declaring that "Point C," as shown on exhibits entered by Lake County was the only point that would satisfy the statutory descriptions of Park and Lake Counties as laid down by the territorial legislature of 1861 and subsequent legislatures which revised these statutes, Judge Henry J. Hersey of Denver, last night decided the Lake County-Summit County line in favor of Lake County.

Judge Hersey's decision brings to an end, for the time being at least, the controversy which has raged since 1917 between Lake and Summit Counties, and it gives to Lake County approximately six square miles of territory along the disputed line. This territory includes the mining camp of Climax and the rich molybdenum deposits of that district owned by the American Metal Company. . . .

Lake County was eager to assess its territorial prize, for Leadville rumors pegged the Climax valuation as high as $1.5 million. Climax attorneys quickly branded that figure as "absurd." The Lake County assessor examined the Summit County tax rolls, finding that $300,000 seemed to be a more realistic figure.

If Summit County wasn't pleased with the court's decision, neither was the Climax Molybdenum Company, for Lake County imposed a much higher mil levy. Company attorneys noted with interest that the new county line, which would soon be upheld in appeals court, ran right through the middle of the old Molybdenum Products Company mill at Buffehr's Spur. Climax attorney Barney Whatley declared that unless Lake County agreed to a more equitable tax arrangement, Climax would move its mill "lock, stock, and barrel" 200 yards north right back into Summit County. Whatley's threat somehow revived hope that the mine would reopen, even if it was in Summit County. Unemployed Leadville miners again flocked to Climax, only to find that the last six Climax employees had begun mothballing the mill for "a long shutdown."

As the winter of 1919 locked Fremont Pass in six months of ice and snow, the battles of the past few years ended. The Allies had won in Europe, the Climax Molybdenum Company had won Bartlett Mountain, and Lake County had won Climax. The German metal cartel was broken, and the federal government finally auctioned off the seized German-owned shares of The American Metal Company to Charles D. Barney & Company, a New York brokerage house, for $5.3 million.

Investors had sunk more than $1 million into Bartlett Mountain. The big loser was the Molybdenum Products Company, which sold its assets to the Climax Molybdenum Company for less than ten cents on the dollar. The Pingrey Mines & Ore Reduction Company, thanks to the efforts of Otis Archie King, actually made a little money, and would make more in the future from the Ceresco Ridge claims that it still retained.

As mining in Lake and Summit counties sank ever deeper into the postwar depression, the Colorado & Southern Railroad cut back its service over Fremont Pass to just one freight and two passenger trains each week. Climax again became a water stop where "nobody got on and nobody got off."

Faces long familiar at Fremont Pass were seen no more. When Otis Archie King took Max Schott's check for $200,000, he fulfilled the option-purchase agreement with Charles Senter for the Gold Reef claims. Senter, the old Indian fighter and prospector, took his $40,000 check and settled into a comfortable retirement in Denver. King, still a young man, also moved to Denver to resume a career in business. Max Schott, after suffering a near-fatal attack of influenza in Denver, moved into semiretirement in California. And former Nebraska banker Hugh Leal also took his retirement in California.

Hugh Leal, Ed Heckendorf, John and Sam Webber, and Dr. John Harris ended up exchanging their claims for Climax Molybdenum Company stock. Any Leadville merchant knew exactly what Climax stock was worth. When offered certificates in trade, most merchants grimaced, pushed them back across the counter, and shook their heads no—gestures that clearly indicated a dismal outlook for the Climax Molybdenum Company.

4
The "Anti-Climax" Molybdenum Company 1920-1928

So, Phillipson, is anything good—or anything at all—happening at Freeload Pass?

—A director of the
Climax Molybdenum Company
to Brainerd Phillipson, 1926

In 1920, the Climax Molybdenum Company consisted of a president, a board of directors, a secretary, and an office in the headquarters of The American Metal Company, Ltd., in New York City. Its assets included a huge low-grade molybdenite deposit in Bartlett Mountain, a mothballed mine and mill, and 125 tons of molybdenite concentrate. On the other side of the ledger, the company had a million-dollar debt, not a single customer, and little hope of finding one in the foreseeable future.

The future of the Climax Molybdenum Company, if indeed it had one, rested solely upon one man, Brainerd F. Phillipson. Phillipson had earned a chemical engineering degree in 1913, after a distinguished academic and athletic career at New York's Columbia University. In 1916, when Max Schott took his first look at Bartlett Mountain, Phillipson was a salesman in the Ore Department of The American Metal Company at the New York headquarters, a position from which he closely followed developments at Climax while familiarizing himself with molybdenum.

Phillipson's interest in the metal persisted, even after the Armistice and subsequent collapse of the molybdenum market. He saw

1920. A panoramic winter view of the Upper Camp and Lower Camp from the portal of the Leal Tunnel.

Brainerd Phillipson, president of the Climax Molybdenum Company from 1919 until 1930.

an opportunity to become more closely involved with the metal when Henry Bruére, the first president of the Climax Molybdenum Company, resigned in January 1919. He asked for the office and his approval was a mere formality, for no other candidates had announced any desire to captain what most believed was a sinking ship.

Phillipson had unbounded faith in molybdenum's future, believing that if he could develop or demonstrate peacetime industrial uses for the metal, demand would surely grow. He had few precedents to follow, for, historically, mining companies did not create markets, but simply supplied existing markets. Two major problems confronted Phillipson: First, the conservative American steel industry was content working with such standard alloying metals as tungsten, vanadium, chromium, manganese, and nickel; second, his directors had no intention whatever to fund a major in-house metallurgical research program.

Phillipson began work with the only material resource at his command—the 125 tons of molybdenite concentrate sitting in dusty barrels in a Pittsburgh warehouse. He offered the concentrate—free—to any American steel company willing to experiment with it.

Then Phillipson began sculpting the image of molybdenum as a uniquely American metal. Foreign mines supplied all other alloying metals; only molybdenum was available from a secure domestic source—the "mountain of molybdenum," as he referred to Bartlett Mountain. In Phillipson's mind, the Bartlett Mountain deposit was so large that he would eventually be able to guarantee unlimited supplies at the lowest possible price.

Finally, the young president of the Climax Molybdenum Company associated molybdenum and its steel alloys with victory in World War I and the military uses that had most captured the public's attention, namely the tough armor plate of the Renault "baby" tanks and the high-stress components of the already-legendary NC-4 Liberty aircraft engine.

When steel producers showed little interest in molybdenum, Phillipson turned directly to the American automotive industry. But Henry Ford again turned down molybdenum in favor of his carbon steel alloys. After several other rejections, Phillipson made the acquaintance of an automotive engineer named C. Harold Wills.

Childe Harold Wills, a close associate of Henry Ford since 1902, had been instrumental in developing the phenomenally successful

*Arthur Storke (left)
and John H. "Jack" White
at the Matchless Mine in
Leadville, June 1920.
White had returned for a
visit after the Climax Mine
had been shut down.*

Ford Model T. But by 1919, Wills felt his engineering creativity and
freedom stifled. He resigned, cashed in his Ford stock for $1.6 mil-
lion, and set out to design and manufacture his own automobile.
Taking some Ford engineers along with him, he founded C. H. Wills
& Company and built a modern assembly plant at Marysville, Michigan, to assemble advanced luxury automobiles. Unlike Ford vehicles,
which achieved durability through weight and mass of carbon steels,
Wills demanded newer alloys that would provide the same durability
with less weight, thus opening the door to better performance and
fuel economy. And the alloy Wills wanted was molybdenum steel.

Production of the Wills Sainte Claire Model A-68, popularly known
as the "Gray Goose," began in spring 1921. Every component of the
engine, power train, frame, and suspension system subject to even
minimal stress consisted of molybdenum steel. The Gray Goose, a
superb balance of beauty, style, performance, and advanced engineering, immediately captured the public's attention. Unfortunately,

that was all it captured, for its $3,000 price tag made it affordable only to the wealthy.

Brainerd Phillipson, meanwhile, formulated a direct advertising campaign, another metal-marketing innovation. His first poster-type ad depicted a muscular steelworker stripped to the waist and ladling molten steel; the background was a stark battlefield scene filled with tanks, aircraft, trucks, and artillery. The caption wasted no words:

OUT OF THE FURNACE OF WAR–MOLYBDENUM STEELS
Climax Molybdenum Company, 61 Broadway, New York

Phillipson then placed a more sophisticated series of ads, not in the trade and technical journals one might expect, but in nationally circulated, mainstream publications, including *The Saturday Evening Post*, *Literary Digest,* and *Scientific American*. Bold print read "Mo-lyb-den-um Steel," with the word *molybdenum* syllabled and accented to aid in pronunciation and spelling. The ads billed molybdenum as

Brainerd Phillipson's first advertisement appeared in 1919 and connected molybdenum with durable wartime steels.

79

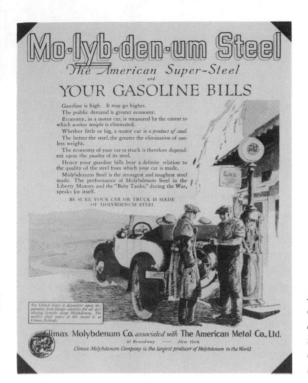

Many of the Climax advertisements of the early 1920s were related to automobiles. This one emphasized the increased fuel economy made possible by the weight-saving advantages of tough molybdenum steels.

"The American Super-Steel," and their texts carried a strong patriotic theme:

> Molybdenum Steel is the strongest and toughest steel made. The performance of Molybdenum Steel in the Liberty Motors and the "Baby Tanks," during the War, speaks for itself. . . .
>
> Molybdenum is the *only* steel alloying element mined in sufficient quantities in this country to take care of our fast growing industries. A mountain of Molybdenum ore at Climax, Colorado, makes the United States independent of the rest of the world in the production of the finest alloy steels. . . .
>
> With faith in the great future of the automotive industry and with no regard for temporary conditions, Climax Molybdenum Company is continuing to create a broader national atmosphere around its product and trying to do its share in making the motor car of greater economic value, with the belief that the domestic industry will continue to give its support to *the only American alloy.*" . . .
>
> BE SURE YOUR CAR OR TRUCK IS MADE OF MOLYBDENUM STEEL

Phillipson's advertisements led many to believe that the molybdenum market was alive and well, and that industry already clam-

80

ored for "the only American alloy." In truth, exactly the opposite was happening; in 1922, the molybdenum market hit rock bottom. Some analysts no longer bothered quoting molybdenum prices, which wallowed just above fifty cents per pound.

To make matters worse, C. Harold Wills, facing heavy debt and slow sales, suspended production of the Wills Sainte Claire. Wartime molybdenum stockpiles were still high; of the millions of tons of steel produced worldwide in 1922, a mere 20,000 tons contained small amounts of molybdenum. And at the "mountain of molybdenum" at Climax, Colorado, general superintendent Robert Merriam resigned, leaving mine superintendent James Welsh in charge of six watchmen.

The directors of the Climax Molybdenum Company, watching their investment slip ever further away, offered Brainerd Phillipson little support. The boardroom jokes—"So, Brainerd, how are things going with the *Anti-Climax* Molybdenum Company?"—did little to encourage anyone.

By 1923, however, Phillipson noted some cause for cautious optimism. When a restructured C. H. Wills & Company resumed production, Phillipson created an unusually effective ad depicting a rakish Wills Sainte Claire convertible superposed against a drawing of Bartlett Mountain—Phillipson's "mountain of molybdenum." "WILLS SAINTE CLAIRE," the ad announced, "The First ALL Mo-*lyb*-den-um Steel Car." Although still unaffordable to the average driver, the new Wills Sainte Claire automobiles quickly became synonymous in the public mind with quality, performance, and, most of all, remarkable durability. In the enormously popular coast-to-coast races of the era, grueling endurance runs over the worst imaginable roads, the Wills Sainte Claire was often the only automobile to finish. Salesmen for competing makes noted prospective customers occasionally inquiring whether their models were built of "mo-lyb-den-um" steel or "ordinary" steel.

The free concentrates Phillipson had handed out to steel companies also began paying off. Metallurgists discovered they had been adding too much molybdenum to many steels, and that reduced amounts—as little as one-quarter of 1 percent—produced enhanced levels of strength and durability.

Another discovery related to molybdenum's indirect role in hardening steel. Steelmakers hardened most standard steels by re-

Phillipson's most successful advertisement emphasized the use of molybdenum steel alloys in the Wills Sainte Claire automobile.

petitive tempering and quenching, a process that also tended to increase brittleness. Although molybdenum alone did not harden steel, researchers learned that the metal, used properly, could repress development of brittleness, thus permitting more extreme tempering to produce greater hardness.

Steelmakers added molybdenum to molten steel in the form of ferromolybdenum, a crude fifty-fifty molybdenum-iron alloy, which was both expensive to produce and difficult to mix uniformly. But in 1923 an independent researcher, Alan Kissock, devised a cheap chemical process to produce calcium molybdate, a compound of calcium, molybdenum, and oxygen that was far better suited for alloying use. Steelworkers could simply toss pre-weighed sacks of calcium molybdate—sack and all—into the molten steel; the calcium, oxygen, and ash formed an easily removable slag, while the molybdenum dispersed uniformly throughout the steel, literally on an atom-by-atom basis. Development of calcium molybdate alloying additives represented a major breakthrough in molybdenum metallurgy, and

The "All Mo lyb den um" Wills Sainte Claire was instrumental in promoting molybdenum steels. This vehicle is displayed at the Henderson Mine. –Stephen M. Voynick

Alan Kissock became the first permanent research associate with the Climax Molybdenum Company.

In 1924, annual world production of molybdenum steel doubled to a still-modest 45,000 tons, while slowly increasing consumption depleted the wartime molybdenum stockpiles. The Wills Sainte Claire coast-to-coast racers remained a traveling, highly visible endorsement of molybdenum steels, which industry could no longer ignore. Industrial giants such as the Studebaker Corporation, Timken Roller Bearing Corporation, and Hyatt Roller Bearing Corporation began specifying molybdenum steel in certain stock "blanks." The two leading American specialty alloy manufacturers, the United Alloy Steel and Central Alloy corporations, finally began ordering molybdenum in quantity. And when General Motors Corporation joined the growing list of industrial molybdenum consumers, Phillipson's 1925 projection for molybdenum steel consumption jumped to 150,000 tons, which would require at least 1.5 million pounds of elemental molybdenum.

Since projected demand would require 2,000 tons of concentrate, Brainerd Phillipson wanted to reopen the Climax Mine immediately. But the directors shared none of their young president's confidence. As majority stockholders in the "Anti-Climax" Molybdenum Company, the directors complained again that their only "dividend" in nearly seven years had been the recurring obligation to issue more stock, then buy it themselves to keep the company afloat. Reopening the mine would demand still more capital, while offering no certainty of profit. And if current demand for molybdenum fell flat, financial disaster was inevitable. To a man, the directors of the Climax Molybdenum Company argued for delaying any reopening of the Climax Mine for several years to better gauge long-term market trends.

Brainerd Phillipson wouldn't consider a delay. He had promoted molybdenum to industry on the basis that Climax could supply it when needed and in whatever quantity needed. Restricting supply at this critical juncture would jeopardize both the industrial future of the metal as well the opportunity for Climax to establish itself as the world's primary supplier.

In too deep to turn back, yet fearful of moving ahead, the directors of the Climax Molybdenum Company reluctantly left the decision to their president. In August 1924, Brainerd Phillipson ordered James Welsh to prepare for the reopening of the Climax Mine.

In Leadville, still mired in the postwar economic depression, no news could have been better. With the first rumors, out-of-work miners jumped Colorado & Southern freight trains, hitched rides, rode horses, and even walked to Climax to put their names on the hiring list. On August 21, 1924, the *Carbonate Chronicle* confirmed the rumors:

> The mine and mill of the Climax Molybdenum Company will soon be in active operation, according to reports reaching the city. During the past week, some of the buildings have been put in shape for the accommodations of men, and the big flotation mill will start as soon as sufficient ore has been broken. . . . High officials of the company are expected at Climax during the week to inspect the plant which is ready for operations.

The "high officials" were Brainerd Phillipson, making his first visit to Climax, and general manager Harry Brown. As an engineer, Brown knew, contrary to newspaper reports, that reopening the

Climax Mine would entail much more than unlocking doors and throwing a few switches. In his inspection report, Brown wryly commented that the decision to reopen was indeed fortuitous, for in a few more years there might not be anything left to reopen. For five years, howling winter blizzards had driven snow through every crevice, while summer thunderstorms had drenched buildings with torrents of water that cascaded into the interiors wherever boards had cracked and shrunk. Lightning had repeatedly struck and damaged the aerial tramway, mill pipes had corroded and burst, mice and chipmunks had nested in switch boxes and chewed through electrical insulation, and the timbers and rock in the Leal and White Tunnels needed immediate attention. Brown believed that minor repairs might put the mill back in operation, but how long it would remain operating depended on how much money the Climax Molybdenum Company was willing to commit to more substantial repairs and replacement of equipment.

After makeshift repairs, the aerial tramway creaked to life and mules hauled the first ore cars out of the White Tunnel. On August 24, 1924, the *Herald Democrat* headlined the reopening.

RESUMPTION OF OPERATIONS AT CLIMAX MINE AND MILL
AN IMPORTANT EVENT—COMPANY FINALLY SUCCEEDED
IN DEVELOPING SATISFACTORY MARKET FOR ITS PRODUCT—
MANY LEADVILLE MEN FIND EMPLOYMENT AT CLIMAX PLANT!

Brainerd Phillipson brought in J. T. Matson, an engineer from The American Metal Company's Pecos Mine at Terrero, New Mexico, as general superintendent. He also appointed H. D. Bemis as mill superintendent and ordered James Welsh, now in his eighth year at Climax, to resume his duties as mine superintendent.

Matson's initial monthly reports reflected the haste of the original construction and subsequent deterioration during the long shutdown:

Considerable repair work on water, steam and sewer lines was necessary. . . . I will say in passing that the electrical transmission has been put in by careless, or ignorant workmen. The material is for the most part good, but badly installed, or unwisely chosen. . . . We found many feet of charred insulation that was easily picked off with the fingers, and all of it burned to some extent. Water actually ran out of the conduits when we opened them. We were not surprised that they gave trouble, but it is hard to understand how we were able to run the mill at all. The rehandling of coal incidental to accumulating against the blockade season on the railroad is a nuisance. If the fellow who laid out

85

this coal bin endwise to the cars had to shovel the stuff back so as to make room for another car, I doubt he would build that way again.

The workforce that reopened the Climax Mine in 1924 included fifty miners and twenty-five mill hands. An additional fifty men dismantled the old Molybdenum Products Company mill and aerial tramway, salvaged the usable timbers and parts, converted the small buildings for storage and living use, and shipped everything else out as scrap to the Colorado Iron Works in Denver. Crews next dismantled the Climax upper tramway and double-tracked more of the White Tunnel.

Matson took receipt of a 3.5-ton, battery-powered electric haulage motor, ordering it hauled up to the White Tunnel portal. Teamsters loaded the motor onto a reinforced freight wagon hitched to team of eight horses. The one-mile trip up the steep mine road took two days. Then Matson arranged a system of mule haulage on one side of the double-tracked White Tunnel, and electric haulage on the other, to carefully compare the costs of each.

A blizzard blocked the Climax-Leadville road in early December, triggering a mass resignation of miners who chose unemployment to spending the winter at Climax, and leaving Matson to ponder what for decades to come would be a major problem at the Climax Mine—an extraordinary labor turnover rate. In his monthly report Matson wrote:

> A serious shortage of competent machine miners, or for that matter, machine miners of any ability at all, was badly felt during the month. Of a total of 51 men on the mine payroll, 21 left during the month. The general result has been that development raises have not been advanced as they should have been, and in some cases the stopes were underdrawn. . . .

During the last four months of 1924, Climax mined and milled an average of 170 tons of ore per day. The average ore grade had fallen off to .086 percent, but with mill recovery increased to 85 percent, total recovery amounted to 160 tons of molybdenite concentrate grading 75 percent. Matson, noting that electric haulage was much more cost-efficient than mule haulage, ordered another electric motor. When that motor arrived in early 1925, Matson retired the last of the Climax underground haulage mules. Most encouraging of all, mining and milling costs for one pound of contained molybdenum amounted to just fifty-two cents, against a market price of $1.00.

A sintered disk of metallic molybdenum, a metal rarely seen or used in its pure form. Metallurgists developed many important alloying applications for the metal in the 1920s.
—Stephen M. Voynick

Meanwhile, the Wills Sainte Claire, still overpriced for the mass automobile market, ran into trouble again in 1925. C. Harold Wills would soon discontinue production, but the "All Mo-*lyb*-den-um Car" had been invaluable in pioneering, proving, and promoting molybdenum steels, which continued to gain industrial acceptance.

More encouragement appeared on other fronts. The U.S. Bureau of Mines published *Molybdenum, Cerium and Related Alloys*, an obscure technical publication, but the first government paper to consider molybdenum as an accepted alloying metal, not as a metallurgical oddity. More important, the Association of Automotive Engineers formally recognized the "4100 Series" of chromium-molybdenum alloys as standard industrial alloys.

The Climax Mine produced 350 tons of concentrate during 1925. Repair and replacement costs remained very high, much to the chagrin of the directors of the Climax Molybdenum Company, but Phillipson was nevertheless encouraged as total production costs for one pound of contained molybdenum dropped to forty-five cents.

Denver businessman Otis Archie King, who still controlled all of Ceresco Ridge, had noted with great interest the Climax reopening, the strengthening molybdenum market, and the fact that Climax was

1926. The Climax Upper Camp.

not alone in the business of molybdenum mining. The Molybdenum Corporation of America, a subsidiary of Dr. George Sargent's Electric Reduction Company, was busy developing a smaller molybdenite deposit at Questa, New Mexico. King, still looking for a buyer for his Ceresco Ridge claims, had talked Sargent into taking an option on Ceresco Ridge for $6,250. But Sargent's metallurgists detected traces of copper, as chalcopyrite, in samples. Fearing the copper might interfere with the milling process, and probably also concerned about the problem of going head-to-head with Climax at Fremont Pass, Sargent dropped the option.

In January 1926, with molybdenum demand continuing to increase steadily, King again set out to market his Ceresco Ridge claims. In Detroit, Edsel Ford informed King that the Ford Motor Company purchased what little molybdenum it needed from the Dominion Molybdenite Company of Canada. In Marysville, Michigan, King learned that C. H. Wills & Company, in dire financial straits and about to close, was no longer a potential molybdenum buyer. King then approached the Central Alloy Corporation and the Timken Roller Bearing Corporation, only to hear that both had favorable contracts with the Climax Molybdenum Company.

Finally, King stopped at the offices of the United Alloy Steel Corporation, but Brainerd Phillipson had been there, too, with a contract that guaranteed not only supply, but price reductions when warranted by volume. King realized then that Climax had tied up the market. There was only one place to sell his Ceresco Ridge molybdenite properties—the Climax Molybdenum Company at 61 Broadway in New York City.

King recalled that February 1926 visit in his book *Gray Gold*. He was favorably impressed with Brainerd Phillipson's pleasant, almost shy demeanor, but not so with Metal Company consulting engineer Dr. Otto Sussman, who King noted had "thick hands, broken English, and the stolidity of the German, the cunning of the fox." Sussman initially expressed no interest whatever in Ceresco Ridge, stating brusquely, "We have all the molybdenum we will ever want, and besides, now that we own all of the available water rights, your ore is worthless." But after some negotiating, Sussman did make a substantial offer—$300,000, take it or leave it.

King took it, and the Climax Molybdenum Company gained control of Ceresco Ridge, consolidating the entire Bartlett Mountain molybdenite deposit. The Pingrey Mines & Ore Reduction Company, through King's efforts, had done well on its Bartlett Mountain venture: It had taken a decade, but the company ultimately realized a 400 percent return on its original investment. When Otis Archie King, now out of the molybdenum business for good, left New York on that cold February day, he regretted not pressing Phillipson for 10,000 shares of Climax Molybdenum Company stock. For what it was then worth, he probably would have been glad to get rid of it.

In 1926, the Climax Molybdenum Company leased a plant site in Pennsylvania from the American Zinc and Chemical Company, an American Metal Company property, and refitted the facility to convert molybdenite concentrate. The plant eliminated the need for costly outside "toll" conversion and enabled Climax to produce its own alloying additives, including calcium molybdate, ferromolybdenum, and molybdic acid, to supply its customers directly.

Meanwhile, European economic recovery presented another marketing opportunity, and Climax exported its first shipments to Belgium and France. During 1926, Climax mined and milled an average of 475 tons of ore per day, recovering one million pounds of contained molybdenum—75 percent of world production.

Although the Climax Molybdenum Company had begun to look better, at least on paper, 1926 and 1927 would be its darkest years.

The directors, now more than $2 million in debt with still no fore-seeable hope of a profit, continued to exchange bitter jokes about "Freeload Pass" and "moly-be-damned." They talked seriously of "pulling out," mentioning George Sargent's Molybdenum Corporation of America as a potential buyer. The directors' greatest fear was that some prospector would sink his pick into another "mountain of molybdenum," probably in a foreign country where cheap labor could easily undercut production costs at the Climax Mine.

Brainerd Phillipson explained repeatedly that his efforts and policies would pay no dividends in the short term, but would indeed, with patience and perseverance, pay off handsomely in the future. In response, the directors demanded to know when Phillipson's vague "future" would arrive. Phillipson himself didn't know the answer, but promised that when it did arrive, there would be no question in anyone's mind.

The directors didn't disguise their gloomy visions of the company's future or their failing confidence in its president. Board meetings often opened with cryptic comments and thin smiles: "So, Phillipson, is anything good—or anything at all—happening at Freeload Pass?"

"Throwing money" at Bartlett Mountain had tested the limits of both the personal financial resources and patience of the disgruntled directors of the "Anti-Climax Molybdenum Company." Summoning Phillipson to a board meeting, the directors demanded a decision one way or another: Either pull out now and cut the losses, or raise prices to generate a long overdue profit.

Phillipson's response drew groans of disbelief. He would not pull out, but, yes, a price adjustment was in order—but it would be a *downward* adjustment. Phillipson remained adamant: The future of the Climax Molybdenum Company depended not on high prices, but on high volumes at low prices. Phillipson persevered, and in November 1926 Climax lowered the price of its molybdenum to ninety-three cents, undercutting the market by 10 percent.

In late 1926, Arthur D. Storke took over the duties of general superintendent of the Climax Mine, with the new title of resident superintendent. Storke, an engineering graduate of Stanford University and the University of Colorado, was familiar with the mine. He had worked as a surveyor and construction foreman under Jack White in 1917 before enlisting with the 27th U.S. Engineers to serve in

France. But by the time his unit demobilized in 1919, Storke's Climax job had disappeared with the mine shutdown.

Storke's first job as resident superintendent was to install a new mill unit to boost capacity to 750 tons per day. His second task was far more critical, and required him to immediately address a problem that was beginning to panic the directors.

When miners drove the White Tunnel in 1918, geologists were surprised that the workings did not pass through molybdenite ore. In fact, ore wasn't even encountered until raises were driven upward to within sixty feet of the Leal Level. No one was then concerned, for with production at 150 tons of ore per day, the Leal Level reserves seemed immense. But miners had already taken out 400,000 tons of ore, and were currently mining 600 tons each day. Accordingly, Climax engineers and geologists arrived at a very disturbing conclusion: The economic limits of the Bartlett Mountain ore body were already in sight.

There was ore in Ceresco Ridge, of course, but geologists, with sampling limited to the 350-foot-length of the Bear Tunnel, knew little about the deposit. More expensive exploration would be costly and risky; even if enough ore was present to warrant mining, another aerial tramway would be needed. Ceresco Ridge simply was not a practical alternative. Geologists would have to find more ore

Unloading tram buckets at the mill tramway terminal at the Lower Camp in the late 1920s. Each bucket held one-half ton of ore.

The diamond drilling program of 1927, directed by Arthur Storke, dramatically expanded ore reserves at a critical juncture in Climax history.

in Bartlett Mountain—and quickly—or the Climax Mine and the Climax Molybdenum Company would go down among the bigger fiascoes in American mining history.

Neither the value of Climax stock nor confidence in the company could sink much lower. Directors deeply regretted having let Brainerd Phillipson "lead them in over their heads." Climax stock listed at $1.00 per share, but traded for much less. To save cash, the company strongly encouraged employees to take part of their pay in stock. When Climax miners who did so needed a new pair of mine boots or a bottle of whiskey, or ran short of cash, they found out just how little a share was worth in trade. Market value depended on how desperate for cash the shareholder was. When miners were broke and payday was a week away, they traded their shares for as little as ten cents.

In February 1927, Arthur Storke and Dennis Haley ordered an around-the-clock diamond drilling exploration program. Storke believed that fault displacement had terminated the Leal ore body to the west, but that another ore body had to exist lower in the moun-

92

tain. By July, 3,000 feet of core drilling—which some directors roundly criticized as yet another nonproductive expense—proved Storke correct. Drilling located more ore northwest of the Leal ore body, increasing reserves for immediate mining; more important, "down cores" revealed a far larger ore body at depth. Geologists now began to understand the composite nature and immense size of the Bartlett Mountain molybdenite deposit.

After a collective sigh of relief in New York, Brainerd Phillipson called an August meeting at Climax to plan future development. Present with Phillipson and Storke were Alan Kissock, Dennis Haley, Harry Brown, and William Coulter, the man chosen replace Storke as resident superintendent. Also in attendance was Max Schott, making his first visit to Climax since 1919.

Storke announced that he would extend the White Level beneath the newly discovered Leal Level ore body, patent one-half square mile of claims to the west and north, and speed up the diamond drilling to delineate the much larger, deep ore body. The primary purpose of the meeting was to discuss development of the new level that would replace the White Level when its projected six-year life was through. Phillipson wanted the "New Tunnel," as the proposed project was named, to be the biggest mine tunnel ever built in the United States, with a haulage capacity more than ten times that of the White Tunnel.

Engineers suggested that Bartlett Mountain, with its large, uniform ore bodies, was an ideal candidate for block cave mining. In the block cave system, large-scale undercutting would literally allow large parts of the entire mountain to collapse upon itself, theoretically making available huge volumes of ore at very low cost. High tonnage and low cost were exactly what Brainerd Phillipson wanted. From August 1927 on, the top priorities of the Climax Mine were pushing diamond drill exploration to delineate the deep ore body and designing the New Tunnel to serve a massive block cave mining system.

In October 1927, Arthur Storke moved on to an American Metal Company property in Africa, leaving William Coulter as resident superintendent. Coulter was a hardrock miner from the old school; his father had mined in South Dakota and Idaho during the 1880s, and he followed in his footsteps. Working in mines in Nevada and Montana, Coulter put himself through Washington State College, graduating in 1914 with an engineering degree. He put in twelve years as a mining engineer in Alaska, then joined The American Metal Company as superintendent of its Pecos Mine in New Mexico. Accompanying Coulter was Joseph Domenico, another Metal Company man from the Pecos Mine, who took over as accountant and manager of the Climax Mine office staff. In the coming decade, Bill Coulter and Joe Domenico would be the two most familiar faces "on the hill."

In 1928, Climax added another 250-ton-per-day mill unit, increasing mill capacity to 1,000 tons per day, roughly equal to the production capacity of the mine and the transport capacity of the tramway. Milling efficiency reached a record high, thanks to Arthur Weinig, an independent metallurgical consultant to Climax since 1918. Weinig realized that only very fine grinding, a process too slow and costly to be practical, would liberate all the molybdenite particles present in the ore. The Climax flotation process floated off only the free molybdenite; it dropped both the gangue and middlings—the composite grains containing both gangue and molybdenite—and piped both to the tailings pond. Weinig modified the flotation circuits to first float the free molybdenite, then to separately float the middlings, even middling particles containing as little as 1 percent molybdenite. He routed the recovered middlings to a regrind unit, then put them right back into the flotation circuit. At minimal additional cost, Weinig's modification boosted mill recovery efficiency to 89 percent.

By the end of 1928, even the directors of the Climax Molybdenum Company grudgingly admitted that Brainerd Phillipson's ideas on volume, production costs, and price might work—if they could keep coming up with enough money. World production of molybdenum steel now topped 300,000 tons annually, far above the 20,000 tons of 1922. Phillipson's low prices were beginning to undercut certain competing alloy metals. As more metallurgists substituted molybdenum wherever possible in alloys, orders from domestic and foreign steel producers rolled in to the Climax Molybdenum Company.

During 1928, Climax mined and milled 300,000 tons of ore—nearly 900 tons per day—to recover a record three million pounds of contained molybdenum. The Climax Molybdenum Company also recorded its first operating profit—$100,000. It was a "paper" profit only, and the directors and other investors didn't see a penny, for Brainerd Phillipson put it all into further development of the Climax Mine.

No one knew it yet, but the "Anti-Climax" Molybdenum Company had survived its darkest years.

5
That Hellhole Near the Sky
1929-1935

◆

Midst molly dust and dynamite
Where money is the brains
There's a future there as black as nite
Where Old King Coulter reigns
　　　　　　　　—anonymous Climax miner, 1935

◆

By 1929, production at the Climax Mine had become an established system, not yet smooth and routine, but increasingly efficient. Miners "dropped" ore from the Leal and White Level stopes to the loading gates just above the White Tunnel haulage level, where muck crews chuted it into new, 4.5-ton-capacity ore cars. Motormen on 3.5-ton, battery-powered electric motors hauled four-car muck trains to the portal. As stopes became exhausted, miners undercut the pillars between them, allowing entire sections of the Leal Level to collapse into the White Level stopes.

The mine worked two shifts daily, while the crusher, tramway, and mill operated around the clock on three shifts. Improved mining, crushing, tramming, and milling practices cut production costs for one pound of contained molybdenum to thirty-three cents. Mill hands packed concentrate bound for the Climax Molybdenum Company's Langeloth conversion plant in 100-pound jute sacks; foreign shipments of concentrate went into 600-pound oaken barrels. All concentrates "went out" on the Colorado & Southern Railroad, which had itself become a major concern.

Construction of the No. 2 Mill nears completion in September 1929.

C&S operations were vital to the Climax Mine, for the railroad delivered all incoming materials and shipped out all the concentrates. But the lingering post-World War I economic depression had led the C&S into hard times. With 90 percent of Lake and Summit County mines inactive, the railroad hadn't earned a profit since 1918.

As early as 1926, C&S officials hinted at abandoning the South Park and Leadville "High Line," or, as the C&S termed it, the Waterton-Leadville line. When, as expected, Lake, Summit, and Park counties objected vehemently, the C&S offered to give the line, along with "a generous amount of equipment and rolling stock," to any county willing to operate it. There were no takers, for the counties wanted rail service, but not the headache of providing it. By 1928, Climax was the only "paying" station on the entire line. But Climax freight revenues alone didn't warrant continued operation; accordingly, the C&S filed a petition for abandonment with the Interstate Commerce Commission. In New York, the Climax Molybdenum Company directors, barely recovered from the ore-shortage scare, again sat nervously on the edges of their boardroom chairs.

The only alternate route to Climax was the Leadville-Breckenridge road. In 1918, the State Highway Department had designated the Climax leg of that route as State Highway 91. But a full decade later, State Highway 91 was still a "highway" in name only. The road was

Late April 1930. Looking along the aerial tramway toward the Upper Camp. When the tramway ceased operation in May 1931, its buckets had traveled an estimated ten million miles.

June 1930. The original Climax tailings pond. The Upper Camp and abandoned portal of the Leal Tunnel are visible in the center of the photograph.

1930. A long Colorado & Southern freight, aided by a helper engine, tops out near Climax after the steep haul up Tenmile Canyon.

an unimproved, rough, dirt track closed by snow throughout the long winter; during the remaining months, washouts, mud, and ungraded ruts made it impassable for weeks at a time. Clearly, operations at the Climax Mine depended upon continued operation of the Colorado & Southern Railroad.

Brainerd Phillipson personally testified at the Interstate Commerce Commission's abandonment hearings in Denver. On February 5, 1929, the Associated Press carried a story that reflected the growing national importance of the Climax Mine.

MOLYBDENUM IS ESSENTIAL
GRAVE DANGER IN CUTTING OFF SUPPLY FROM CLIMAX
IF SOUTH PARK IS SCRAPPED—GOVERNMENT IS INTERESTED—
EXPERTS TO TESTIFY

Denver, Feb. 5.—To stop the supply of molybdenum from the state of Colorado might result in a dangerous situation to the nation in times of national defense.

This testimony was presented today by B. F. Phillipson, president of the Climax Molybdenum Company of Climax, Colorado, before the Interstate Commerce Commission hearing the request of the Colorado and Southern Railroad to abandon the Waterton-Leadville branch of their road. . . .

Phillipson said he returned from New York to testify. The cause of molybdenum will be taken before the Interstate Commerce Commission in Washington soon. Testimony before that body as to the value of the product will be used as an argument against the Colorado and Southern Railroad request to abandon its Waterton-Leadville line.

Molybdenum is used as a substitute for tungsten in the making of defense implements. Climax, it is testified, produces about 85 percent of the supply used by the government. A radiogram received from [Assistant Secretary of War G. B.] Robinson stated:

"In case of emergency, a large deficit of tungsten may seriously impair the national defense. Molybdenum can be substituted for tungsten in many uses, reducing the tungsten deficit to a small amount.

"The Assistant Secretary of War, therefore, is vitally interested in maintaining an available production facility intact. Climax Molybdenum Company is the most important source of supply."

The Interstate Commerce Commission denied the first petition for abandonment. But in the coming years, the C&S would file repeatedly, and the Climax Mine would lead the fight to keep the line operating.

Diamond drillers completed their eighteen-month-long exploration program early in 1929. After studying 13,000 feet of drill cores, Climax geologists determined the grades and delineated the configu-

Surveying the portal site of the New (Phillipson) Tunnel in March 1929.

In April 1930 the largest piece of mobile, mechanized equipment at the Climax Mine was this new steam shovel.

ration of the new ore body. Using core drill data and geologists' reports, engineers completed design of the New Tunnel.

Resident Superintendent Bill Coulter waited impatiently for the weather to break to begin construction of the portal. The C&S delivered a heavy steam shovel specifically to speed portal preparation. Crews off-loaded the dismantled steam shovel on April 15, assembled it in just three days, then found the big machine couldn't move in deep snow. After three days of towing, pushing, and swearing, a twenty-man crew succeeded in moving the shovel only 300 yards from the rail siding.

Although Coulter had envisioned a rapid, mechanized start to construction of the nation's largest mine haulage tunnel, he ran out of patience on April 22. He sent eight miners with picks and shovels to a surveyed site at an elevation of 11,463 feet, where they spent the day in a biting wind digging through six feet of frozen spring snow. The next day, they finally reached the frozen overburden. One week later, they erected the first timber set at the portal of what would be the future of the Climax Mine—the New Tunnel.

Determined to meet his tight development schedule, Coulter placed his new mine superintendent, C. J. "Jack" Abrahms, a University of California mining engineering graduate with fourteen years of experience, in charge. But Abrahms's April report told of a disappointing start in difficult conditions:

> The cost of this work is necessarily very high, due to the character of the ground, it being necessary to drive both top and side spiling and breastboard the face. Water from melting snow gives no end of trouble. . . .

Abrahms reported little improvement in May:

> Progress in the tunnel has been very slow. . . . The character of the ground is changing and by the middle of June the tunnel should be in fairly solid rock. Fourteen sets were put in during the month. The mucking machine will be put in service in early June. This should help speed up the work. . . .

During June, the rate of advance actually slowed. The shallow surface gradient above the tunnel required a long lateral distance before miners passed the loose glacial overburden and drove into solid rock. During the day, icy water poured into the tunnel in torrents, then froze solid at night. Mining the loose ground was actually faster with picks and shovels than with drills and dynamite. By the end of June, after two months of laborious hand mucking and hand tramming, the tunnel had advanced only 140 feet from the portal—

April 1929. After digging through six feet of frozen snow, a Climax crew begins excavating the portal of the New (Phillipson) Tunnel with picks and shovels.

101

June 1929. Moving a new nine-ton trolley haulage motor to the portal of the New (Phillipson) Tunnel. Two tractors and a steam shovel required four days to move the motor one-half mile.

an average advance of less than 3 feet per day. Miners then encountered a strange mix of silt, gravel, rock, and boulders locked in a matrix of blue ice that "took to neither pick nor drill." Abrahms's mine crews were driving through permafrost in the subterranean remnants of 20,000-year-old alpine glaciers.

As summer warmth melted more snow, the overhead ground became soft, or in miners' parlance, "heavy." Timbers broke, and crews retreated to replace the shattered sets. Miners advanced only seventy-three feet in July, the month that Brainerd Phillipson officially renamed the New Tunnel. It became the Wills Tunnel, in honor of Childe Harold Wills and his now defunct "All Mo-lyb-den-um" Wills Sainte Claire.

The new name did nothing for the fortunes of the mine development crews. During August, they formed and poured the portal in concrete, but advanced the tunnel a mere ten feet—one-third of a foot per day. Abrahms offered no excuses in his monthly report: ". . . nothing can be said for the Wills Tunnel other than we are doing our best."

1929. Resident Superintendent Bill Coulter at work in his office. Coulter oversaw development of the Phillipson Tunnel and initiated many new company managerial policies.

Bill Coulter, busy overseeing production, a major tunnel development project, and the summer construction program, began delegating more responsibility to his management team, only to learn that many individuals weren't up to the job. In June, Coulter fired eight shift bosses and two foremen, explaining his actions to Phillipson in a detailed letter that established many future Climax training and operating policies:

> Realizing that in the not too distant future the mine will be called upon for much greater production, organization is being planned toward that end. As you know there has been a complete change of bosses. The new bosses are all engineers. Mr. Romig, the new foreman, has broad experience in mining.
>
> I am firmly convinced that the boss with engineering training (other qualities being equal) is superior to the boss who has not had that training.
>
> In a few words we are selecting and training our shift bosses to be mine foremen. The mine foreman must have qualities that fit him into the superintendency. Bosses who cannot fit this scheme are not of much use to us.
>
> To properly train our bosses we are starting a system of charts which will keep before them the daily costs, status, and the relative efficiency of the operations under their control. . . .

To eliminate the possibility of anyone being "left in the mine" when the shift goes off, each shift will have a board on which is hung a white tag for each man giving his name and number. When he comes on shift he takes his brass tag off the board and when he goes off his brass tag is hung up over the white one. IF THE BRASS IS NOT TURNED IN the shift boss must hunt the man up.

I realize I have gone into the question of the mine organization to perhaps a monotonous extent. But we all realize that we progress or we fall by the organization we have. The building up of the mine organization, as I see it, is our most important problem. . . .

In his spare time, Coulter attended to an array of problems that adversely affected everything from production and cost control to morale. One problem was the aerial tramway, which engineers described as "a mile-long lightning rod." During July, lightning from regular afternoon thunderstorms caused seventy-five hours of down time from power failures and tram "wrecks." Another concern was the poor condition and frequent outages of the 13,000-volt Public Service Company power line coming in from Kokomo. Every power failure jerked the tram to an abrupt halt, leaving dozens of wildly swinging, fully loaded ore buckets severely stressing the cables. Abrahms's engineers finally devised a "sliding clutch" that permitted further cable travel after the motors stopped, dramatically decreasing the frequency of broken saddle bars and parted cables. August 1929 was the first month without a major tram wreck.

Coulter also "straightened out" the Upper and Lower Camp boardinghouses, where the stewards never seemed to make a profit. Personally investigating, Coulter noted that most miners ate four or five meals each day, but were charged for only three. When Coulter instituted a control system, boardinghouse profits shot up to $1,600 per month.

Realizing that life at Climax was difficult at best, Coulter put his summer construction crews on twelve-hour shifts to build some needed community additions, including six four-room houses and a new schoolhouse. The school, with two big classrooms and quarters for two teachers, was also designed to serve as a dance hall, movie theater, and recreation center. The building had a coal furnace and steam heat; like the rest of the camp, it was supplied with water from a horse-drawn wagon. Coulter inaugurated the new schoolhouse-recreation center with a Thanksgiving Day party and dance that drew 100 people from Leadville.

1929. The newly poured concrete portal of the New (Phillipson) Tunnel belied the difficulty of driving the tunnel through the Mosquito Fault.

To help speed development of the Wills Tunnel, Coulter ordered a new nine-ton trolley haulage motor. A C&S reinforced flatcar delivered the motor bolted atop a heavy timber skid. With two tractors pulling and the ponderous steam shovel pushing, crews needed four days to move the motor a half-mile from the freight siding to the Wills Tunnel portal. Electric muck haulage aided development, and November's 146-foot advance was a record. But as cold weather set in, ice built up several feet thick as far as 250 feet from the portal. Several miners worked full-time breaking ice in the drainage ditches and building fires to prevent freeze-up in the drill water lines. By Christmas, eight months of backbreaking work had advanced the Wills Tunnel only 900 feet from the portal—far behind Coulter's original schedule.

While too much water plagued development of the Wills Tunnel, the mill suffered an annual winter water shortage. With virtually all surface water frozen, mill hands rarely had enough water to mix with the ground ore to properly prepare a slurry to pipe to the flotation tanks.

Nevertheless, production rose again during 1929, when Climax mined and milled an average of 1,200 tons of ore per day, recovering and shipping 3.5 million pounds of contained molybdenum. But, as expected, the record production level soon slowed. Two days be-

105

fore deepening snow closed the Leadville road, one-fifth of Coulter's workforce—forty-one men—"walked," promising, as usual, to be "back in spring."

January 1930 began on an ominous note when a fire broke out on the Upper Camp ore conveyor belts. With no water available in the subzero temperatures, crews resorted to dynamite to save the big timber ore bins. Fire completely destroyed one conveyor and dynamite knocked the other so far out of alignment that five days of production were lost.

Meanwhile, in New York, Brainerd Phillipson worried about the suddenly weakening molybdenum market. Demand for all metals began falling after the stock-market crash of October 1929 triggered a rapidly worsening international business and industrial recession. Most American mines had already closed, and numerous banks and businesses failed every day. When the steel industry cut back production, Phillipson watched helplessly as his domestic sales fell flat. But the Climax Mine continued operation, thanks to its growing export business. Packing-plant hands noted how little molybdenite concentrate went into jute sacks, and how much more went into 600-pound oaken "export" barrels.

The greater concern of those associated with the Climax Molybdenum Company was not the deepening Depression, but the health of Brainerd Phillipson. When Bill Coulter wrote a lengthy technical article about the Climax Mine and sent it to Phillipson for perusal, he received this reply, dated March 4, 1930:

> Dear Bill,
> I don't believe you can imagine my surprise and pleasure when I received your most beautifully gotten up article. . . . Even my children took great delight in looking it over.
> It reached me at an especially opportune time as I had been in bed seventeen days last month and home a good bit besides and it brought back some great memories of past visits to Climax as well as an inspiration for the future. . . .

Only a week later, Phillipson ordered Coulter to cut production back to 900 tons per day, a level "more in keeping with the economic situation." When Coulter expressed his displeasure with the limits imposed on his newly expanded mill, Phillipson responded again on March 28, 1930.

Dear Bill,

I am dropping you this line from home. I have not been in the office since early February. I have been laid up with Pertusis [sic]. Better ask Doc Evans what that means and it will be several more weeks before I am up and around again.

Miss Fonden comes in to see me about three times a week and I manage to get off a few letters now and then. I have just read your letter of March 17th. Of course you would like to have us take the lid off but do you have any idea how very rotten business is? As a matter of fact, Climax is very much better off than most of the enterprises connected with the Metal Company right now and we should be thankful that we can not only keep going at all but that we can install a new crusher. Of course this will not last forever but nobody can tell when it will stop.

Best wishes to all at camp.

Yours very truly,

B. F. Phillipson [signed]

That was Brainerd Phillipson's last letter to the "camp." His condition steadily worsened and, on May 8, 1930, Phillipson died of diffused meningitis at age forty. In a brief obituary, *The New York Times* acclaimed Phillipson "a pioneer in the development and the use of molybdenum."

In New York, Dr. Otto Sussman replaced Phillipson as interim president of the Climax Molybdenum Company. At Climax, the Wills Tunnel, formerly the New Tunnel, received the permanent name by which thousands of miners would know it in the decades to come—the Phillipson Tunnel.

In his tunnel development report for May 1930, Jack Abrahms noted:

> During the month of May the heading was advanced 290 feet. On June 1st the tunnel was in 2,190 feet. The advance was much less than in April, and the cost was higher, due to the nature of the ground. All during the month the formation was intermittently Weber Grits, Porphyry and Gouge Seams. . . . It required timbering right up to the face and in places the ground was very heavy. On June 1st this condition still existed and the only hope we have for better ground is to reach the Mosquito Fault which should not be very far ahead.

Miners had driven both the Leal and White tunnels through the hard, altered granite east of the Mosquito Fault. But the Phillipson Tunnel portal was located 2,300 feet west of the fault in far less stable

Driving the Phillipson Tunnel in 1929 and 1930 was a brutal job made more difficult by water, bad ground, and inexperienced miners.

Precambrian sediments, and the tunnel would pass directly through the Mosquito Fault, where geologists were uncertain about the nature of the shear zone separating the east and west crustal blocks. Most likely the rock would be completely oxidized, wet, and dangerously unstable.

For the miners who performed the drilling, blasting, mucking, and timbering, advancing the Phillipson Tunnel was a grueling job. Rockfalls and injuries were frequent, water remained a problem, and the twelve-inch-square timbers sometimes groaned audibly under the enormous weight of the unstable Precambrian sediments. In just ten months, miners replaced 200 of the 340 timber sets because of collapsing, cracking, or sagging. Miners called the Phillipson Tunnel a "bad tunnel" in "bad ground," and some flatly refused to work in it. Many complained that the timber sets, usually spaced on standard ten-foot centers, provided insufficient protection. Others disliked management's urgency to advance the tunnel as quickly as possible.

The only hope miners voiced for the tunnel, if the geologists and engineers could be believed, was that the rock would improve greatly once they had driven through the Mosquito Fault. But the fault itself remained a mystery, and underground rumors warned that driving through it was "gonna be hell."

Climax had a reputation of being a reasonably safe mine. The first fatality had occurred in 1925, when Ike Jones, a Leadville teamster hauling winter supplies to the Upper Camp, fell from his horse-drawn sled, later dying of his injuries. The first fatality directly related to mining occurred three years later when August Schemerling, a thirty-seven-year-old miner working only his fourth shift at Climax, broke his neck in a thirty-foot fall down a White Level raise. By the safety standards of the 1920s, two fatal accidents in more than six years of operation of a fairly large mine was certainly acceptable. Miners considered Climax a "good" mine, an assessment that would soon change as the face of the Phillipson Tunnel approached the Mosquito Fault.

When miners finally reached the Mosquito Fault, they found the ground even worse than expected. Early on the morning of June 7, shift boss Archie Wilson and five miners were doing their part to get through the exceedingly unstable ground of the shear zone. Ralph Port and Fred McMahon worked at the foot of the fourteen-foot-wide face, drilling the last holes of a round, as Leon Burton and Sherman Frazier loaded powder from a scaffold. Wilson, anxious to fire the round before quitting time, stood nearby with Edward Parker, a new hand working his third shift, who passed up sticks of powder.

As carbide lamps cast flickering shadows on timbers and the rough rock walls, the tunnel reverberated with the deafening thunder of the big drill. Suddenly fifty tons of rock burst loose, shattering timbers and crashing down on the working men. Parker remembered being knocked backward by a timber. When he got to his feet, he was alone; he heard the hiss of escaping air, then realized that his carbide lamp was the only one still lit. Parker saw Archie Wilson pinned beneath some timbers and dragged him free, then raced back for help.

Mechanics telephoned Bill Coulter, who ordered every available miner to the tunnel. But before rescue work could begin, miners had to erect timber sets right to the still-crumbling face. Four hours later, crews carried the bodies of four miners, crushed beyond recognition and identifiable only by their numbered brass discs, from the portal of the Phillipson Tunnel. Shift boss Archie Wilson died a short time later.

109

The site of the rockfall and cave-in of June 7, 1930, in the Phillipson Tunnel that killed five miners in the most tragic single accident in Climax history.

The Leadville *Herald Democrat* held up publication to run this front-page headline:

FOUR ARE INSTANTLY KILLED AT BREAST OF CLIMAX BORE
WHEN ROCK AND TIMBER FELL—ACCIDENT OCCURRED
EARLY THIS MORNING IN TUNNEL BEING DRIVEN BY CLIMAX
MOLYBDENUM COMPANY—SHIFT BOSS WILSON PROBABLY
FATALLY INJURED—VICTIMS WERE BURIED UNDER MASS OF
ROCK AND LAGGING—INQUEST TO BE HELD MONDAY

Before a packed Leadville courtroom, the coroner's inquest focused on timbering practice. Miners testified how they often objected to the company policy of erecting timber sets on standard ten-foot centers. They said the company ordered five-foot-centers only when the ground was "very bad," but always returned quickly to the cheaper and faster ten-foot-centers whether the ground improved or not. The nine witnesses called from Climax included Bill Coulter and Jack Abrahms. The next day, the *Herald Democrat* reported the verdict:

110

**COMPANY FAILED TO GIVE PROTECTION TO MINERS SAYS VERDICT
CORONER'S JURY AFTER VISITING TUNNEL AT CLIMAX
CRITICIZES CHARACTER OF TIMBERING USED THERE**

. . . that it is the verdict of the jury that the timbering of this tunnel should be in at least five foot sets given this character of ground.

Also that this tunnel is improperly timbered.

Also that the company failed to take proper precautions to protect the lives of these men.

Testimony went beyond matters of safety, drawing attention to such problems as morale and the high labor turnover rate.

. . . Joseph Domenico, mine accountant who has been with the company since July, 1927, was questioned with regard to the average turnover of the men employed. He stated that off-hand he could only say that the general turnover of men in the tunnel would not exceed forty percent. When asked the cause of this, he said it was generally due to the altitude, some didn't like the work, some didn't like the shift boss, and some leave by request. He stated that when the men leave he generally asks them why they are leaving and he had heard no complaints about the tunnel being a bad place to work. This statement brought a snicker from many of the men in the audience.

Miners no longer considered Climax a "good" mine. Its tarnished reputation worsened when a widely disliked company foreman dismissed the inquest proceedings with a callous, "Men are cheaper than timbers." The comment, neither original nor opportune, worsened the deteriorating relationship between management and miners. For the first time, miners began referring to the Climax Mine as "the hellhole on the hill."

When mining resumed in the Phillipson Tunnel five days later with orders that timber sets be erected on five-foot centers, Abrahms couldn't find enough miners for a full shift. When ordered into the Phillipson Tunnel, many miners quit on the spot, driving the June labor turnover rate to an astounding 156 percent. The big reason, of course, was the extreme danger in "cleaning up the mess" left by the fatal rockfall. The fault ground was so loose that miners fired the round that was being loaded at the time of the accident six times, then fired the next round four times. Advancing the Phillipson Tunnel just twelve feet through the worst of the Mosquito Fault shear zone took eleven days and five lives. But after miners finally fired the second round, geologists noted the first traces of altered granite and molybdenite.

East of the shear zone, rock stability improved, but now icy water cascaded into the tunnel at a rate of 200 gallons per minute. As working conditions at the face remained difficult and dangerous, miners "came and went" with such frequency that inexperience became its own serious hazard. Abrahms now had difficulty finding miners "who had worked here last week."

Just two weeks after the "big accident," a Phillipson Tunnel shift boss was breaking in a new hand on a pneumatic mucking machine. While walking forward to inspect the face, the boss slipped down the steep muck pile, wedging his foot beneath the machine's bucket. The operator, working his fourth shift, panicked; instead of easing the bucket control handle back, he slammed it forward, dropping the heavy steel bucket and shattering his shift boss's leg.

Another serious accident occurred outside the Phillipson Tunnel, where muck trains crossed a temporary timber trestle leading from the portal to the crusher. Crews had just replaced part of the trestle with a permanent earthen bank. But as a loaded, nine-car muck train rumbled toward the crusher, the new embankment settled, derailing and overturning the entire train. The nine-ton motor rolled directly over the motorman, who miraculously emerged unscathed. But the motorman had "seen the elephant"; with his face ashen, he walked directly to the general office building, quit, collected his pay from Joe Domenico, and without turning around began walking the thirteen miles down the hill to Leadville.

During July, miners used five-foot-center sets all the way to advance the Phillipson Tunnel another 140 feet. On July 20, Coulter detailed two men to set a bronze plaque into the concrete above the portal. It read:

PHILLIPSON LEVEL 1929

Miners entering the portal to start their shift glanced up at the new plaque and commented cynically, "Well, at least they got that up without killin' anybody."

By September 1, 1930, miners had advanced the Phillipson Tunnel 2,701 feet from the portal, completely clear of the shear zone of the Mosquito Fault. Jack Abrahms reported:

> At last the character of the rock has changed in the tunnel. Since early August the rock encountered has been very hard and required no timbering. The tunnel has been brought down to rock section size of 9'x12' which materially decreases the amount of muck to be handled.

112

Summer labor turnover rates exceeded 100 percent every month because of the June accident, bad ground, and icy water, which at its peak poured through the workings at a rate of 675 gallons per minute. The watercourse in the Mosquito Fault was both a blessing and a curse. Abrahms noted that "men could not, or would not, work efficiently in it." But the mill no longer faced its usual critical winter water shortage.

The labor turnover rate dropped sharply in September. One reason was the "good rock" in the Phillipson Tunnel. Another was that the nation was entering the darkest days of the Great Depression and 90 percent of all American metal mines were shut down. Word had spread to Kansas, Oklahoma, and Texas that "some outfit" in the Colorado mountains was still working and might be hiring. Joe Domenico noted that the C&S freight trains arriving at Climax usually had several men riding the rods, hoping to rustle a job.

But in November the economic situation became so bad that Coulter was instructed to reduce production from 900 to 600 tons per day. Climax remained open only because of its foreign orders, which now accounted for 75 percent of all concentrate shipped. Coulter cut back to two shifts and a four-day week, but couldn't avoid laying off sixteen men. To prevent further layoffs, Coulter announced that he would rotate crews on a three-day work week. No one argued. Nor was there the usual seasonal exodus of employees when a blizzard closed the Leadville road on December 17.

As Climax settled in for the winter, bitterly cold weather quickly froze the water flowing down from the high cirque. The Upper Camp's only other available water came from a diamond drill hole that penetrated a watercourse. With the camp road closed by snowdrifts and the drill-hole flow diminishing every day, crews at the lower crusher loaded emergency blocks of ice aboard the "up-bound" ore buckets of the aerial tramway. Upper Camp cooks thawed the ice to provide water for drinking, cooking, and, occasionally, a bit of "sponge bathing."

On Christmas Eve 1930, the company served a free turkey dinner at both the Upper and Lower Camp boardinghouses. Miners and mill hands enjoyed the dinner by lantern light or candlelight, for a howling blizzard had knocked out electrical power for ten hours. The 110 employees on the Climax payroll were thankful that dark

1930. Wearing their best, the kitchen crew of the old Climax boardinghouse pose for a group photograph.

winter night for more than just a "company meal"; unlike many other Americans, they still had jobs.

With the main haulage section of the Phillipson Tunnel complete, Jack Abrahms's mine crews turned to development of an elaborate and extensive pattern of haulage drifts, loading stations, laterals, and chute and ventilation raises encircling the barren core of the Upper Ore Body and extending beneath the ore body itself.

Coulter realized that large-scale block cave mining demanded a steady, experienced workforce, and that decent housing was the best way to reduce the extreme labor turnover rate. The two boarding-houses were the best living quarters, but they were suitable only for single men, who often earned a quick stake and then quit. Quarters for more reliable married men were, in Coulter's words, "wretched." In January 1931, Bill Coulter made his housing concerns clearly known to the New York office:

> As you know we are badly in need of family houses and if it can possibly be provided for, I think we should plan to build at least five two-family apartment houses during the coming summer. This would take care of ten families and while these houses would by no means meet demand, they would considerably help the present congested conditions. To illustrate how far employees have gone to have their families with them, it might be well to state where some of them are living. Five families are living in the old Buffehr bunkhouse which has

114

virtually been turned into an apartment house. The company has not spent money for improvements to this building and living conditions are anything but good. These families at present, and as many as five, have made their homes in the Buffehr's bunkhouse and outbuildings below the tailings dam. Coal is sold to the families in both of the Buffehr's Camps. Many of these families have small children of school age and while they make very creditable attendance records during the winter months, it is truly pathetic to see these little youngsters trudging back and forth in some of our winter storms, especially from the lower Buffehr Camp. Two families with children have been living in the shacks built by King on the railroad track next to the barn, another family over the office, another makes their home in the lean-to of the guest house and Joe Wood, our construction boss, and his wife live in the old electrical shop below the warehouse, and the tractor is housed in the lower part of this building. Outside of the human consideration for furnishing housing for our employees we find that the married men are our best workmen, they are steady, reduce the labor turnover and are actually an asset to the company that can be measured in dollars and cents. Provision for homes for ten families would be conservative so far as demand is concerned and I believe should be given serious thought for the immediate future. . . .

1930. Part of a shift enjoys a meal at the old Climax boardinghouse.

Coulter's graphic description of the misery of life at Climax had its desired effect. When interim president Otto Sussman agreed to allocate funds for improved family housing, Coulter announced construction would begin in spring. News of a housing program "up the hill" elicited a strong reaction in Leadville, where most mines remained closed and unemployment was rampant. Since company housing would only further isolate Climax and its payroll dollars, Leadville merchants thought it was time to establish closer economic ties to the Climax Mine. And the best way to do it would be with a well-maintained, all-season road. On March 27, 1931, a *Herald Democrat* editorial suggested that Climax was Leadville's only immediate economic hope, and, while a road might be a start, the city should begin thinking even more seriously about its relationship with the growing mine:

> . . . But a stretch of highway between the two places will not of itself accomplish much, unless there is a definite program worked out by Leadville to provide homes for the men who can be expected to change their residences.
>
> It does not appear to have occurred to those who are building such high hopes on this road, that the Climax Molybdenum Company has plans of its own as to the housing of its employees. They don't fit into the plans of Leadville, because Leadville has no concerted plan. . . . We can become a town for Climax, or we can sit back and watch as Climax will surely build its own town.

Development of the Phillipson Level now moved rapidly under the guiding hand of engineers like C. Carl Cunningham. A former Purdue University professor of agricultural engineering, Cunningham, along with his wife Gladys, came to Climax in October 1929. He learned quickly that engineering at Fremont Pass was a bit different than in the Indiana farm country. On his first assignment, he surveyed a new street and a few building sites, marking his lines with foot-long stakes. But by morning, to the great amusement of those in the Climax engineering office, two feet of fresh snow had buried the stakes. After that, Cunningham, like veteran Climax engineers, used only six-foot-high stakes when surveying outdoors between September and June.

In 1931, Cunningham, now chief engineer, supervised the sinking of a critical ore pass connecting the White Level with the Phillipson Level. The ore pass was not a simple job; with a sixty-five-degree declination and a length of 465 feet, it would connect two precise points on two different levels, one of which, the White Level, had "highly questionable" original surveying. A total linear traverse of 9,000 feet left plenty of room for error, which would be not only costly in time and money, but embarrassing for the chief engineer. For three months, Cunningham shot angles and checked his calculations repeatedly, virtually resurveying the White and Phillipson workings up to the connection points, and taking a lot of kidding in the process. When the long-awaited breakthrough was near, Cunningham, on the White Level, could hear the drills of the Phillipson Level miners reverberating through the solid rock, but could not determine their distance or direction. "At least you're in the same mountain," the other engineers laughed.

In March 1931, as miners hopefully drilled the final round, Coulter assembled his staff and their families at his home in the evening. After the round was fired, Coulter and Abrahms left the gathering to venture through the smoke and gas for a quick look. When they returned, Coulter brusquely ordered Cunningham's wife to "pack your bags because the damned thing missed by a mile." Gladys broke into tears, and even Cunningham thought he had been fired. Finally, when Coulter had had enough fun, he put an arm around Gladys and announced that the breakthrough showed no

Climax surveyors at work in winter 1929. New surveyors soon learned to use six- and even ten-foot stakes in their winter work.

117

discernible error whatever. Cunningham recalled the rest in an interview many years later:

> Bill Coulter said, "We're gonna celebrate. It was a satisfactory breakthrough." So he locked us all in the house and kept the keys. We couldn't leave and everyone else started drinking. I couldn't drink and couldn't stand the smoke (they all like Havana cigars and they really lift your hat!). I finally got out for some air and they locked the door behind me. I was locked out!
>
> I hammered on the door but they wouldn't let me in. It was cold March weather, too. Finally I found the basement coal chute window not locked. I crawled in, over the coal bin, and came upstairs all covered with coal dust. Some evil-minded guy hollered, "He's been down there in the basement with the maid!" (They had a Mexican maid who stayed in the basement.) Oh, they were having lots of fun!

The following day, after the powder smoke, coal dust, and hangovers had cleared, a precise survey showed the cumulative lateral error to be just over one inch; the grade showed no error at all. When the report reached New York, disbelieving staff engineers of both the Climax Molybdenum Company and The American Metal Company insisted that Coulter swear to those figures.

With an operating ore pass, the days of the Upper Camp were numbered. Crews began stripping track, pipe, steel, and timbers, moving all salvageable materials down to the Lower Camp. Coulter declared the Leal Level abandoned, as much of it had already caved into the White Level stopes. Mining continued in the White Level stopes, with ore being dropped down the ore pass to the Phillipson Level for haulage.

On May 12, 1931, the aerial tramway creaked to a halt for the last time, its job finished. Over nine years of operation, the Big Tram had survived hundreds of lightning strikes while conveying 2.3 million tons of ore from the Upper Camp down to the mill. In their gently swinging ascents and descents of Bartlett Mountain, the buckets had traveled an estimated ten million miles. The gentle, creaking whine of the cable wheels and tower runners that had been a part of Climax life was replaced by the low rumble of seventeen-ton haulage motors pulling strings of ten-ton Granby muck cars out of the portal of the Phillipson Tunnel.

In September 1931, Dr. Otto Sussman stepped down as interim president of the Climax Molybdenum Company to become chairman of The American Metal Company. The directors elected Sussman's replacement unanimously, installing him in office with the clear understanding that things would be done his way, an unusual concession for the directors, most of whom were still close associates of the consensus-minded Metal Company. The new president was Max Schott, now fifty-five years old and eager to take over where Brainerd Phillipson had left off.

Phillipson had relied primarily on salesmanship to expand his markets during the 1920s, but Schott emphasized in-house research to develop new uses for molybdenum. Schott quickly established an in-house metallurgical research laboratory in Detroit, placing it under the direction of William Park Woodside, the former chief of the Studebaker Corporation's Department of Materials and Standards. Woodside's metallurgists turned immediately to finding new uses for molybdenum and molybdenum compounds in steels, lightfast color dyes, catalysts, and most important, in cast irons.

Schott next lured James Thorpe away from U.S. Steel Corporation, assigning the alloy expert to restructure the Climax sales force into a small core of just a dozen men, each of whom would be a graduate metallurgist or engineer, as well as an experienced salesman. The new Climax president continued Phillipson's advertising program promoting molybdenum steels, aiming ads specifically at the aircraft, rail, marine, and petroleum industries, all of which were potentially large consumers of molybdenum. Schott's ads retained "mo-lyb-den-um" as a spelling and pronunciation aid, and also introduced "moly" (pronounced "molly"), a term long used by miners.

But neither promotion nor in-house metallurgical research could overcome the economic devastation of the Great Depression. By 1932, domestic molybdenum orders had nearly ceased. In July, Schott ordered Bill Coulter to make further cuts in both production and employment. Climax Mine production dropped to only 200 tons per day, just enough to keep the mill operating ten days each month. Coulter reported:

> . . . The crew was reduced from 130 to around 50. As far as was possible, the mine divided work among employees on a 50-50 working time basis so that the men on the payroll [numbered] considerably more than actual straight time workers. In view of the fact that most of the crew were old-timers and long in the employ of this company, that many of them were either married or had dependents, and that

119

there was little chance of them getting employment elsewhere during these times, this arrangement appears to be the very best we could do under the present conditions.

The Climax warehouse overflowed with a huge stockpile of 1,500 tons of concentrate with 1.5 million pounds of contained molybdenum. During the last four months of 1932, the Climax Mine didn't make a single domestic shipment. But foreign shipments continued to increase. Every week, the C&S shipped out 600-pound export barrels of concentrate bound for places now familiar to the packing-house crews: Hamburg, Osaka, Marseilles, Liverpool, and Antwerp. During 1932, exports accounted for 85 percent of all concentrate shipped from the Climax Mine.

Although Climax came precariously close to shutting down, it remained one of the few mines in the United States to operate continuously through the Great Depression. By March 1933, the Climax Molybdenum Company had weathered the worst of the economic hard times. With the warehouse stockpile down to 60,000 pounds

Packing-plant hands fill a 600-pound oaken "export cask" with molybdenite concentrate. Foreign orders alone kept Climax working through the Great Depression.

of contained molybdenum, Schott finally gave Bill Coulter the green light to step up production.

As word spread that the Climax Mine was hiring, hundreds of destitute men showed up at Fremont Pass to "rustle" jobs. Joe Domenico gave preference to the 80 men he had laid off eight months earlier, then hired another 40 to bring total employment up to 175. Most "rustlers" arrived on C&S freights; others walked for days, sometimes arriving at Climax weak from hunger, fatigue, and cold. Although Domenico had to turn hundreds of men away without a job, he never turned them away without a good meal. Sometimes the bitterly disappointed job seekers, with the help of a little end-of-Prohibition-era alcohol, vented their frustrations and things became ugly. The *Herald Democrat* reported one such incident in early April 1933.

NEAR RIOT AT CLIMAX WHEN BUNCH
OF RUSTLERS START FIGHT
SHERIFF BRINGS IN TRUCKLOAD

Rocky Mountain moonshine apparently mixed with class pride was the cause of a mild riot at Climax early last evening, when a group of rustlers who had arrived there during the morning on the C&S freight train, after consuming a considerable amount of liquor, bore down on the occupants of the bunkhouse in an attempt to avenge themselves for not having obtained employment. A large number of the rustlers, it was stated, were easterners and after the liquor had numbed their clear thinking capacities they developed a "grudge" against the Texans, a large number of whom are on the payroll of the Climax Molybdenum Company.

Using fists for weapons they attacked the occupants of the bunkhouse, threw mattresses out of windows and made themselves a nuisance generally. Several blows were exchanged between employees of the company and the rustlers, resulting in a few black eyes and bruises. Officers of the local Sheriff's office were notified about 6:30 last evening that 35 men had taken possession of the Climax bunkhouse and Sheriff Walsh and Undersheriff Traverson set out immediately to quash the riot taking with them the county's tear gas gun.

Officials went to Leadville for a truck in which to haul the prisoners to Leadville and while awaiting this means of transportation, the rioters were fed on sandwiches, pie and coffee, obtained for them by J. Domenico, bookkeeper in charge of the company's office and "Tex" Romig, one of the company's foremen. . . .

Various tales of hardship were told by the men during their ride back to Leadville last night, before they were booked at the jail close to midnight. One fellow, an ex-service man, was said to have wept bitterly when officials offered little sympathy.

121

During the "Anti-Climax" era of the 1920s, Brainerd Phillipson had rejected opportunities for short-term financial gain, instead directing his efforts and aiming his policies toward a vague "future." He always coaxed more money from the directors, while reinvesting the company's few paper profits into development of the Climax Mine, building toward that ill-defined day when high volume and low prices would finally pay off. The impatient directors of the Climax Molybdenum Company had often asked their young president pointedly, "And just when, Phillipson, is this future of yours?" Phillipson, of course, could not provide a day, a month, or even a year, but promised that when the future did arrive, every man in that boardroom would know it.

Phillipson didn't live to see the future he had worked toward, but most of the directors of the Climax Molybdenum Company did. And when they looked back in their later years, they realized what their young president had meant. For the future of the Climax Molybdenum Company arrived quite clearly on May 24, 1933, fourteen years and four months after Brainerd Phillipson had taken over the sinking Climax ship.

With production back up to 1,200 tons of ore per day, all attention was on an event of paramount importance: "Shot No. 1," a huge underground blast that would undercut the pillars supporting the stopes in a 150-by-450-foot area above the Phillipson Level. If successful, the shot would initiate the caving sequence that had been six years in planning and development; the entire ground mass above the stopes would settle, and its own great weight would fracture an enormous volume of ore. Shot No. 1 would mark the transition from conventional, small-scale shrinkage stope mining to massive block cave mining, which, Phillipson had promised, would dramatically slash production costs. But if the shot failed, or if the ground mass failed to react as expected, things were going to be, in Bill Coulter's words, "a disaster."

Mine crews needed two weeks to load the 120,000 pounds—sixty tons—of dynamite and "tie it in" with 5,000 feet of detonating cord. Mine superintendent Jack Abrahms and mine foreman Tex Romig personally supervised the best shift bosses Climax had—Walt Palo, Alex Martin, Gus Miller, and George Sharp. On May 25, 1933, the *Herald Democrat* dramatically reported:

BARTLETT MOUNTAIN SHIVERED AS ITS HEART WAS TORN BY RECORD BLAST OF DYNAMITE

A low rumble, a slight shiver of the earth, and a mass of snow jarred loose from a rocky slope above Climax provided the sole spectacle on the surface as sixty tons of dynamite exploded in the heart of Bartlett Mountain.

. . . In the opinion of the representatives of DuPont and Hercules Powder companies who were present it was the largest blast in the history of underground mining.

Toward 6 o'clock, Chief Electrician Frank Garrabrant and his corps of assistants made the final countdown and at 6:06 he pulled the switch that sent the electric current into the wires and exploded the electric blasting caps.

"I'm just tickled to death it's over and I can get some sleep," said the grimy-faced electrician as he came out of the tunnel. He had been going day and night for the past two weeks, and the slightest miscalculation might have spelled disaster.

The results of Shot No. 1 exceeded even the best expectations. In conventional mining, a single pound of powder broke about 200 pounds of rock; in Shot No. 1, the same pound of powder broke

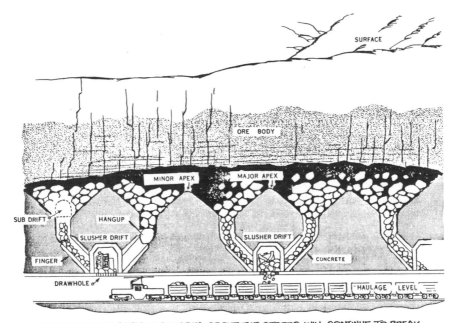

THE FRACTURED ROCK IN THE AREA ABOVE THE STOPES WILL CONTINUE TO BREAK AND SPALL DUE TO ITS **OWN WEIGHT**
...THIS ROCK CREATES A GRINDING AND BREAKING PROCESS ALL ITS OWN AS IT FALLS AND IS FED TO THE HAULAGE LEVEL BY THE **FORCE OF GRAVITY**

A schematic drawing explaining the block cave mining system. —drawing by Ted Mullings some 36,000 pounds—eighteen tons—of rock. The big shot shattered 700,000 tons of ore immediately and 1.3 million more in the slow caving action that followed. Within days, muck crews began drawing broken ore, and new, nineteen-ton haulage motors, each pulling fifteen ten-ton Granby muck cars, arrived at the crusher every thirty minutes. The ore in a single muck train equalled the total daily production of the Climax Mine in 1918.

When new mill units came on line in September, daily production topped 4,000 tons. Most important, the total mining and milling costs for one pound of molybdenum contained in concentrate plummeted from thirty-five cents to seventeen cents. With the Climax Mine about to rewrite the books on cost-efficient underground mining, Max Schott, in a move that would have pleased Brainerd Phillipson, cut the price of molybdenum to eighty-three cents per pound.

With employment at a record 300, Bill Coulter knew a general store would make living and working at Climax much more attractive to both single men and families. Another point Coulter considered was that, during the long months of winter isolation, a general store could be a financial bonanza. And Coulter knew just the man to run such a store—his brother George. In summer 1933, with Bill's ready assistance, George Coulter leased seven acres of land from the Climax Molybdenum Company. The plot was located atop Fremont Pass, directly across the railroad tracks and dirt highway from the Climax general office building.

George Coulter owned and operated the Fremont Trading Company, doing business as the Fremont Trading Post, a private venture. Nevertheless, it was essentially a company store, offering the best and worst of the company store concept. George erected a sprawling wooden building to house the general store, offices, warehouse, bar, gas station, and, within a year, an automobile dealership. The store stocked groceries, hunting and fishing gear, clothes, shoes, and everything a Climax miner would need for the job, including "hard-boiled" leather safety hats, carbide lamps, tool belts, rubber mine boots, and the rugged work clothes the miners called "diggers." The bar, which miners quickly named the "Slop Chute," provided card tables and slot machines for after-shift "recreation."

George Coulter made certain that the Fremont Trading Post offered convenience. Any man with a Climax payroll number didn't need cash, for credit was available on his signature. George and Bill Coulter got together to provide another convenience—a direct Climax payroll-deduction plan to quickly "zero" a miner's "tab." George issued his own company currency—paper chits in dollar denominations and "Good in Trade at the Fremont Trading Post," available in books worth $5.00, $10.00, and $20.00. George also circulated brass tokens, stamped out in the same sizes and denominations as standard U.S. coinage, which conveniently fit his slot machines.

During the late Depression years, many men arrived at Climax with literally nothing more than the shirts on their backs. If hired, they moved into the comfortable boardinghouse, where they received three square meals per day. They bought their mine gear and perhaps a beer or two, with all the costs deducted against their first paycheck. George Coulter's easy credit was both wisely used and sadly abused. For some penniless men, the easy credit represented opportunity, finally, to begin meaningful lives and careers. But others plunged into debt and never saw that first paycheck or any other paycheck, and would always, as the words of the song later bemoaned, "owe their souls to the company store."

And if a miner needed cash, he simply signed for a book of chits, then sold it to someone else—at the appropriate discount, of course—for "cash money." The chits and tokens made fine poker chips and were circulated and exchanged as cash in Climax, the Tenmile camps, and Leadville. When Leadville saloon keepers cleaned out their slot machines, half the take was often Fremont Trading Post tokens. Between chits, tokens, credit, and cash, George Coulter did a booming business, and the Fremont Trading Post quickly grew into one of central Colorado's largest-volume general stores. George's prices were high—miners wryly blamed a "high altitude tax"—but there was nowhere else to go, especially during the four or five months each year when Fremont Pass was snowbound.

During 1934, the first full year of block cave mining, average production reached 5,000 tons of ore per day. Mill studies revealed that "good metallurgy," or milling that achieved a 90 percent molybdenite recovery rate, was not nearly as cost efficient as "poor metallurgy," or milling that recovered only 78 percent of the molybdenite present in the ore. When engineers adjusted mill regrinding and flotation circuits, production costs of one pound of contained

125

1930. Mill hands at the flotation tanks.

molybdenum dropped to fifteen cents. Even though average ore grade had now declined to 0.65 percent, Climax recovered 8.3 million pounds of contained molybdenum worth $7.5 million—ten times the combined production of all other Lake County mines.

With Climax rapidly gaining recognition as a leader in mining efficiency and milling technology, Bill Coulter was besieged with requests for tours, visits, technical information, photographs, articles, and special courtesies to be rendered to Climax customers. A sampling of Coulter's correspondence in late 1934 shows how the resident superintendent's duties now extended beyond supervision of mining and milling. Bill Woodside, director of the Climax Research Laboratory in Detroit, wrote to Coulter:

> . . . Mr. McGraw is president of the Braeburn Alloy Steel Corporation and they buy all their molybdenum from us.
> He is a very good friend of mine and I know you will make him feel at home, especially when you meet him for he is a real fellow. Ask him to tell you the story about his telephone conversation with a friend and his wife mistaking the word "swimming" for "women." . . .

From Coulter, in reply to a request for a class tour from the University of Colorado Geology Department:

> Ordinarily we would not have any objections to granting you this privilege, but this time of year the smoke and gas is bad on the Phillipson Level. In addition to this we are running a heavy tonnage and we do

126

not think it advisable to permit a group of 20 inexperienced boys going around the level in a group. . . . If you care to come up and look through the mill and the crushing plant, this will be satisfactory.

To Coulter, from Dr. P. G. Wodehouse, Professor of Geology, University of Colorado:

I have just been talking with Mr. H. L. Brown about an article for Popular Mechanics Magazine. The title will be "Mining a Mountain" and I am using Climax as the main subject.

I have most of the facts I need but am up against it for pictures and understand you are quite a photographer. . . .

To Coulter, from the Big Sandy High School District (Clendenin, West Virginia) Chemistry Club to Molybdenum Climax Co. (sic):

. . . We will have a chemistry exhibit. We would appreciate it very much if you would send us any charts, exhibits, or chemicals. If necessary, it will be returned.

To Coulter, from Max Schott in New York City:

Enclosed you will find copy of letter with regard to a visit to Climax by Mr. G. A. Lukashin, Mining Engineer representing the U.S.S.R. . . .

The Russians are looking all over the world for molybdenum. Our suggestions to you are that you give Mr. Lukashin every opportunity to see the mine and mill and to familiarize himself with our problems and operating methods but that you avoid, as tactfully as possible, revealing anything about our costs. . . .

The growing success of the Climax Mine in the early 1930s attracted much outside attention, such as this field trip for engineering students from the Colorado School of Mines.

When Max Schott felt the requests for tours and information had become too frequent, particularly from foreign mining companies and governments, he advised Coulter:

> ... Our operations have had a great deal of publicity and it is quite natural that parties figuring on handling low grade deposits of molybdenite should wish to study our methods. We have been more than liberal in our policy and I believe it is time that we should be more particular with regard to visitors.
>
> We should find out who the people are who wish to see our property and what their object is. Anyone going to Climax without a letter from this office or from Denver should have to satisfy you before being given permission to go through the works. Detailed information should not be given to anyone except on request from here or Denver unless the information asked for is harmless by nature.

Meanwhile, in New York, several nationally circulated general-interest and financial magazines, led by *Fortune*, demanded interviews with Max Schott, the president of what was suddenly acclaimed as the most successful American company of the Depression era. Climax had become newsworthy not because it had survived the Depression, but because it had emerged in a remarkable position of strength.

Foreign orders, which had carried Climax through the Depression, rolled in faster than ever as Europe and Japan stepped up armament production. The domestic steel industry, however, remained sluggish, working at 50 percent of its 1929 level. But by 1935, Max Schott's research and development program had paid off, for U.S. steelmakers now used molybdenum in one-third of all steels and cast irons, resulting in a net increase in domestic molybdenum consumption.

Climax enjoyed the most enviable position of any mine in the world: It had a new production level, an extraordinarily efficient mass mining system, enormous ore reserves, dirt-cheap production costs, and a market for every pound of concentrate it could produce. The Climax Mine now accounted for 86 percent of world molybdenum production, and competitors couldn't begin to match its price. *Fortune*, with few fortunes to cover during the Great Depression, wasn't about to let this story get away. Max Schott finally agreed to cooperate with *Fortune* writers for a feature story.

The *Fortune* article focused on Climax Molybdenum Company stock, which had become Wall Street's rags-to-riches story of the decade. During the "Anti-Climax" days, a share listed at $1.00, but traded for as little as ten cents. Shortly after the first $100,000 paper profit of 1928, the directors had voted to split the stock ten-for-one. High mine development costs consumed the modest annual operating profits that followed. The 1931 operating profit of $109,000, as an example, didn't cover the cost of driving 900 feet of the Phillipson Tunnel. The directors finally declared a modest quarterly dividend in June 1933, but only after Shot No. 1 had proven that the block caving system would work. It was the first token return that any Climax stockholder had ever received.

The low cost and high volume of block cave mining took effect in 1933, suddenly pushing the net earnings of the Climax Molybdenum Company to $900,000. Net earnings doubled in 1934 to $1.8 million, then nearly doubled again in 1935 to $3.2 million. Between 1931 and 1935, net earnings rocketed from 7 percent of gross sales to 51 percent—a Depression-era record unmatched by any other American company. The directors split the stock again, this time three-for-one, and by June 1935 Climax Molybdenum Company stock, now bona fide "blue chip," traded on the New York Stock Exchange for $42.00 per share. A single share of Climax stock worth $1.00 in 1928 had appreciated in value to $1,200 by 1935. Every pound of molybdenum—and the Climax Mine produced ten million pounds of molybdenum in 1935—represented thirty-two cents in clear profit.

Six families owned half of what *Fortune* magazine called "the Climax fortune." The Bernard Hochschild family owned 280,000 shares, the families of Carl M. and Julius Loeb 375,000 shares, Dr. Otto Sussman 140,000 shares, the Max Schott family 200,000 shares, and Braincrd Phillipson's widow and family 55,000 shares. The American Metal Company, the final major shareholder, held 225,000 shares.

Many individuals held—or had held—the remaining shares. Some profited handsomely, others cursed their luck for selling out too soon. Sam Webber, one of Ed Heckendorf's partners on the Leal claims in 1916, sold his shares to buy into a wildcat oil venture and lost everything. Others bought at just the right time. Attempting to liquidate an estate in 1928, a Denver bank considered itself lucky to find a British speculator willing to take a chance on 5,000 shares of Climax stock at the listed price of $1.00 per share. Seven years later, that same speculator cashed in his $5,000 investment for $6 million.

To conserve cash during its lean years, Climax encouraged employees to take part of their pay in stock. The original owners still held some shares, but most had been passed on to merchants and

Climax Molybdenum Company stock performed better than any other American stock issue during the years of the Great Depression. From 1928 to 1935, a $1.00 share of Climax stock appreciated in value to $1,200.

saloon keepers, or even to Coyote Annie, one of the few Leadville prostitutes who accepted shares of Climax stock in trade.

One Climax employee made a killing on company stock—without even knowing he owned any. Art "Doc" Sloan was an orphan who had known nothing but poverty. A solitary bachelor, he found his first steady job at Climax in the 1920s and took up residence in the boardinghouse. When silicosis prevented him from working underground, he became a mine dry janitor, sweeping floors, emptying garbage, and handing out aspirin to the miners before shift and bandages after, the latter duty leading to his nickname. Never having had many pennies, Doc never wasted any. When miners discarded worn-out diggers, he collected them, sewed the holes, and wore them himself. Over a decade, Doc managed to save several thousand dollars. Since there were no nearby banks, Doc asked Joe Domenico to keep his cash savings in the company safe. Domenico obliged, issuing Doc receipts and storing the envelope of cash.

During the lean years, the New York office insisted that Bill Coulter request special company authorization for all extraordinary cash expenses. Coulter's requests, which were troublesome and time-consuming, were often refused. On one occasion, particularly pressed for time and cash, Coulter quietly borrowed Doc Sloan's life savings. Later, when Coulter realized just how awkward it would be to request a cash authorization to replace Sloan's money, he replaced it instead with an equal value of Climax stock at $1.00 per share—and forgot the whole thing.

In 1935, when Doc Sloan finally retired, he turned in his cash receipts. Joe Domenico, puzzled to find no cash in Doc's envelope, brought the matter to Bill Coulter's immediate attention. The resident superintendent remembered what he had done, sorted through the contents of the safe, and withdrew a stack of old Climax stock certificates that he had made out in Sloan's name. While Doc Sloan waited nervously in the outer office to take receipt of his $4,000, Domenico counted the shares and scribbled some quick calculations. Without saying a word, Domenico showed the results to Coulter.

The following day, Coulter asked Joe Domenico to accompany Sloan to a Denver brokerage house to oversee the stock sale transaction. Doc Sloan, who had never earned more than $5.00 per day in his life, took receipt of a certified check for $120,000. Doc used his Climax stock windfall to repay what he imagined to be his only

131

"debt." He contributed most of the money to the Missouri orphanage where he was raised.

In September 1935, Max Schott promoted Bill Coulter to general manager working out of the Climax Molybdenum Company's new Denver office. But Jack Abrahms, Coulter's intended replacement, disrupted Schott's management plans. Abrahms resigned on short notice to take a position with a Denver iron company. That left only one man with Climax managerial experience who was somewhat qualified to fill the demanding position of resident superintendent—mine superintendent W. E. "Tex" Romig. Miners with firsthand knowledge of Romig's notorious temper called him the "Wild Man."

As Bill Coulter's last act before handing over the superintendency of the Climax Mine to Tex Romig, he created the new position of assistant resident superintendent. The new position reflected the growing and increasingly complex supervisory responsibilities of running a much larger mine. Some also suspected that Bill Coulter believed Tex Romig would need all the help he could get.

Shortly after moving into the "Mansion," the new resident superintendent's residence, Romig constructed two additions: One was a ten-foot-high fence to hold his two vicious chows, the other was a shed to house the big, black Harley-Davidson motorcycle on which he toured the mine property. Miners debated which to fear more—the chows, the Harley, or Romig himself. When all three appeared at once, they agreed, trouble was a sure thing.

Early one September morning, Romig woke to the sound of sheep being herded over Fremont Pass. He was not particularly enamored of sheep, but knew that sheepherders often used the dirt road atop the pass to move their flocks between the alpine meadows. Peering out his bedroom window, Romig saw 1,000 sheep, not on the dirt highway where they belonged, but milling around the general office building, the rail siding, and the packing plant. He quickly dressed and set out on the Harley, his two chows following in the dust, to get to the bottom of things.

But the thunder of the Harley, the snarling chows, and Romig's curses created chaos. When the chows headed straight for the sheep, a pack of tough shepherd dogs went right at the chows. Then the sheepherder appeared, livid with rage, pointing a rifle at the chows and threatening to "blow 'em both to hell!" Romig, not known for

1935. The newly constructed resident superintendent's home, known as "the Mansion."

negotiating skills, gunned the Harley and roared straight for the sheepherder, shouting, "Over my dead body!" Apparently perceiving some merit in that thought, the sheepherder pointed the rifle at Romig. As cooler heads from the packing plant rushed in to defuse the situation, 1,000 sheep scattered through the Climax property, down both sides of the Continental Divide, and into the timberline forests of two counties.

The sheepherder filed charges, then had a Leadville attorney send Romig a bill for 1,000 sheep at $2.00 each. When Climax attorneys advised paying the bill, Romig advised his employees that any and all sheep seen near Fremont Pass were "Climax sheep" to be shot on sight and brought to the boardinghouse kitchen. Romig took a lot of kidding about his "sheep war," even during graveyard shift, when motormen aboard the rumbling muck trains bound to and from the crusher would pass the Mansion where Romig was sleeping, cup their hands to their mouths, and shout, "BAAA-AAA-AAA!"

For those who worked at the Climax Mine during the early 1930s, Climax didn't mean stock appreciation, engineering achievements, or magazine publicity—it meant a job they probably wouldn't have found elsewhere. Considering the combination of elevation, climate, personal health, and brutal mine conditions, not everyone could hold a job at Climax. Among those forced to leave was chief engineer C. Carl Cunningham, whose chronic low blood pressure sometimes caused him to black out when he bent over to tie a shoelace. While surviving four years at Climax, he forgot his condition just once. Bending over to pick something up, he blacked out and fell eighty feet down an ore pass. He managed to climb back up to a pocket just seconds before ten tons of muck thundered by. When Bill Coulter heard of the near-tragedy, he demanded Cunningham's resignation, declaring simply, "You're not going to die on this job!"

But for many of those who could take the work, Climax was a turning point in their lives. One was John Slifka, who found work on a Climax muck crew two weeks before Christmas 1935. Many years later, Slifka recalled that as his best Christmas ever. "The Depression was still being felt and jobs were hard to come by," he said. "But when they put me on at Climax, I went over to the store and got me a new hard hat and carbide lamp. On the way home, I sneaked up the alley and hid my hat and lamp in the coal bucket out back so I could surprise my wife and kids with the news of a new job. But Ruthie, our youngest daughter, spied the hat and lamp in the bucket and came running into the house laughing and crying, 'Daddy has a job!'" Slifka, who would retire from Climax thirty-three years later, also recalled that on that Christmas Eve in 1935 he took home a $10.00 company bonus.

Few men would forget the experience of working on the Phillipson Level during its early years. Although the level was a model of block cave mining and haulage efficiency, it had two big problems. One was the dangerous "bulldozing" procedure needed to clear "hang-ups" on the chute-and-grizzly loading system. When big rocks blocked the grizzly bars and "bottlenecked," shift bosses ruthlessly pushed their men to clear the bars to keep the muck moving. Miners, carrying dynamite, cap, and fuse, edged precariously out onto the grizzly bars, "plastered" the offending rock with powder, inserted the cap, lit the blackwick fuse, and scrambled back across the bars to remove themselves from harm's way. Falling on the eighteen-inch-center steel bars meant certain injury; falling *through* the bars into the ore pass below usually meant death.

But poor ventilation was the Phillipson Level's biggest problem. After a caving shot, clouds of gas, smoke, and rock dust lingered for days. The daily routine of bulldozing, developmental blasting, and chute loading often limited visibility to only a few feet. Miners coming on shift rode open, gondola-like mantrip cars into the mine, then walked to their working places holding their carbide lamps low at their sides so the light would gleam off the rails as a guide. And on days when the air was very bad, miners recognized their working places by groping for familiar patterns of spikes hammered into timbers.

Many miners finished their shifts with splitting headaches from the nitroglycerin fumes generated by the daily underground detonation of 3,000 pounds of dynamite. Much worse, however, was the rock dust churned up by the detonations and daily chute loading of 750 big muck cars. Miners with only a few years on the Phillipson Level could develop pulmonary problems ranging from decreased lung capacity and shortness of breath to increased susceptibility to a host of pulmonary complications, all of which were aggravated by climate and elevation. Many miners became "dusted" or "rocked up," that is, contracted silicosis, an industrial disease caused by inhalation of rock dust that ultimately resulted in irreversible petrifaction of delicate lung tissues.

Given the bad air, poor visibility, and shift bosses that relentlessly pushed crews for "more muck," increased injury and fatality rates became inevitable. There had been no fatalities for two years following the "big accident" of June 1930. Then Climax recorded a death in 1933, two more the following year, and three in 1935. But growing safety problems never stood in the way of production. From supervisors down to foremen and their shift bosses, the order was always for more muck.

Shortly after Brainerd Phillipson's death in May 1930, his ashes were buried at a grave site just above the portal of the big tunnel that carried his name. A black iron fence protected a four-foot-high stone obelisk bearing an engraved bronze plaque testifying that Phillipson's "Genius, Devotion and Indomitable Courage Guided This Enterprise to Success." As mantrips filled with miners going on shift rumbled toward the portal of the Phillipson Tunnel, many would wink and say to their partners, "Gotta give 'er hell today." Gesturing toward the little grave site, they'd add, "He wants more muck."

One anonymous miner who "did his time" at Climax expressed his feelings in rhyme. His poem, handwritten on a faded scrap of paper, follows verbatim. The identifying names were added later.

> *I just came down from Climax*
> *That hellhole near the sky*
> *And now my beer bill is all paid up*
> *It leaves me high and dry*
>
> *Midst molly dust and dynamite*
> *Where money is the brains*
> *There's a future there as black as nite*
> *Where Old King Coulter reigns* [Bill Coulter]
>
> *A penitentuary bunk house*
> *A Finlander shifters curse* [Walt Palo]
> *And a beer dump by the roadside* [the Slop Chute]
> *That waits to snatch your purse*
>
> *There is plenty of gas and powder smoke*
> *And farmers breaking rock*
> *A Texas longhorn skipper* [Tex Romig]
> *How I'd like to stop his clock*
>
> *A caving system quite unique*
> *A place to end this call*
> *In the office there's a freak* [Joe Domenico]
> *That gives advice to all*
>
> *I heard the freight train whistle*
> *And it's time to say good-bye*
> *Forever to Dear Old Climax*
> *That hellhole near the sky*

1935. Bartlett Mountain, the Upper Camp, and the now-inactive aerial tramway. The subsidence appearing on the shoulder of the mountain is the first surface sign of block cave mining in progress below. That subsidence would eventually grow into the famed Climax Glory Hole.

6
Growing Pains
1936-1939

*... there was a snowdrift in the living room. The
bathroom was about as wide as my shoulders.
When I saw the shower mounted directly over the
toilet, I told Romig I didn't need any job this bad.*

*—James Richardson, recalling a job interview
with Resident Superintendent Tex Romig,
winter 1936*

In January 1936, as 400 Climax employees mined and milled a
record 4,000 tons of ore daily, Tex Romig pondered how to maintain the employment level in the dead of winter, when the Climax
labor turnover rate traditionally peaked. Romig first sought the help
of the Colorado Employment Bureau, then began newspaper advertising. Advertising for employees was so unusual at the end of the
Depression that the Associated Press reported it as a wire news
story appearing in newspapers throughout Colorado and much of
the Midwest:

MACHINE OPERATORS WANTED AT CLIMAX

CANON CITY, January 24—(AP)—A request for hardrock machine
operators was received Saturday by Miss Evelyn Easton, Canon City
representative of the Colorado State employment bureau.

The machine operators are wanted at the Climax Molybdenum
mine at Climax, Colo. Wages paid range from $4.50 to $6 per day and
living accommodations for families may be secured there, it is said.
Jobs will probably be permanent for qualified men, altho the men must
be of sturdy physique to work at the Climax altitude, 11,000 feet above
sea level. . . .

But response was slow, for few men, even those desperate for work, would journey to Fremont Pass in the middle of winter. Some of those who did took one look and left; others who hired on lasted less than a month.

As Romig tried everything to hire and hold workers at Climax, Max Schott was busy in New York studying projected demand for molybdenum. Considering the political and military situations in Japan and Europe, Schott was convinced that war was just a matter of time. A major war would create an unprecedented demand for molybdenum that the Climax Mine, at its present production capacity, could never hope to meet. Accordingly, Schott directed Romig and Coulter to immediately submit plans and cost estimates to double daily production to 8,000 tons within one year, and to attain daily production levels of 12,000 tons and 20,000 tons within two years.

From his Denver office, Bill Coulter submitted a lengthy, detailed report to Schott emphasizing that the Climax Mine had entered a "new era." The traditional Climax approach of "tacking on" mill circuits and "scraping around" for additional living facilities was inadequate and outdated. The Climax Mine now needed a radically expanded infrastructure and organization, for higher production would affect everything from employment levels, water supply, and housing facilities to projected life of the tailings pond. Climax had difficulty holding 400 employees, and would never retain more unless Schott committed himself to upgrading salaries, pensions, and, most important, housing and recreation facilities. Bill Coulter's recommendations would reshape life at Climax.

> HOUSING: . . . For 8,000 tons per day we will expect to employ 650 men, and for 12,500 tons we will require 900 men per day. In either case, additional hotel accommodations are necessary, and more houses for married employees are required. We are already experiencing trouble holding skilled employees, particularly miners, on the present tonnage, and to build up our crew to double or triple this scale of operation and hold them, makes the housing of both our single and married employees of the first importance.
>
> RECREATION FACILITIES: So far very little has been done by our Company to provide and supervise recreation for our employees. The camp is isolated, and Leadville is not capable of furnishing desirable or healthy recreation for this number, and other mining and industrial companies employing a fewer number of employees have found it necessary to deal seriously with the problem of recreation in order to hold their men and keep them contented. The competition for a good

class of labor is already becoming apparent, and unless we do something at Climax to provide attractive recreation for our employees when they are off work it is going to be difficult to get and hold the type of men we want and must have. We feel that provision for good housing, good board and good recreational facilities for the men and women of our community will have a more favorable effect on reducing labor turnover, securing the best class of labor, and keeping them satisfied and content than higher wages. With a larger community, more or less isolated, and located in a high altitude where there is six months of winter, we believe the matter of providing adequate recreation facilities is also a problem of the first importance. We have in mind a recreation building, moving pictures, swimming pool, basketball, tennis court, golf course, baseball grounds, a pool hall, bowling alleys, gymnasium, and perhaps a skating rink. The nature of our work and location calls for young, active, healthy men in our organization. It is natural for them to want and demand these different forms of recreation during their hours of leisure, and if we don't furnish them, they are going where they can get them. . . .

Coulter also noted that increased production would accelerate depletion of ore reserves and thus the life of the mine itself. Climax should therefore consider conservation of the Bartlett Mountain mo-

The Climax Molybdenum Company aimed its advertisements of the 1930s directly at industrial consumers.

lybdenite deposit, halting "poor metallurgy" mill practices in favor of the highest recovery rate possible. The tailings pond, built in 1917 near the mill, was filling rapidly, necessitating a new and much larger pond at Robinson Flats lower in the Tenmile Canyon. And even if that pond covered an entire square mile, 20,000-ton-per-day production would fill it at the rate of six feet per year.

Finally, Coulter estimated the physical haulage limits of the Phillipson Tunnel at 12,000 tons per day. High production would mandate either widening the tunnel for double trackage or driving a second parallel tunnel. Coulter believed the wiser alternative would be to begin exploration immediately, either in Ceresco Ridge or deeper within Bartlett Mountain in preparation for a new level below the Phillipson. Coulter concluded that costs to double production within one year would be $800,000; going to 12,000 tons per day would require $1.5 million. And if Schott was serious about 20,000 tons per day, he could begin figuring at $10 million.

The housing situation was already critical, for Climax provided living accommodations for only 180 of its 400 employees. Others lived in old buildings in Robinson and Kokomo in the Tenmile Canyon and in strings of squalid shacks strung down the Arkansas River toward Leadville. About 125 Climax employees lived in or near Leadville.

Keeping State Highway 91 open between Leadville and Climax in the winter was imperative. Tex Romig, backed by a committee of Leadville merchants, pressured the county commissioners, who in turn asked for assistance from the state highway department and the federal Bureau of Roads. By mid-January 1936, the weather had become a serious problem. In his monthly report Romig wrote:

> . . . The weather was very severe throughout the month; twenty-six days with snow and wind, with five fairly good days, but there was some snow on all days. The temperature was as low as 31 below zero. . . .
> The State Highway Department has been plowing the road between Climax and Leadville daily, in spite of which the day shift has been very late three mornings, and once neither the graveyard nor the day shift could get through until the following afternoon. . . .
> Five cases of Scarlet Fever have developed during the month. The Mine Superintendent, Mr. Weidman, developed a streptococci infection. He has been removed to the D&RGW hospital in Salida. His condition is very serious due to toxic poisoning from the infection. There

142

was one case of mumps at the Boarding House. A large number of men are off each day with heavy colds and the flu. Joe Woods [construction superintendent] has been off three weeks because of stomach trouble. Joe Domenico has taken a thirty-day leave because of nervous indigestion. . . .

Romig's troubles were just beginning. In the following five weeks Leadville reported five feet of snow, while twenty-two feet fell at Climax. On February 14, the *Herald Democrat* announced:

BLIZZARDS MAROON RANCHERS, MINERS AND RAILROAD MEN

The headline was even more ominous the next day:

LOCAL SNOW CONDITIONS BRING CRITICAL SITUATION
INDUSTRY THREATENED; EQUIPMENT IS BROKEN DOWN

When two more feet of snow fell on February 17, Leadville declared a snow emergency. Numerous avalanches and twelve-foot drifts blocked the C&S, bringing service to a halt. The last train from

1937. A Colorado & Southern rotary snowplow keeping the rails clear to Climax.

143

Denver took two full days to reach Climax; even though it was double-headed for extra motive power, it became snowbound on the way to Leadville. The C&S sent two locomotives to help out, then soon had a train and four locomotives "out of water and coal, drifting over and freezing solid." The crews were lucky to make it to Leadville on foot.

A big rotary plow from the Bureau of Roads worked around the clock to keep the Climax road open. But on February 23, the Bureau of Roads suddenly reassigned the plow to open the Berthoud Pass road for Denver skiers. The next day, a massive avalanche blocked the Leadville-Climax road. Twenty Climax men crossed the 400-foot-wide avalanche on skis and snowshoes to reach company trucks waiting on the other side. Climax trucks ran day and night to keep that section of the road open. But trains had not reached Climax in a week, and the mine ran low on gasoline, diesel fuel, coal, and food. February 26 brought more snow and this *Herald Democrat* headline:

CLIMAX ROAD STILL IMPASSABLE
MOLYBDENUM WORKERS HOLD MASS MEETING AND SEND
PETITION TO GOVERNOR FOR HELP

Mickey Rossi, a Climax timberman and former professional boxer, assembled more than 100 Climax miners at the Lake County Courthouse, where he delivered a fiery speech attacking the politicians who had diverted the federal rotary plow to accommodate "a bunch of damned skiers." The crowd signed a petition and Rossi fired off this telegram to Governor Edwin Johnson:

> Highway 91 between Climax and Leadville blocked. 450 men on payroll facing immediate loss of employment. Climax Molybdenum Mine must close unless relief is furnished at once. Rotary has been over road just once this year. Miners have practically kept road open by own efforts with 150 cars per day plus freight and company trucks. Present trucks of Bureau hopeless and inadequate. Insufficient drivers furnished. Food and fuel exhausted at Mine, no accommodations for Climax residents if mine is closed. Road can be opened with proper equipment. Need rotary and bulldozer. Situation urgent.
>
> Mickey J. Rossi
> by direction of employees of Climax Molybdenum Company

Then the weather broke; skies cleared, temperatures plummeted, and for the next three days the highest temperature recorded at Climax was eight degrees below zero. Romig cut mill heating as much as possible to conserve his dwindling coal supply and still avoid a disastrous mill freeze-up. With flour the only staple available in quantity, boardinghouse cooks served pancakes at all three meals.

Mickey Rossi, now something of a Climax hero, received a telegram in reply from the governor.

> Am having conference with Bureau this morning. We are planning on bringing in a tractor and other equipment from Pueblo. Please keep me posted. We will get Colorado 91 open. Thanks for your help.
>
> Edwin Johnson
> Governor

The promised equipment finally arrived, but railroad crews needed three days to remount a standard-gauge Denver & Rio Grande Western rotary plow on the C&S narrow-gauge rolling stock. The *Herald Democrat* reported more problems with the rotary highway plow:

> CLIMAX SLIDE CLEARED BUT ROAD NOT OPEN YET
>
> There was much disappointment among Climax miners this morning owing to their inability to get to Climax. The state highway department rotary successfully negotiated the slide but burned out a bearing about three miles from Climax. . . . Some of the men made their way on foot this morning to Climax over the three miles of snowdrifted road yet to be opened by the rotary.

As eight heavy trucks loaded with coal and food waited in Leadville, a Climax bulldozer, burning the last of the available diesel fuel, slowly worked its way down from Fremont Pass, finally meeting the repaired rotary plow to open the road. The trucks reached Climax on March 2; crews immediately unloaded the coal and food, then loaded molybdenite concentrate bound for the D&RGW freight terminal in Leadville. Meanwhile, C&S rail rotaries, each pushed by three locomotives, worked both sides of Fremont Pass to clear the track to Climax. On March 10, the first train in three weeks—two locomotives and two freight cars—crept into the Climax yards. The snow had drifted so deep that State Highway 91 wouldn't open for automobile traffic between Climax and Frisco until May 1.

"I hope these conditions," Tex Romig wrote in his monthly report for March 1936, "emphasize the need for complete housing at Climax."

That summer's construction program, by far the most ambitious ever undertaken at Climax, began on May 1. Community construction included 100 houses of three to six rooms each, forty-three apartment units, a 171-room hotel, a 326-seat dining room addition to the old boardinghouse, a "first-class" hospital, and a school. Despite the high construction costs, Max Schott never intended for the new Climax community to operate at a profit. Its sole purpose was to attract and hold a stable workforce for the mine. The three-room houses would rent for $12.00 per month, including heat and utilities; the big, six-room houses would rent for $24.00 per month. Single men would pay only $1.50 per day at the hotel for room and board.

Schott matched his community development projects with an equally ambitious plant expansion program. Crews at Robinson Flats built high earthen dams to contain a new one-square-mile tailings pond and a 2,500-acre-foot reservoir. Timbermen erected a three-mile-long trestle supporting an open wooden trough to carry tailings slurry from the mill to the new pond. In operation, solid tailings would settle out, while pumps piped the water first into the adjacent reservoir, then back up to the mill as needed. The closed system, which reclaimed and recycled industrial water, would be vital for high-tonnage operation, especially during the winter water shortages.

A new mill, designated "No. 2 Mill," boosted milling capacity to 15,000 tons per day. Climax consulting metallurgist Arthur Weinig replaced the distilled pine oil that had been the standard Climax flotation agent since 1918. The new agent was Arctic Syntex M, an antifreeze-like, sulfurated monoglyceride manufactured by the Colgate-Palmolive-Peet Corporation, which provided better flotation for the critical coarse middlings. Using "good metallurgy" milling practices, molybdenite recovery soon reached 92 percent.

Meanwhile, on the Phillipson Level, engineers realized that the chute-and-grizzly loading system was suited neither for higher tonnages nor the character of the ore. Constant bulldozing on the grizzlies so weakened the ground that entire chutes were lost. Engineers tested a new slusher system employing angled fingers for draw control, learning that the slushers were cheaper to operate, required less development and maintenance work, and improved safety and ventilation. But the original rigid slusher buckets that scraped muck from the fingers to the loading drawholes were notoriously inefficient. Two young Climax engineers, Bob Henderson and Bill "Mac" MacLaughlin, invented a slusher bucket with a folding blade to permit rapid, one-directional scraping. The design represented a major advance in mining technology. It was so successful that Climax soon phased out the chute-and-grizzly system and switched completely to a slusher operation.

The force of 250 construction workers enclosed all the new buildings by October. The big recreation hall had a gymnasium-auditorium, card rooms, four bowling alleys, a poolroom, writing room, two lounges, and a library with 1,000 volumes. The staff of the twenty-bed hospital included a director and associate physician, a head nurse with four assistants, a medical technician and an assistant, and a clinical records clerk. When the hospital opened in December, Climax provided full medical and hospitalization insurance to all residents for $18.00 per year.

The Max Schott School replaced the old two-room schoolhouse. The modern, two-story brick building had fourteen rooms—half designed as regular classrooms, the others as laboratories, libraries, shops, and even a photographic darkroom. Staff included a superintendent, eight experienced graduate teachers, and a custodian. The Department of Education of the University of Colorado granted the Max Schott School full academic accreditation before the first classes were ever held, an unusual move that reflected the school's modern facilities and the faculty's superb qualifications.

As Bill Coulter had warned, construction, especially if "done right," wouldn't be cheap. Community construction and plant expansion during the hectic summer of 1936 cost $4 million.

With the new mill on line, production reached 7,000 tons per day by December. During 1936, Climax mined and milled two million tons of ore to recover fifteen million pounds of contained molybdenum, generating net earnings that easily covered the expansion and construction costs. Employment rose to 600 and, for the first time, the Climax Mine annual payroll surpassed $1 million.

Block cave mining on the Phillipson Level had already yielded five million tons of ore, and the caving effect had reached the surface of Bartlett Mountain. A small, craterlike subsidence formed just west of the old Leal claims, the first visible indication of the massive scale of mining being conducted within the mountain. Miners called it the Glory Hole; in time, the slowly growing crater would become not only a symbol of the Climax Mine, but the dominant feature of Bartlett Mountain.

With record production, the Climax Mine depended more than ever on the Colorado & Southern Railroad. In a typical month, Climax shipped seventy twenty-five-ton carload lots of concentrate. During summer construction, three freight carloads of building materials, cement, timber, steel, and mill supplies arrived every day. But the C&S, which had tried for a decade to abandon its South Park line, was finally on the brink of bankruptcy. In January 1937, the C&S again petitioned the Interstate Commerce Commission for abandonment. Since the C&S was unable to give the South Park line away, and was now financially incapable of continuing service, the commission had no alternative but to grant approval. The announcement caught many by surprise: On or about April 8, 1937, the Colorado & Southern Railroad would terminate service on and abandon its South Park line.

Climax attorneys, along with the attorneys of Park, Summit, and Lake counties, fought for an injunction. Climax, county, and C&S attorneys, state and federal judges, and representatives of the Interstate Commerce Commission negotiated in round-the-clock meetings, even on April 10, when the last C&S passenger train departed Leadville for Climax and Denver. At Climax, Tex Romig contracted for every heavy truck he could find between Denver and Pueblo.

But on April 15, the parties hammered out a compromise. The C&S could abandon all of its South Park line east of Climax, but must continue to operate the fourteen-mile-long section between Climax and Leadville. On April 16, 1937, the *Herald Democrat* reported the agreement.

COURT ORDERS CLIMAX LINE TO CONTINUE ITS OPERATIONS
STEPS TAKEN TO PREVENT INTERFERENCE
WITH OUTPUT OF MOLY CAMP

The federal court took a hand in the litigation growing out of the abandonment of the South Park Branch of the Colorado and Southern. . . .

With the railroad having ceased to operate between Climax and [points east], it remains the only connecting link to Leadville and any interference with this would have serious consequences to the moly camp now pouring out 8,000 tons of ore daily . . .

The South Park Railroad, a newly formed subsidiary of the C&S, took over the Leadville-Climax right-of-way, the last surviving remnant of the historic South Park line. With all Climax freight now routed through Leadville, the Denver & Rio Grande Western's Leadville yards bustled with activity. But the Leadville yards were an inefficient transshipment point: All freight bound to or from Climax had to be manually transferred between the South Park Railroad's narrow-gauge cars and the D&RGW Railroad's standard-gauge rolling stock.

With rail service assured, Climax grew rapidly during 1937, mining and milling 10,000 tons of ore per day. Decent housing made a big difference, and employment doubled in just one year to 1,270, raising the annual payroll to $2.5 million.

As early as 1932, when the Climax Mine had only 100 employees, Bill Coulter foresaw that increased employment would make attempts at unionization inevitable, perhaps by such undesirable and radical groups as communists and the "Wobblies," the Industrial Workers of the World. Coulter was staunchly antiunion, and in correspondence suggested two approaches to discourage unionization at Climax: "Keep 'em happy" with recreational opportunities, and maintain a large stockpile of concentrate as an advantage in any protracted labor dispute.

The first serious attempt to unionize Climax workers came in fall 1937, when a group of forty employees formed Local 435. They petitioned the International Union of Mine, Mill, and Smelter Workers, affiliated with the Congress of Industrial Organizations, for a charter, and began actively seeking broader support. Rumors flew that Max Schott was adamantly opposed to unionization and would not tolerate union supporters on the Climax payroll. When several other Colorado unions voiced support for "suppressed" Climax workers, Schott clearly stated his position in a letter mailed to every Climax employee.

> Due to the fact that during the past year we have greatly increased our working forces, it is quite probable that many of our employees are not familiar with the policy of the company. . . .
>
> The Climax Molybdenum Company is and always has been willing to meet with any employee or group of employees to discuss matters relating to the welfare or working conditions of its employees.
>
> You are already informed the representatives of the Company will soon enter into discussions with the representatives of the Interna-

tional Union of Mine, Mill and Smelter Workers. I wish to make it plain that employees of this Company will neither be favored nor discriminated against because of union membership. To join or not to join any union is a matter which each employee has a right to decide for himself. . . . To this I wish to add that regardless of any union affiliation the policy and purpose of this Company has been and will continue to be to give its duties the fairest and fullest consideration while at the same time insisting upon its rights.

Like the Company, the employees have rights and duties. I can assure you that the Company will do its part, and that this, together with the full and faithful performance of your duties, will promote and preserve the interests of all concerned more than anything else. . . .

Schott emphasized that wages and hospital, hotel, and recreational facilities at Climax were superior to those of other mining districts, that family housing would be expanded further, and that the Climax store was neither owned nor controlled by the company (Schott was correct about the store—technically). On the matter of the already legendary Climax labor turnover rate, Schott commented:

One of the principal reasons for the large labor turnover at Climax has been the lack of sufficient housing facilities. The Company is doing everything possible to correct this situation. In addition to this some of the men who are hired find they cannot stand the altitude and quit. During the past few years, however, the major cause for the large turnover has probably been the rapid increase in our working forces. We have found that under such circumstances a great number of the men hired are subsequently found to be unfit for the work or too inexperienced for their own good and the other man's safety. . . .

In our relations with our employees it is our main desire and interest to maintain industrial peace. We realize that such a state can be maintained by having an economically and socially contented labor force under the safest conditions which can be attained in order to reduce accidents and to assure their physical well-being. Accordingly, our policy will continue to be directed toward contributing to those ends and toward improving existing conditions wherever need for improvements is indicated.

In May 1939, in a company-wide vote, Climax workers rejected unionization.

Recreation facilities at the Climax Mine were the best in central Colorado. Twice weekly, the big gymnasium in the recreation hall became the Climax Fox Theater, which screened both first-run films and popular classics. Climax hired Ralph Hargrove as full-time rec-

150

reation director. A former professional basketball player, Hargrove organized dozens of activities, from pick-up-sticks and Monopoly to Ping-Pong, bowling, and volleyball tournaments—even tennis tournaments on one of the nation's first regulation indoor courts.

Hargrove also supervised the recreation hall library, where his first job was to catalogue and shelve a shipment of 300 new books, a personal gift of Mr. and Mrs. Max Schott, who had asked a personal friend—the chief librarian of the New York City Public Library—to select appropriate titles.

An especially popular form of recreation took advantage of a natural winter resource that Climax had in abundance—fine, deep, powder snow that offered world-class skiing. Climax always had a number of cross-country skiers, and in fall 1936, construction foreman Scott Gorsuch and fellow employees John Petty, Scotty MacGregor, Bill Spencer, Jim Proctor, and Chuck Pooler asked Tex Romig for permission and assistance to establish a small downhill ski area on the east slope of Chalk Mountain just north of the summit of Fremont Pass.

Using wire and lights "borrowed" from the mine, Gorsuch's team of volunteers worked into the nights clearing trees and burning stumps. By January 1937, the downhill runs were ready. There was no lift, so only well-conditioned, hard-core skiers would—or could—make more than three runs per day. Nevertheless, the little ski area became so popular that the first Climax Ski Meet, held on April 25, 1937, drew a crowd of 300, half from Climax and the remainder from Leadville and the Tenmile camps.

Climax held its first social event in the new recreational hall on January 15, 1938. It was a joint safety rally and dance with a live band, free refreshments, and a guest speaker from the U.S. Bureau of Mines. Dress was surprisingly formal for Fremont Pass; men wore ties and many women appeared in full-length gowns. Among the 700 people attending was Leadville *Herald Democrat* cub reporter Norman Miller, who was assigned to interview the guest of honor, the famous Mr. Max Schott. Miller's article told of the reporter's difficulty in interviewing the president of the Climax Molybdenum Company.

> Max Schott, president of the Climax Molybdenum Company, is a "regular guy." I found that out Saturday night when Mr. Schott submitted to an interview in the "privacy" of the Recreation Club gymnasium.

151

He is a little, stockily built, gray-haired man, kindly and with no desire for the limelight. When he speaks it is in soft tones and he wastes no words. . . .

At first I was told that Mr. Schott refused to grant an interview, that he was to leave the following morning and that he was tired. I hung around the dance floor until I spied Schott and his party mixing with the Climax men and women in an informal fashion.

No, he had nothing to say, the company supplied all the information, he said modestly, and there was little he could add. Newspapers generally exaggerated stories and he wasn't seeking publicity.

"But, Mr. Schott, this is different, I can't go back to my newspaper without an interview from you. I'll be fired."

"Well, that's different," he said. "Won't you sit down?" But before questions could be asked [the band music] brought a beautiful lady before us. . . . Soon Mr. Schott and the gazelle-like creature were whirling away over the floor, while I was left to meditate over some of the advantages of being a company president.

When Schott returned to the reporter, he spoke of a bright future for both molybdenum and the improving national economy. He also answered a question of recent concern in Leadville: Considering the tremendous expansion of the last two years, was Climax attempting to displace Leadville as the biggest and most important city in Lake County? Certainly not, Schott assured the young reporter; Climax was concerned only with the immediate needs of its employees and was not, nor would ever be, in competition with Leadville.

The grand opening of the recreation hall with a safety rally proved ironic, for mine safety at Climax had reached critical levels. Climax had attained the 12,000-ton-per-day production level that Max Schott had ordered nearly two years earlier, but the increase in production and hiring brought a sharp decline in mine safety. Although no fatal accident was recorded in 1936, five occurred the following year.

In February 1938, Climax employed 1,400 largely inexperienced workers. That month a miner timbering bad ground died of a fractured skull suffered in a rockfall. By July that was the year's only fatality, and the newly formed Safety Department had high hopes that 1938 would be a "good year." But then the real trouble started, and the *Herald Democrat* reported a string of fatalities.

MINER DIES IN MISHAP AT CLIMAX
OLAF OLSON IS KILLED WHEN POWDER UNEXPECTEDLY EXPLODES
Finished loading thirteen holes with powder, preparatory to blast-

March 26, 1938. Climax engineers pose for a group photograph in front of the Phillipson portal.

ing in a stope of the Climax mine, the fourteenth dynamite-filled hole he was tamping suddenly exploded at 3:45 o'clock this morning, killing Olaf Olson, 31, of Leadville, almost instantly, and sending his helper, Leonard Doddon, of Climax, to the Climax hospital suffering lacerations of the head and face and shock. . . .

The tragic news continued for the remainder of the 1938. In August:

TWO LOCAL MEN LOSE LIVES IN MISHAP AT CLIMAX

Two Leadville men, Leonard McMahon, 21, and Clyde Miracle, were found dead at 7:15 o'clock this morning in Drift No. 360-15. Coroner James J. Corbett, who investigated the accident, pronounced their deaths due to gas which accumulated after blasting during the night. . . .

Fatal accidents also occurred in September, October, and November. Then, in December:

1937. An underground toolroom on the Phillipson Level.

TWO LOCAL MEN CRUSHED IN SLIDE OF ROCK EARLY TODAY

At 5:30 this morning, the crushed bodies of Kenneth G. States, 24, and Chester Johnson, 27, both of Leadville, were found in Raise 16-5, D finger East, of the Climax mine, by their boss Don Shafer, who had last seen them alive at 3:30 o'clock. . . .

In 1938, nine Climax miners died, eight within a five-month period. Coupled with forty-six "lost time" accidents, many involving broken bones and crushed limbs, Climax compiled the worst annual safety record of all major underground metal mines in the United States. Miners gave "the hellhole near the sky" another nickname— "the slaughterhouse." The only good thing about safety at Climax, miners said with derisive laughs, was where the company chose to build the hospital—just 100 yards from the portal of the Phillipson Tunnel. Miners loaded the frequent "basket cases" on the nearest motor for quick delivery to waiting doctors and nurses.

The frightening number of fatal accidents at "the slaughterhouse"— twenty-five fatalities in just nine years—played heavily upon the imaginations of superstitious miners. Some believed that in the last moment before the rock came down, the powder detonated prematurely, or the gas reached asphyxiation levels, a doomed man saw another miner, dressed as he was in dirty diggers and hard hat, but

154

A miner "taking five" in a Phillipson Level powder room. From a popular postcard series of the late 1930s.

wearing spotlessly clean white boots. Some said his face was expressionless, but most thought the "Man with the White Boots" wore a faint, knowing smile. No one was certain, of course, for miners who had come face-to-face with the "Man with the White Boots" weren't around to answer questions. When shift bosses assigned their miners to unusually dangerous jobs, they'd caution, "Be careful, you don't want the Man with the White Boots walkin' in there."

Climax had issued its first safety manual in 1932, but didn't begin an organized safety program until 1935. During those years, the Climax attitude regarding safety generally reflected that of the mining industry: Safety is fine, but don't let it get in the way of production. The Climax bonus system to speed development and production on the Phillipson Level was the very antithesis of a safety program. First, the company paid mine and muck crews a tax-free cash bonus for all footage or tonnage recorded above "standard" levels. Many miners doubled their wages but weren't satisfied, resorting to every trick in the book to further boost footage and tonnage, often at the expense of safety.

When accident rates rose sharply, the company modified its incentive program by setting aside a fixed amount of bonus money to be claimed by crews based on their performance. That provided

1936. An outside dispatcher controlling the movement of haulage trains through the Phillipson Tunnel.

imaginative crews with another route to a fat bonus besides working harder for more footage or tonnage—sabotaging their competition. Miners thought nothing of handicapping the other crews by slashing air hoses, cutting slusher cables, and hiding or stealing drill bits and tools. Both safety and production suffered further when several underground fights broke out over use of drills and mucking machines.

The company next experimented with a bonus system that deducted accidents and injuries against footage and tonnage numbers. Now, injured miners refused to report accidents for fear of reducing their crew's bonus. Some miners were literally carried off shift, only to report for work the next day limping or with arms in slings hidden under bulky shirts.

In yet another attempt to lower accident rates, Climax eliminated all footage and tonnage bonuses and offered one based solely on safety. Reporting injuries became mandatory and miners were paid for recuperation time. Footage and tonnage numbers soon plummeted as miners lined up to report injuries, both real and imagined. Many were lower back injuries that, while purportedly causing immobility and pain, were difficult for doctors to diagnose and treat. The company abruptly terminated that program when "recuperating"

Climax miners turned up working at other mines—and collecting two paychecks.

The rising accident and fatality rates exerted measurable adverse effects on mine development and production. Labor turnover increased and production dropped immediately following every serious accident. After all of the company's safety-production bonus-incentive systems had failed, Climax put the problem in the hands of its first full-time safety director, James K. Richardson.

Richardson recalled his first visit to Climax early in the winter of 1936. He arrived in Leadville just as an avalanche blocked the Climax road. Richardson walked across the slide to a waiting Climax truck that took him toward Fremont Pass. But by then the road had drifted over below the pass, forcing him to walk the last steep mile through deep snow.

After an interview, Tex Romig showed Richardson the house where he and his wife would live. "The house hadn't been lived in for a while," Richardson recounted. "Romig opened the front door and there was a snowdrift in the living room. The bathroom was about as wide as my shoulders. When I saw the shower mounted directly over the toilet, I told Romig I didn't need any job this bad." But a year later, after Climax built seventy-eight new houses, Richardson returned and took the job.

Richardson found that Climax miners and shift bosses harbored a deep disrespect for safety directors and safety inspectors. Miners labeled anyone wearing a white hard hat a "school of mines punk." By late 1938, Richardson suspected that the best safety men might be shift bosses with relatively safe work records. He organized a program requiring every shift boss, on a rotating basis, to join the Safety Department for six months as a safety inspector. Bosses unable—or unwilling—to complete their safety training and assignments forfeited all chance for advancement. Those who completed the training returned to their production and development crews. Miners were far more receptive to accepting safety advice and instruction from shift bosses, men who had drilled, blasted, timbered, and mucked, who understood their problems, and who spoke their language. For the first time, safety education and practice began making a difference at the Climax Mine. Safety was further improved in late 1938 by introduction of such modern equipment as steel-toed rubber mine boots, metal hard hats, and, most important, rechargeable electric cap lamps.

157

Smoke after lunch - Climax Mine

1937. A smoke break after lunch on the Phillipson Level. The carbide lamps would soon be replaced by battery-powered electric cap lamps.

Both safety and industrial hygiene also improved when engineers finally designed effective ventilation for the Phillipson Level. The first mechanical fan, installed in 1934, had little effect on the clouds of dust, smoke, and gas. Three more fans installed in 1936 helped, but real improvement began when Climax hired Leo Glanville as full-time ventilation engineer in 1937. Glanville became a familiar figure around Climax, with his clipped British accent, spit-shined, knee-high, leather riding boots, and love of reciting Rudyard Kipling to the Max Schott School students.

After a year of ventilation studies, Glanville concluded that the Phillipson Level needed to double its existing air flow for satisfactory ventilation. He designed an integrated ventilation flow pattern for the entire level, controlled air flow with automatic air doors and powerful intake and exhaust fans, and installed mechanical humidifiers to help control dust. After Glanville's work, Phillipson Level miners no longer stumbled to their work places in clouds of gas, dust, and powder smoke that once took days to clear.

In just over two years, Climax had tripled production and employment, built a respectable community, established an effective safety program, and substantially improved working conditions. The expansion and construction had not been cheap; Climax had spent $9 million and suffered 13 fatal accidents in 1937 and 1938 alone. But Max Schott had wanted more muck, and he had gotten more muck. By December 1938, the Climax Mine was mining and milling 12,000 tons of ore per day.

Meanwhile, exploration progressed from the Phillipson Level through a 500-foot-deep shaft and a half-mile-long pattern of narrow drifts that engineers designated the 500 Level. Diamond drilling revealed more molybdenite at depth, and geologist David Le Count Evans supervised the core studies that would determine the size and configuration of the new ore body. Evans was among the very few men ever to come to Climax to work at a lower elevation. Previously he had worked at Potosí, Bolivia, where mine elevations exceeded 15,000 feet.

By the late 1930s, a colorful culture had evolved at Climax, both in the mine and the community. Miners routinely spoke in an underground patois that new hands had difficulty understanding. Specialized underground job classifications included "nippers,"

A Phillipson Level miner operating a "buzzy" drill. From a popular postcard series of the late 1930s.

"whistlepunks," "car whackers," "woodpickers," and "powder monkeys"—all mine jargon for jobs involving, respectively, delivering mine supplies, positioning muck cars under drawholes with the use of whistle signals, blasting frozen or packed mud from the bottoms of muck cars, manually picking bits of wood and steel from crushed ore, and servicing the many underground powder magazines.

Life in the Climax community was a unique experience, and residents devised numerous tricks to cope with the winter. With some 300 inches of seasonal snowfall, many children skied to their classes at the Max Schott School. Climax road maintenance crews didn't blade streets clear, but simply compacted the snow. By February, roads were buried under a five-foot-thick layer of hard, compacted snow. By then, most drivers gave up and simply parked their cars. With additional snow falling nearly every day, many cars weren't seen again until April. Since the snow didn't melt evenly, experienced Climax car owners took great care to brace their vehicles with timber stulls to assure they would settle on their wheels and not, as sometimes happened to the cars of first-year residents, on their sides.

Since early electric refrigerators were still troublesome and expensive, Climax families relied instead upon "Okie iceboxes," wooden powder boxes mounted outside kitchen windows. Experienced Climax homemakers preferred DuPont powder boxes over the Hercules type because of their sturdier construction. Temperature control meant opening the kitchen window just enough to allow the right amount of warm air to exhaust into the box. Two "Okie iceboxes" were a status symbol, for the family could ostensibly afford the groceries to fill both.

All the groceries that filled the "Okie iceboxes" came, of course, from the Fremont Trading Post, where business was booming. George Coulter had learned that just selling tokens and chits was quite profitable. George had sold tens of thousands of dollars worth of chits, not all of which were exchanged in trade. Some became lost, others were literally worn out by being pushed across the beer-stained poker tables in the Slop Chute, and still more vanished forever in the pockets of departing miners who contributed to the high labor turnover rate.

George Coulter always encouraged sales by reminding folks that his chits weren't just a substitute for cash; as far as he was concerned, they were exactly the same as "cash money." George wasn't outsmarted often, but he met his match in 1939 when a miner bought a new Chrysler from his automobile dealership at the Fremont Garage. When the miner turned in his old Ford as a trade-in, George asked how he'd be paying the remaining $800. "Cash money," was the answer, which was just what George wanted to hear. But then the miner opened the trunk of the old Ford and withdrew a cardboard shoe box filled to the brim with torn, faded, folded, beer-stained Fremont Trading Post chits. "Here you are, George, cash money," the miner said. "Even counted 'em out for you." George hesitated for a fleeting second, then took the box without a word. For months, the miner had bought every chit he could find in Leadville and Climax, paying cash at a big discount. Years later he still told his friends at the Slop Chute that he hadn't gotten nearly as much pleasure out of that new Chrysler as he had gotten from the look on George Coulter's face.

1937. A welcome sight for a Phillipson Level miner—coming out of the Phillipson portal at the end of a shift.

7
Beyond Reasonable Limits
The 1940s

Climax has been working at maximum stress and at seven days per week during the past year. . . . We are working at top speed and at the limit. Under such conditions we certainly cannot overlook the dangers that accompany increasing pressures to the breaking point of both men and equipment in our desire to achieve maximum production of molybdenum.

—Bill Coulter, in a letter to the War Production Board, January 1943

Foreign sales of molybdenite concentrate generated the revenues that enabled the Climax Mine to survive the Great Depression and expand so rapidly in the years that followed. In the late 1930s, all primary foreign customers—Great Britain, France, Germany, the Soviet Union, and Japan—prepared for war and bought huge amounts of molybdenum. Export sales boomed; by 1938, the Climax packing plant shipped 3,000 export casks, each filled with 600 pounds of concentrate, every month. The sturdy export casks were still constructed of oak, with the exception of those bound for Osaka. Since 1936, Japan had specified steel drums for all shipments in order to obtain every bit of metal possible as part of its national war-materials acquisition program.

The approaching war's first effect on the Climax Mine was not to increase molybdenum production, but to decrease it. Early in 1939, President Franklin D. Roosevelt summoned Max Schott, along with top executives of other American exporting companies, to meetings in Washington. Roosevelt asked for a voluntary "moral embargo" of war-related materials to nations then using aircraft to bomb civilian

163

populations. Those nations were Germany, Japan, and the Soviet Union—the Climax Molybdenum Company's three biggest foreign customers.

Max Schott complied with the president's "request" immediately, terminating export shipments of molybdenite concentrate to Hamburg, Osaka, and Leningrad. The embargo wiped out about one-quarter of the Climax market. But before leaving Washington, Schott met privately with Roosevelt, extracting a promise that the president would use his power to encourage the War Department's ordinance-development researchers to consider molybdenum steels more closely.

Schott had a clear understanding of exactly what global war would mean for Climax. He had based his 1936 order to triple production within two years upon his personal conviction that global war was inevitable. The following year Schott began setting aside $100,000 per month as a company "war fund." He earmarked the fund not to help increase production, but to carry the company through the hard times that inevitably followed every major war.

Compliance with Roosevelt's "moral embargo" left Schott no choice but to cut back production at the Climax Mine from 12,000 to 8,000 tons per day. Instead of ordering layoffs, however, Schott redirected manpower to two areas that would have great consequence in the near future: continued development of broken ore reserves, and massive concrete reinforcement of the Phillipson Level slusher workings.

At Climax, the Mine Department accelerated its program of big caving shots until broken ore reserves measured in the tens of millions of tons. Engineers directed much attention to excessive wear of the bare rock slusher workings. Heavy, repetitive hang-up blasting had fractured many fingers; others were reamed out to dimensions that threatened draw control.

To save the fingers, engineers first tried timber and steel reinforcement, but without success. In 1939, they placed concrete rings at badly worn finger points. When results were encouraging, they formed and placed entire fingers with a foot of concrete. But the concrete still failed to withstand the long-term stresses of hang-up blasting and ore movement. Engineers finally found an answer in steel-reinforced concrete. Although costly, steel-reinforced concrete finger sleeves withstood the severe stress, improving draw control and reducing the wear and friction that caused most hang-ups. Ole

Lee, the first Climax concrete foreman, supervised the placing of 80,000 cubic yards of concrete to greatly extend the life of the Phillipson Level and prepare the mine, just in time, for coming wartime production.

But before the war began, Max Schott became entangled in two important court battles, the first of which dealt with a question that originated in 1916 when Schott, then the director of western operations for The American Metal Company, first visited Bartlett Mountain. The Associated Press carried the story nationally in June 1939.

SUIT DEMANDS TITLE TO SHARE OF CLIMAX

NEW YORK, June 23.—(AP)—Court action demanding the transfer of title and two-thirds interest of the $81,000,000 Climax Molybdenum Company to the American Metal Company, Ltd., has been started by the American Metal minority stockholders against the present and past directors of the American Metal Company, it was disclosed today.

The suit charges "conspiracy" dating back to 1916 under which molybdenum was claimed to have been seized without payment. . . .

It was no secret that American Metal Company people, expertise, and money had launched the Climax Syndicate in 1916. But when the Climax Molybdenum Company was founded in January 1918, the Metal Company directors took most of the Climax shares in their own names, leaving the Metal Company with only a 10 percent interest. No one had questioned that distribution, certainly not after the mine shut down in 1918 or during the "Anti-Climax" years when the future of the Climax Molybdenum Company was in grave doubt.

But after *Fortune* magazine publicized the Climax Molybdenum Company in 1935 as the darling of Wall Street, the Metal Company's minority shareholders were no longer content with a corporate-diluted, 10 percent share of the huge Climax profits. Together, the minority shareholders filed suit in December 1938, contending that without the Metal Company's substantial financial and technical contributions, Climax never would have gotten off the ground. The suit demanded proper compensation and asked the court to award title and two-thirds of all interests of the Climax Molybdenum Company to The American Metal Company.

Early in 1940, the case concluded favorably for Max Schott and the Climax Molybdenum Company. The court ruled that the Metal Company had not shared in the considerable risks and expenses of the 1920s, also pointing out that the certificate of incorporation of The American Metal Company, Ltd., specifically excluded active participation in mining ventures.

Max Schott often said that granting the *Fortune* interview in 1935 had been a big mistake. After that article hit the newsstands, he had been besieged by publications demanding interviews. They ranged from *The Wall Street Journal*, which wanted access to financial records to determine just how low Climax production costs really were, to men's adventure magazines seeking sensational accounts of "treasure hunting" in Bartlett Mountain. Schott finally halted the interviews in January 1938 and, with the exception of an occasional *Herald Democrat* reporter, barred journalists from the Climax property.

But as Schott suspected, the damage was already done. More legal trouble started when John Seaman, chairman of the Colorado Tax Commission, studied the *Fortune* article. If that article were even half true, Seaman declared, then the Climax Molybdenum Company was "getting away with murder" on its tax obligations. Seaman advised Lake County to take a much closer look at the Climax Mine's 1938 valuation of $4 million. When the Lake County assessor did just that, he quadrupled the valuation to $16 million in 1939. The sharply increased valuation nearly tripled the Climax Mine's annual county property tax bill from $100,000 to $280,000, raising its share of Lake County's total annual property tax revenues from 46 percent to 74 percent. Lake County Attorney Eugene Bond declared, "Since God Almighty put the mineral wealth down in Lake County, then the county is entitled to a share of [the Climax Mine's] 50 percent profits."

Climax received its revised tax bill in August 1939, but made only a partial payment while its attorneys reviewed the matter. But Lake County refused to accept a partial payment, citing that legal precedent in tax disputes was to pay the entire bill first, then contest any irregularities later. Climax attorneys promptly withdrew their partial payment and refused to pay anything.

Climax attorneys noted two main points of "gross inequity": One was duplicate assessment of certain assets in Summit and Eagle counties; the other was the assessed value of the Climax concentrates. Climax claimed the concentrates had no value until converted into usable forms. But Lake County contended those concentrates were the basis of the well-publicized Climax profits. Furthermore,

166

the Lake County assessor determined that the Climax warehouse contained 7,500 tons of 90 percent concentrate with a tax-purpose valuation of $3 million. Climax then announced that if the courts accepted the $3 million valuation, it would build a new warehouse and move every pound of concentrate one-half mile north into Summit County. But the Colorado Tax Commission thwarted that option by ordering equal valuation not only in Summit County, but also in nearby Eagle County should Climax think of heading that way.

The "tax war" dragged on for a full year. Climax steadfastly refused to pay a penny, while Lake County was rapidly running out of money. On August 2, 1940, the *Herald Democrat* announced Lake County's new strategy.

PAYMENT OF CLIMAX TAX IS DEMANDED BY COUNTY
THREAT OF SEIZURE AND SALE OF MINE IS DENIED

The Lake County commissioners cautioned the press that seizure might be "somewhat premature," yet insisted that Max Schott personally attend the upcoming tax hearing in Denver. The county commissioners then tossed Schott a "carrot"—a modest reduction in the assessment. Schott not only refused to attend the tax hearing, but denounced the assessment reduction as "illegal and absurd."

Lake County couldn't afford to argue the matter indefinitely, for Climax was its biggest single source of tax revenue. Desperate, the county made one last attempt at settlement by "generously" reducing the total Climax tax bill by $51,000. When Climax flatly refused to consider the new offer, Lake County filed for an emergency state loan until "a compromise could be worked out." But the Colorado Tax Commission ruled that request illegal on the grounds that tax regulations were laws not subject to compromise.

Finally, Lake County threatened to formally charge Climax with tax evasion through fraudulent misstatement of its production values. Climax replied that production values were a moot point; if necessary, the company would never again store another pound of molybdenite concentrate anywhere in the state of Colorado.

The tax war had political undercurrents, with two of Lake County's three commissioners up for reelection. Incumbents Thomas J. Starr and B. A. Swansen, both Leadville businessmen, campaigned on a "make Climax pay" ticket. They lost to Cy Pierce, a Climax employee, and George Burke, a pro-Climax railroad man, who swept the Climax precincts by twenty-to-one margins. But Starr and Swansen were still commissioners until January 1, 1941, more than enough time, they vowed, to "make Climax pay." Four days after the election, the *Herald Democrat* headlined their next move.

CLIMAX PROPERTY MAY BE SOLD FOR TAXES

The commissioners directed Lake County Treasurer Frank E. Kendrick to secure a court distraint order to seize the Climax property for nonpayment of taxes. But a court distraint order had to be handled delicately. First, it might require the awkward posting of a seizure writ on the front door of the Climax general office building. Second, exercising a distraint order could make the county responsible for operation and maintenance of the multimillion-dollar Climax mine and mill. But of most concern was a third possible consequence, for closing the mine and throwing half the county out of work would be the ultimate political disaster.

Kendrick chose a low-key approach, as if Climax were no different than any other tax-delinquent residential or business property. He advertised the Climax property at tax sale, placing advertisements in major newspapers, including *The New York Times*. The Climax Molybdenum Company countered with its own newspaper advertisements, warning that anyone attempting to buy the tax certificate would also "buy himself a lawsuit."

On December 9, 1940, the Climax Mine, together with all associated features and structures located in Lake County, was called for tax sale at the Lake County Courthouse. It was the fourth property called, following two vacant houses and an empty lot. The Lake County deputy treasurer needed eight minutes to read the legal property description, which included 3,000 acres of land, approximately twenty miles of underground workings, seventeen electric haulage locomotives, a reservoir, office, school, numerous living facilities, tram trestles, tailings pipes and ponds, substantial water rights, and much more, all with an estimated real value "somewhere in excess of $20 million."

Seventeen witnesses waited in silence as Frank Kendrick opened the single sealed bid—and withdrew a $10.00 check from one George Malott of Indianapolis, Indiana. When the chuckles subsided, the deputy treasurer moved on to the next tax-delinquent property, an unimproved half-acre field.

The Climax Mine remained on the block for another week while two additional bids came in. The first was for $1.00, the other for a more substantial $10,000. Calling all the bids "ridiculous," Kendrick explained he would accept none until the basic tax certificate, then up to $294,000, including the county-imposed penalties, had been satisfied. On December 21, 1940, *Business Week* ran the story nationally.

HOLE IN A MOUNTAIN
TAX FIGHT FOCUSES SPOTLIGHT ON COLORADO MINE
WHICH PRODUCES TWO-THIRDS OF WORLD
OUTPUT OF ALLOYING ELEMENT

... between giant ridges on Colorado's Highway No. 91, suddenly you come upon a square mile of white and blowing desert sand, laced by high spidery wooden trestles. You round the next bend, and there, a quarter mile from the highway, a red mountain is being disemboweled. The mountain seems to be groaning, but this is the noise of the mill, grinding 12,000 tons of ore per day to the fine white tailings that spread along the valley.

This is the huge and prosperous plant of the Climax Molybdenum Company, source of two-thirds of the world's output of the precious alloying element, and estimated to have 90 percent of the world's supply. It is now in the national news because this whole property was recently offered at forced sale for delinquent taxes.

Lake County's seat is historic Leadville, which produced nearly half a billion dollars in gold and silver—but its future values are deep in drowned pits, and it is a semi-ghost city. . . .

The company says it won't fight in print, but will wait for the courts. It asserts that the tax claim is excessive and will never be paid.

Lake County, Climax, and a state judge finally reached an agreement in July 1941, and the Climax Molybdenum Company settled its tax bills. A state district court order eliminated duplicate assessment: Lake County would assess all future production; Summit County, and to a smaller extent, Eagle County, would assess most water and tailings holdings. The court reduced the total three-county assessed valuation of the Climax property from $20 million to $13 million. With the tax war over, the Climax Molybdenum Company turned its full attention to preparing to meet emergency production demands for a world war that was about to engulf the United States.

In 1939, Jack Abrahms had returned to Climax to take over as resident superintendent. In February 1941, Max Schott ordered production stepped up to 12,000 tons per day, but Abrahms found that maintaining high employment levels, especially of experienced workers, was increasingly difficult. Competing with a military draft and steady hiring at many defense-related construction projects, the mining industry petitioned the War Department for draft exemption as a vital war-production industry. But even before the War Department acted on the petition, Schott ordered Abrahms to boost production to 15,000 tons per day—which everyone at Climax agreed was the physical limit of both the mine and mill.

The bombs fell on Pearl Harbor on December 7, 1941. The United States formally declared war on Japan on December 10, and on Germany and Italy on December 11. Under authority of the Executive War Powers Act, President Franklin D. Roosevelt placed American industry under the direction of the War Production Board, a quasi-military agency empowered to control material supply and distribution and to maximize industrial production. The Climax Mine fell under direct jurisdiction of Brigadier General Paul B. Clemens, Commanding General of Supply Services, Seventh Service Command, headquartered in Omaha, Nebraska.

Global war made foreign supplies of such alloying metals as tungsten, chromium, nickel, manganese, and vanadium scarce and unreliable, and the ready availability of tough molybdenum steels was obviously vital to victory. But molybdenum was unique from the standpoint of supply, for no other metal in the world was so utterly dependent upon a single mine source.

The War Production Board summoned Max Schott to Washington in January 1942, serving notice that it had assigned the Climax Mine the highest operating priority of any mine in the United States. By order of the War Production Board, the Climax Mine would immediately achieve and maintain maximum production. At the time, the order seemed a mere formality, for the Climax Mine was already operating at its physical production limit and would produce a record twenty-five million pounds of molybdenum per year.

But on February 5, 1942, Max Schott received this letter from H. K. Masters, chief of the Molybdenum Branch of the War Production Board in Washington.

> In view of the present and certainly very greatly expanded demand for molybdenum and the probability that during 1943 stocks will be exhausted and the capacity of existing production facilities

will be overtaxed so that an actual shortage may result, we request that you let us know under what conditions your company will be prepared to increase its output by at least 10,000,000 pounds [of molybdenum] yearly and how long it will take to reach the increased production figure. As a basis for calculation we are assuming a production from your company of about 37,000,000 pounds during 1942. . . .

At Climax, Jack Abrahms met with Bill Coulter and engineer Dennis Haley to decide how to increase production. A new mill unit would come on line in three months, but the obvious production bottleneck was the mine itself, which was already operating just above its design capacity. Abrahms outlined the alternatives: widen and double-track the Phillipson Tunnel, drive an identical haulage tunnel parallel to the Phillipson Tunnel to access the same level, push development of the lower 500 Level, or begin exploration and development in Ceresco Ridge.

Abrahms found none of the alternatives realistic because of the time and cost of new development, the uncertainty of the duration of the war, and the growing shortage of construction supplies, especially of steel and cement. The most pressing consideration was that the War Production Board demanded molybdenum not next year, but immediately. Therefore, any additional production would have to come, somehow, from the Phillipson Level.

Abrahms halted all development work on the Phillipson Level, as well as repair and maintenance work that he personally judged not absolutely essential. He put muck trains on a precise, round-the-clock, to-the-minute schedule of loading, hauling, and dumping. Finally, Abrahms ordered the highest-grade ores to be pulled first, a very risky move that tinkered with the coordinated development necessary to assure critical balance of the entire massive block cave system overlying the Phillipson Level. If balance was lost, the long-term consequence would be a dramatically shortened life for the Phillipson Level. And disrupting balance so as to affect draw control would jeopardize immediate production. An additional risk was perceived in the unfortunate reality that all of Abrahm's emergency measures would be performed by an increasingly undermanned and inexperienced workforce.

Any Climax employee thinking of quitting didn't have far to go for another job. Along the Eagle River only seven miles west of Climax, the U.S. Army Corps of Engineers rushed construction of Camp Hale

171

as a training site for the Tenth Mountain Division, an elite ski-trooper unit that would later distinguish itself in combat in northern Italy. The Camp Hale construction projects offered outdoor summer jobs, good pay, and work that was much safer than in the Climax underground. In April 1942, Climax countered with a fifty-cent-per-day, across-the-board pay raise, but still lost 23 men. During the warmer days of May, Climax hired 146, but 198 quit, resulting in a net employment loss of 75 men in just two months.

Personnel director Adolph Doepke, empowered to do "whatever's necessary" to hire men, listed Climax jobs with state and federal employment agencies, opened a permanent company employment office in Denver, and placed newspaper advertisements in Nebraska, Colorado, Kansas, Oklahoma, Texas, and New Mexico. Doepke succeeded in hiring 254 men in June, but his net gain was a mere 37, for 217 quit. In July he hired 161 men, but 249 quit, giving him a net loss for the month of 88 men.

Despite the steady employment decline, Jack Abrahms pushed production to 18,000 tons per day. To do it, a fifteen-car muck train rumbled out of the Phillipson Tunnel every nine and a half minutes. During July, Climax sent out 5,000 tons of concentrate. The Colorado & Southern shipped it out in 192 rickety wooden freight cars. Valiant little steam locomotives that were already antiques headed the little seven-car trains as they click-clacked and squealed over fourteen miles of worn-out narrow-gauge track. In his monthly report, Jack Abrahms called both the production and the shipping "a near miracle."

In August 1942, Adolph Doepke hired another 146 men, yet recorded a net loss of 157. In September, as cooler weather set in, the net loss dropped to only 8 men, but by then the manpower shortage had become critical. Despite its most intensive recruitment program ever and the offer of double time on Sundays, the Climax Mine lost 60 percent of its workforce in just eight months, dropping total employment to only 406.

Not surprisingly, daily production declined to 15,000 tons. Nevertheless, recovery of contained molybdenum hit a record high of 4.2 million pounds per month because, as Abrahms reported, ". . . we are pulling the best ore left in the mountain." Meanwhile, the big warehouse stockpile of concentrate was about gone. And with few men left to produce more, Climax needed help.

The first help arrived when the War Production Board issued Executive Order L-208, closing all primary gold mines in order to redirect men and mining materials to production of iron, coal, and base and alloying metals. Doepke immediately set up a temporary employment office in Lead, South Dakota, and recruited sixty-one experienced hardrock miners from the Homestake gold mine. Next, the War Department released 4,000 experienced miners from military service. Doepke requested 250, but received only 160 "soldier-miners" in the War Department's largest single allotment. The "soldier-miners" had an option. After a few days at the Climax elevation and a look at the Phillipson Level, they could stay or return to the military. Twenty of them chose to take their chances in military combat. The federal government also shipped eight refugees to Climax from Japanese-occupied Mongolia. All were experienced underground miners, but they spoke not a word of English.

The War Department helped out with an "assigned manpower" program utilizing "borderline deserters" and "misfits" of questionable military value. Climax received a small allotment of those men, who did not have an option. Climax foremen, as advised by officers of the Seventh Service Command, greeted them with a short, to-the-point, "boot camp-style" welcome: "Men, I'm sure some of you would rather not be here, and maybe we'd rather not have you here. But Climax is your home for the duration of this war. So let's make the best of it. Remember, if you quit, you're a criminal, and they're gonna hunt you down sooner or later. Until this war is over, the only way you legally go down this hill is feet first."

Unfortunately, eight men did go down the hill "feet first" in 1942 and 1943. They were the first mine fatalities since Climax adopted an effective safety program in 1938. Their deaths reflected not safety shortcomings, but gross inexperience and production demands in excess of reasonable limits.

The War Department prohibited the Climax Molybdenum Company from releasing any information regarding operations, production, employment, and ore reserves, even in the company's annual report to shareholders. Teams of U.S. Army officers from the Internal Security Division of the Seventh Service Command regularly inspected the Climax Mine to ensure compliance with military standards of secrecy and security. With the mine dry room and mill lunchrooms adorned with "Loose Lips Sink Ships" posters, officers lectured employees not to discuss any company matters off the property. Climax virtually disappeared from newspapers and magazines; after December 12, 1941, not even Leadville's *Herald Democrat* mentioned the mine and mill atop Fremont Pass.

Prior to the war, a half-dozen watchmen had maintained loose security at Climax. But on December 20, 1941, the Internal Security Division ordered Ralph C. Thompson, a former Federal Bureau of Investigation agent, placed on the Climax payroll. Thompson established the Climax Protection Department with ten guards on January 1, 1942. Although originally an internal company security force, the Protection Department was militarized in June. The Climax guards, now numbering twenty-eight, were formally inducted into the civilian branch of the U.S. Army Auxiliary Military Police under command of Lieutenant Colonel James E. Marshall of the Internal Security Command branch headquarters in Denver.

Climax guards took fifty hours of instruction in police fundamentals and methods of plant protection, then trained with pistols, rifles, and shotguns. The guards practiced regularly on an FBI-regulation combat pistol range in the timberline pines near Brainerd Phillipson's grave above the portal of the Phillipson Tunnel. They also rotated to Denver for advanced instruction and training from army officers in the use of machine guns and hand grenades, should "extraordinary measures" become necessary for plant protection. Other courses of military instruction included bomb reconnaissance and disposal, establishment of perimeter defenses, and blackout implementation methods. The army provided the Climax guards with two trained guard dogs, but Jack Abrahms turned down the offer of horses for mounted patrols of the distant tailings ponds.

On duty, the Climax guards were armed, uniformed (at their own expense), and rotated between permanent posts and random patrols. Wartime military authority gave them considerably more power than Colorado county sheriffs. Their primary mission was to prevent unauthorized entry onto the Climax property, and guards who failed to follow orders risked military court-martial for dereliction of duty.

The traditional openness and friendliness that once invited even the curious visitor at Climax disappeared. In its place stood armed guards who challenged everyone and 3,000 feet of eight-foot-high chain-link fence topped with barbed wire. Somber-faced Climax guards took names and license plate numbers of travelers who chanced to stop at Fremont Pass, then ordered them on their way. And at regular intervals on the chain-link fence hung big white signs with bold red letters reading:

WARNING—NATIONAL DEFENSE AREA
PHOTOGRAPHING PROHIBITED BY FEDERAL LAW
NO CAMERAS ALLOWED IN THIS AREA
NO TRESPASSING

To protect against internal sabotage, the Climax guards fingerprinted all individuals entering the front gate and fingerprinted and ran background checks on all employees. Unfortunately, the security policies cost Climax a number of good men.

Some of the steadiest Climax miners and mill hands had simply appeared one day, gave a name which may or may not have been true, and hired on. Always fighting a labor turnover, Climax never asked many questions. If a man, whoever he claimed he was, could handle the work, he had a job for as long as he wanted it. If he couldn't handle the work, it didn't matter anyway. Many men who hired on were private, quiet, and tough; they were trying to escape from things they never talked about. Many had enough trouble and weren't looking for more of it. Because of men like that, there had been little trouble or crime at the Climax hotel or the boardinghouse; Lake

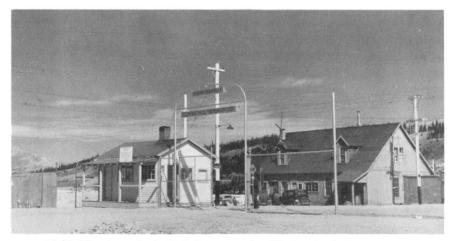

1945. Wartime chain-link fences at the Climax main gate atop Fremont Pass.

175

County sheriff's officers rarely had cause to visit Climax, and that was the way many men liked it. At the hotel, even the most dim-witted would-be petty thief could sense the grave risks that existed, for justice at Climax usually came not from a county judge, but from the end of a drill steel. When the time came for fingerprinting and background checks in the summer of 1942, two dozen men, including veteran miners who helped drive the Phillipson Tunnel, packed their suitcases, collected their pay, and headed down the hill.

The most vulnerable target for a saboteur was the industrial water system, specifically the dams around the tailings ponds and reservoir and the pumps and pipelines that returned water to the mill. Climax guards, with authority to shoot on sight, manned wooden towers with sweep searchlights overlooking the dams. Jack Abrahms and Ralph Thompson often visited Camp Hale to speak to the Tenth Mountain Division ski troopers, urging them to avoid cross-country ski outings that would take them near the headwaters of the Eagle River and the Climax tailings dams, for fear they might encounter the guard dogs or, worse, a rifle bullet.

The Protection Department even recruited the Campfire Girls and Boy Scouts of the Max Schott School into the Climax Defense and Service Corps. Within eight weeks, the Campfire Girls and Boy Scouts collected 16,000 pounds of scrap rubber, iron, brass, and copper—100 pounds per student—for shipment to a national defense scrap depot in Denver.

In the nine months following the bombing of Pearl Harbor, the Climax Mine produced thirty million pounds of contained molybdenum—more than the cumulative production of the mine in its first twelve years of operation. In September 1942, Undersecretary of the Navy James Forrestal sent this letter to Max Schott.

> Dear Mr. Schott,
> This is to inform you that the Army and Navy are conferring upon the mine, mill, conversion plant, and research laboratory of the Climax Molybdenum Company the Army-Navy Production Award for high achievement in the production of war equipment.
> The patriotism which you and your employees have shown by your remarkable production record is helping our country along the road to victory. The Army and Navy are proud of the achievement of the men and women of the Climax Molybdenum Company.
> In conferring this award, the Army and Navy will give you an appropriate number of flags to fly above the mine, mill, conversion

plant, and research laboratory, and will present to every individual within these plants a lapel pin, symbol of leadership on the production front.

May I extend to the Climax Molybdenum Company my congratulations for accomplishing more than seemed reasonable or possible a year ago.

The Army-Navy Production Award, popularly known as the Army-Navy "E" Award, originated as the 1906 Navy "E" Award for excellence in gunnery, and was later extended to engineering and communications achievements. In 1941, the U.S. Navy further extended it to include industrial plants producing naval equipment. After Pearl Harbor, the War Department made it a joint service award to symbolize the unity of the army, navy, and industry in the war effort.

Aware of the need for rallying and "flag waving" in the darkest year of the war, the Internal Security Division lifted the veil of secrecy over Climax for the award presentation ceremony in the rec-

September 1942.
Selected guests received this
formal invitation to attend the
Army-Navy Production Award
presentation ceremony at Climax.

Climax Molybdenum Company
cordially invites you
to attend the ceremony
in connection with the presentation of

The Army-Navy "E" Award to the Company
on Sunday, the fourth of October
Nineteen hundred forty-two
at three-thirty in the afternoon
at Climax, Colorado

Please present this invitation at the gate for admission

Accepting the Army-Navy Production Award are (from left to right): Max Schott for the Climax Molybdenum Company, Stonewall Jackson Parker for the Climax mill, and Michael Verant for the Climax Mine.

October 4, 1942. Hundreds of invited guests gather outside the Climax recreation hall to witness the presentation of the Army-Navy Production Award to the Climax Mine and mill.

178

reation hall on October 4, 1942. Newspapers reported the event locally and nationally. An American flag flew over the main gate, and guards decorated the austere chain-link fence with red, white, and blue bunting. Reporters from four Denver radio stations were present, along with the Army Air Corps band from Lowry Field. Among the 400 invited guests were Max Schott, along with representatives of the Langeloth conversion plant and the Detroit research laboratory. The guest speaker, U.S. Marine Brigadier General Robert H. Denig, described at length the vital role of molybdenum in the manufacture of war materials, then presented the awards. Michael Verant accepted for the Climax Mine; Stonewall Jackson Parker accepted for the Climax mill.

Max Schott, who had really begun preparing the Climax Mine for its wartime role in 1936, delivered only a brief comment. "It's a great privilege to accept this pennant for the employees of the Climax Molybdenum Company," Schott said, reading from prepared notes. "Early in 1940, the Company began preparing for the emergency by bringing production up to the physical limits of the mine. This was possible only through the wholehearted support of the Climax organization, to whom belongs the greater part of the honor of this achievement. The company was fortunate in that its employees early recognized the need for maximum production. This is a war of production as well as arms. The employees of the Climax Mine stand on the production line. Thank you one and all." As Schott stepped down from the podium, the polite round of applause faded into the incessant hum of the mill and the rumble of another muck train rolling out of the Phillipson portal.

By December 1942, the Climax Mine achieved a record production level of 19,000 tons per day. The Protection Department remained as busy was ever, with guards dressed in military winter clothing patrolling the dams, ponds, and pipelines on snowshoes and skis. In one year, the guards fingerprinted and filed information on 3,337 persons, including 1,272 regular Climax employees and 100 subcontractor employees working in the school, store, hotel, and boardinghouse, and on diamond drilling and construction sites. The guards' work often did not endear them to the public, for it included confiscating twenty-one rolls of film from travelers on State Highway 91, travelers who made the mistake of getting out of their cars with a camera in hand.

179

Sixty-six-year-old Max Schott delivers brief comments during the Army-Navy Production Award presentation ceremony at the Climax recreation hall.

On December 14, 1942, the guards mobilized the Climax Civilian Defense and Service Corps for a full-scale test of the plant blackout system. The guards issued all residences detailed blackout instructions and assigned wardens to control every light circuit. Climax maintenance crews had already painted the windows black in the mill, crusher, offices, and other surface facilities. At 8:00 P.M., as U.S. Army inspection teams watched from the summit of Chalk Mountain, all of Climax fell into an eerie darkness. Even with the muck trains, crusher, and mill in full operation, the inspection teams rated blackout effectiveness at 100 percent.

One problem the Climax Mine did not have during the winter of 1942-43 was snow-blocked roads. The Seventh Service Command's

Internal Security Division issued an "operational order" to the federal Bureau of Roads, the state highway department, and the Lake County Road Department. In essence, the order stated that no matter now much snow fell or how many plows it took to move it, State Highway 91 between Climax and Leadville would remain open around the clock. The state highway department erected a big shed atop Fremont Pass to house a powerful new plow, and additional state and federal equipment was assigned permanently to Leadville. Miners late for a shift, whether it had snowed or not, jokingly told shift bosses that they had been "caught in snowplow traffic."

The pressure of emergency wartime production did not dampen enthusiasm for skiing at Climax. Since the first ski meet in 1937, Climax had held annual downhill ski races in conjunction with the Southern Rocky Mountain Ski Association. The annual races developed a name and attracted some seventy expert skiers annually. The Climax Ski Area included downhill runs on the western shoulder of Bartlett Mountain, not far from the portal of the Phillipson Tunnel and precariously near the edge of the deepening Glory Hole. The slalom courses were on Chalk Mountain, where a 600-foot vertical descent on a short 1,400-foot run brought out the best—and the worst—in any skier.

When Climax skiers formed the Continental Ski Club in 1941, they asked the company for help to install a rope tow and lights for night skiing. At year's end, the club opened the improved Climax Ski Area. A diesel engine salvaged from an old Climax dump truck powered a winch to operate an 1,800-foot-long rope tow lift; a few hundred industrial light bulbs strung along both sides of three runs provided light for night skiing.

The Climax Ski Area was open on Wednesday and Friday nights, and all day Saturday and Sunday. The Protection Department assigned an on-site blackout warden to immediately turn off the run lights if an alert were ordered. On weekends, the Climax Ski Area attracted hundreds of skiers from Climax, Leadville, the Tenmile camps, and Frisco, as well as many Tenth Mountain Division ski troopers from Camp Hale. All were warned not to wander outside the ski area because of the guard dogs and armed guards. For the duration of World War II, Climax was clearly Colorado's best ski area.

1943. An underground crew poses for a photograph on the Phillipson Level. Note that one miner still uses a carbide lamp.

In January 1943, with the "E" pennant fluttering from the gatehouse flagpole, the Climax Mine set new production records every week. The production figures looked good on paper, but General Manager Bill Coulter and Resident Superintendent Jack Abrahms knew their ability to maintain emergency production levels grew more precarious every day. With virtually all manpower assigned to production, maintenance fell far behind schedule. Equipment, especially ball mills and rail, was rapidly wearing out, and the War Department refused to allocate steel for replacement. But the biggest fear continued to be loss of block cave balance and draw control, which would be disastrous for production. Satisfied he could do nothing more, Coulter informed the War Production Board that the Climax Mine was operating at the absolute limits of production.

But the War Production Board thought otherwise, and Bill Coulter took personal offense to this letter from E. Franklin Hatch, assistant chief of the board's Ferro-Alloys Branch.

> Dear Mr. Coulter,
> Thank you for your letter of January 5 on the present situation at Climax. We note that you state your production has averaged over 19,000 tons per day for the last two months.
> In that connection a number of engineers have expressed the opinion that Climax can produce in excess of its present output. Mr.

Fred Searles of the Facility Clearance Board, who we understand is well acquainted with Climax, has stated to us that additional molybdenum production should be obtained from Climax.

When I was at Climax in November, mine and mill feed was averaging 20,000 tons per day, which was felt to be approximately average production. Apparently this production is not being maintained.

I would very much appreciate a statement from you as to what may be considered maximum daily tonnage of the mine and mill and, if that is not being produced, the reason therefore. . . .

On January 20, 1943, Coulter fired back a reply that didn't mince words.

Dear Mr. Hatch,

. . . In view of the many inspections and analyses that have been made of our operations during the past year, we are a little surprised that it is felt that we have not done everything possible to conduct our operation at Climax at maximum capacity.

After the experience of operating on the average of 19,000 tons per day in November and December we are satisfied that this is very close to the maximum capacity of the mine, crushing plant and mill, and that in order to maintain such an average tonnage throughout the year of 1943 such things as labor shortage, labor trouble, material shortage, serious breakdowns or major maintenance can have no place in the picture.

1943. A mantrip hauling a shift out of the Phillipson Tunnel.

During the past year we have been able to improve our recovery approximately 1-1/2 percent through metallurgical research involving new reagents. We can improve our recovery further by additional equipment . . . we do not know what success we will have in securing this equipment.

At this time of year particularly we have many problems to deal with in conducting our operation because of climatic conditions that all affect our tonnage and production of molybdenum. As an example, last Friday we experienced one of the worst blizzards in the history of this country in high altitudes and during the day there were ten interruptions of power. Fortunately, but more particularly due to the almost superhuman efforts of the Public Service Company, no major breaks in power of any long duration occurred. Furthermore, for some time past and for the next two months, we have experienced and are experiencing sub-zero temperatures reaching 20 below zero. . . .

I am disappointed to know that there are some who believe that we are not doing everything possible to obtain maximum production, and if you can suggest specifically anything that you think can be done to increase both tonnage and production we will certainly welcome any suggestions. I think however that it is in order for me to tell you that our entire organization at Climax has been working at maximum stress and at seven days per week during the past year. All of our equipment has been operating on the same basis. In other words, we are working at top speed and at the limit. Under such conditions we certainly cannot overlook the dangers that accompany increasing pressures to the breaking point of both men and equipment in our desire to achieve maximum production of molybdenum.

A week later, Coulter received this subdued and understanding reply from E. Franklin Hatch.

Dear Mr. Coulter,

. . . I appreciate the very clear and comprehensive way you have summarized the situation at Climax. . . . I hope you will understand that our repeated inquiries and visits have been due to a natural anxiety to obtain the maximum amount of molybdenum so badly needed in the War Effort.

Also, you will appreciate that we are under continual pressure from numerous directions in connection with the supply of this metal as the stocks of the commodity continue to decline. Consequently, we must assure ourselves, as well as other interested agencies, that everything possible is being done to obtain maximum molybdenum production.

It is unfortunate that at times this pressure results from misunderstanding, or misinformation on the subject.

Climax contributed more than molybdenum to the war effort, and in a way that not even Max Schott, Bill Coulter, or Jack Abrahms were aware of. In 1941, the Climax Molybdenum Company granted permission to Harvard University to build a small astronomical observatory at an elevation of 11,450 feet on the north slope of Ceresco Ridge overlooking the Climax Mine. No one at Climax knew what went on at the little observatory, beyond the fact that a small, secretive team of astronomers and technicians conducted "some type of solar research."

Since the 1840s, astronomers and physicists had observed the sun's corona, a pale, nebulous, greenish-white halo marked by irregular occurrences of scarlet gaseous clouds called prominences. But the obscuring brilliance of normal sunlight made close observation of the prominences impossible, leaving astronomers to study details of the prominences, or solar flares, only during rare total solar eclipses.

During the 1920s, physicists realized that solar flares were linked to the quality of long-range radio communications on Earth. To study the solar flares more closely, French physicist Bernard Lyot invented a specialized telescope that created an artificial eclipse. The Lyot-type coronograph, as Lyot's telescope became known, provided the greatest understanding yet of the nature of solar flares. Harvard University owned one of the three existing delicate, expensive, Lyot-type coronographs. When World War II broke out, the U.S. Navy ordered Harvard to place the instrument in operation as soon as possible.

Harvard assigned Dr. Donald H. Menzel, a Harvard College Observatory astronomer, to find a permanent site for the coronograph. Menzel, a former Leadville resident who favored the high elevations and dry, clear air of the Colorado Rockies, considered three Colorado sites: Loveland Pass, Independence Pass, and Fremont Pass. Although Fremont Pass was the lowest of the three passes, it was accessible in winter and, thanks to Climax, had power and support services. Harvard University and the U.S. Navy jointly asked the Climax Molybdenum Company for permission to use the Climax Mine as a site for the coronograph and a supporting team of scientists on a mission of "considerable importance." Climax not only agreed, but provided construction materials, vehicles, and support and power services, all at company expense, and the Fremont Pass Station of the Harvard College Observatory began operations in summer 1941.

185

Summer 1943. The Fremont Station of the Harvard College Observatory, located on the side of Ceresco Ridge, provided invaluable long-range radio communications reliability data for the War Department during World War II. Bartlett Mountain and the widening Glory Hole appear in the background. –National Center for Atmospheric Research

Dr. Menzel, the first director of the observatory, soon turned supervision over to Walter O. Roberts, a Harvard graduate student about to earn his doctorate. When the United States entered the war shortly after the bombing of Pearl Harbor, ranking U.S. Navy officers visited Climax, inspected the little observatory, and ordered the Protection Department to afford it "the utmost in protection."

From January 1942 on, whenever Walter Roberts or an assistant appeared at the Climax general office building, Jack Abrahms vacated his office to allow confidential use of his private telephone. And on days when blizzards knocked out telephone service, a Climax vehicle and driver waited to drive an astronomer to the Western Union Office in Leadville. As ordered, no one at Climax asked questions or was permitted near the observatory, and it wasn't until May 1943 that Max Schott received the following letter from the Chief of Naval Operations in Washington.

In busy days such as these one can scarcely hope to acknowledge all the help and assistance that various individuals and companies are voluntarily giving to the War Effort. Nevertheless, because you might not otherwise know of its importance, I should like to take this opportunity to express my own appreciation as well as that of the Joint Communications Board for the cooperation that the Climax Molybdenum Company has given to the Fremont Station of the Harvard Observatory. We understand that this station was established and that its continued operation has been made possible only through the help and support of your organization.

We have felt, therefore, that you are entitled to know that the observations from Climax have been playing a unique role in an important phase of the War Effort. The exact uses to which the data has been put must remain, of course, confidential. But we want you and your colleagues to know that your efforts to establish the observatory are appreciated by the Services. The Harvard Station is the only one in Allied hands capable of furnishing us the necessary information. The fact that you had the foresight to assist its establishment has been fortunate, indeed, for us.

Please note that the contents of this letter are confidential. . . .

Only after the war would the U.S. Navy declassify the purpose and operations of the observatory at Fremont Pass. Twice daily from the base of Ceresco Ridge, weather permitting, Walter Roberts and his team created and photographed an artificial solar eclipse. With the photographic plates still wet, Roberts measured and interpreted all detected solar prominences, coded the data, and telephoned it to Leadville for immediate telegraphic transmission to Washington over Western Union's priority government wire. In Washington, military specialists quickly interpreted the data, then recoded it for radio transmission to military theater headquarters in London and Pearl Harbor, which in turn passed the data on to every major Allied command. The solar flare data that Walter Roberts and his team recorded in the little observatory on the side of Ceresco Ridge was vital in accurately projecting several days in advance the quality and reliability of long-range military radio communications. The data figured into the scheduling of every major Allied naval, aerial, and amphibious operation throughout the war.

In June 1943, Climax achieved a remarkable sustained production level of 23,000 tons per day—a wartime record. But the strain had taken its toll on equipment, draw control, and human nerves. When several slusher motors suddenly failed, Ralph Thompson, head of the Climax Protection Department, investigated and found missing

1943. A twenty-five-car muck train has just dumped its load and circles the elevated "loop" to return to the Phillipson Tunnel.

seal rings and oil-tank caps. Suspecting possible sabotage, Thompson followed orders and contacted the Denver office of the FBI, which immediately dispatched an agent to Climax.

After a "brusque" interrogation of fifteen miners, the agent concluded the problem was not sabotage, but "negligent" maintenance, which pointed the finger at chief electrician Frank Garrabrant. Garrabrant wrote a heated response to Jack Abrahms, Thompson, and the FBI agent, noting that he had 1,200 electric motors to maintain "and exactly two underground electricians with more than six months experience" with which to do the job. Meanwhile, the fifteen interrogated miners indignantly refused to "go back in the hole until this whole thing is settled." They returned to work only when the FBI withdrew its agent from the Climax property.

In August 1943, the U.S. Army honored the Climax Protection Department as an outstanding auxiliary military police unit. Max Schott, Dennis Haley, Otto Sussman, and Bill Coulter were present in the recreation hall when army officers presented Ralph Thompson with the award and a military guidon. The Climax guards had indeed done their job. When cars stopped anywhere near Fremont Pass, Climax guards appeared within minutes to check identification and suggest the driver "keep moving." In both Frisco and

188

Leadville, gas station attendants warned visitors headed over Fremont Pass "not to stop anywhere near Climax."

Some of the "assigned manpower" employees ordered to Climax in 1942 had tried everything to leave, most without success. The only valid reason for assigned manpower transferral was physiological inability to handle the altitude. Naturally, assigned manpower employees who wanted to get away from Climax complained frequently of general weakness, shortness of breath, headaches, nausea, and fluttering heartbeat—all the symptoms of altitude, or mountain, sickness. But Abrahms often saw the same complaining employees "playing basketball half the night" in the recreation hall. "This tells me," Abrahms wrote in his monthly report, "that imagination, not altitude, is the greater problem."

One Climax "recreational activity" that didn't suffer during the war, even with restricted supplies of commercial beer, was drinking. Since George Coulter couldn't obtain all the beer he might have wanted, he stocked the Fremont Trading Post with ample supplies of malted grains, hops, and earthenware crocks. With crocks of fermenting beer under most bunks, nondrinkers complained that the Climax boardinghouse and hotel smelled like breweries. Climax home brewers even found something good to say about the altitude; many believed the reduced air pressure together with a properly adjusted mix significantly accelerated fermentation. That was arguable, but another point about the altitude wasn't: At an elevation of 11,320 feet, it took only half the usual amount of beer to put a man flat on his back.

Another wartime change at Climax was the arrival of organized labor. The first attempt to unionize the Climax mine and mill in 1938 had been overwhelmingly rejected by a vote the following year. But the CIO-affiliated International Union of Mine, Mill and Smelter Workers returned for another try in 1943. Climax attorneys attempted to delay a vote until after the war, knowing that the wartime employment turmoil and turnover would make a big difference. But the attorneys failed and the vote was narrowly in favor of the union. Prodded by the National Labor Relations Board, the Climax Molybdenum Company reluctantly recognized the local Climax Molybdenum Workers Union of the International Union of Mine, Mill, and Smelter Workers as the bargaining agent for most of its employees.

August 1943. Colorado & Southern narrow-gauge steamer No. 76 makes one of its last runs. No. 76 made its last run on August 25.

Wartime also brought changes to railroading at Climax. The War Production Board had well-founded fears that the "antique" narrow-gauge rail and rolling stock of the Colorado & Southern Railroad that connected Climax and Leadville might not be up to the job of handling the huge Climax wartime production. Converting to standard gauge would be tricky on the Climax line, for the War Production Board would not permit daily freight service to be disrupted. But to make the job easier, the board also exempted the Climax line from the wartime regulation of retaining one narrow-gauge rail as a steel conservation measure.

Work began in summer 1942, when crews laid longer, heavier cross ties beneath the old narrow-gauge rails without affecting freight service. In early 1943 the War Production Board allocated the C&S thirty miles of standard-gauge rail, enough for "double-rail" conversion of the entire line. Railroad crews spiked down the new rail outside the old narrow-gauge rails, again without disrupting freight service.

On August 25, 1943, with both standard-gauge and narrow-gauge rail in place, C&S narrow-gauge steam locomotive No. 76 made its historic last run. The U.S. Army Internal Security Division lifted security to permit publicity for the event. Witnesses included the editor of *Trains* magazine, a C&S vice president, Associated Press reporters, a *Life* magazine photographer, and many old-time railroaders, some of whom had steamed over Fremont Pass before the Climax Mine even existed. At Climax, Jack Abrahms and thirty other specially invited Climax men and women posed for the obligatory photographs alongside No. 76, in the shadow of its familiar, big "bear trap" spark arrestor. When old No. 76 headed down the hill on the last narrow-gauge run, it headed up a train of fourteen wooden boxcars loaded with another 125 tons of molybdenite concentrate.

The following morning, the locomotive that made steam in the Leadville yards preparatory to its first run up the hill to Climax was C&S No. 641, a much heavier and more powerful standard-gauge steamer. Three weeks later, crews had torn up the equivalent of twenty-eight miles of rusted narrow-gauge rail, all that remained of the historic Denver, South Park & Pacific Railway, shipping it as scrap to waiting steel mills and closing out one of the grand chapters of Colorado mountain railroading.

The Climax Mine earned a star for its Army-Navy "E" pennant in recognition of its performance in 1943, when production continued beyond "what could reasonably be expected." Throughout that year, daily production averaged 22,000 tons of molybdenite ore per day—almost 50 percent above the design capacity of the Phillipson Level. Surface construction crews had also been busy, completing fifty-two new family apartment units, along with a sand and gravel plant to supply underground concrete crews that now placed 15,000 cubic yards of concrete annually to shore up the crumbling slusher workings. Part of the chronic Climax wartime labor shortage had been made up by seventy-eight women, who worked as welders, crane operators, cap-lamp technicians, and even armed guards with the Protection Department.

Even with American industry working around the clock, a full year passed before molybdenite ore mined and milled at Climax could be converted, alloyed into steels, manufactured into armament, and shipped to combat zones. The enormous production of molybdenite concentrate at the Climax Mine in 1943 had exceeded even the prodigious demands of the War Production Board. In April 1944, amid growing stockpiles of molybdenum and with the end of the

191

war in sight, the War Production Board allowed Climax to cut production to 18,000 tons per day. In September, when the War Production Board formally permitted the Climax Mine to "stand down," Max Schott ordered Jack Abrahms to slash production to 8,000 tons per day.

When World War II finally ended in August 1945, the Climax Mine produced only 5,000 tons per day as it headed for the uncertainties of a deep postwar depression. The Homestake gold miners returned to South Dakota, and the furloughed soldier-miners, misfits, and borderline deserters, their tours of duty complete, drifted away. Gone, too, were most of the farmers, cowboys, and truck drivers that Adolph Doepke had recruited from six states. Climax employment plummeted from a record high of 1,290 in late 1943 to just 390 in September 1945.

The War Production Board finally permitted the Climax Molybdenum Company to disclose the wartime production of the Climax Mine. From 1939 to 1945, the Climax Mine produced and shipped 180 million pounds—90,000 tons—of elemental molybdenum contained in concentrate. Production had peaked with 47 million pounds in 1943. Climax had broken, drawn, hauled, and milled 30 million tons of ore, and the physical cost of that emergency production was just now becoming apparent. Most slusher workings, despite being formed with reinforced concrete, were reamed out to uselessness. Broken ore reserves were decimated, and the highest grades of ore were gone. The careful system of mine development, caving balance, and draw control was a shambles. In a detailed report on general mine and mill condition, Jack Abrahms wrote that maintenance "was five years behind" and major crusher components and nearly all the balls mills were "junk."

In August 1946, Max Schott, already seventy years old, retired as president of the Climax Molybdenum Company. Arthur D. Storke, formerly a Climax surveyor and construction foreman in 1917 and resident manager in 1926-27, succeeded Schott as president.

Storke's first job was to meet with Jack Abrahms to plan the rebuilding of the Climax Mine. Storke agreed to hold production at 5,000 tons per day for several years while crews replaced and rebuilt worn-out equipment, restored the Phillipson Level system of development and caving, increased reserves of broken ore, and hired and trained a new force of employees that, hopefully, would be permanent.

192

Two assets would make the rebuilding program easier. First was the emergency postwar fund that Max Schott had started in 1937 and which now totalled $10 million. Second, Climax now had the most effective safety program of any major U.S. underground metal mine. Between 1944 and 1946, Climax had recorded no fatalities and a remarkably low accident rate, earning prestigious safety awards from the U.S. Bureau of Mines, the National Safety Council, and the Colorado Industrial Commission. By late 1946, Climax became the nation's safest major mine of any kind, and was far ahead of many large facilities in industries with considerably less inherent physical risk.

The economic picture facing Climax was not encouraging, for the war had completely disrupted national and international metal markets. Although Storke knew that molybdenum's place in industry was secure, he faced huge stockpiles and weak short-term demand. The biggest foreign prewar molybdenum buyers, Japan, Germany, and the Soviet Union, would spend years rebuilding their shattered industries. Storke also concerned himself with a problem new to the Climax Molybdenum Company—growing competition in molybdenum production.

In 1933, metallurgists at the Greene Cananea Consolidated Company, an Anaconda property in Mexico, identified the shiny gray film in their copper sulfide flotation circuits as molybdenum disulfide. Molybdenum is present in most copper ores in uneconomical trace amounts, but Greene Cananea found that it composed up to 0.5 percent of its concentrates. After Climax had created a market for molybdenum, Anaconda metallurgists designed a final differential flotation step to recover the molybdenite. Initially, Greene Cananea attracted buyers for its molybdenite by packing concentrate in quality oaken drums reusable as wine and whiskey casks.

In 1936, the Utah Copper Company's Bingham Canyon Mine and Arizona's Miami Copper Company also began recovering by-product molybdenite. Above a certain break-even point, molybdenum prices were not of great importance to copper companies, for their by-product sales were supplementary to their basic profit on copper.

But as a primary molybdenum producer, the Climax Molybdenum Company was very concerned about price. Climax, which produced 75 percent of the world's molybdenum supply, remained the dominant influence on market price. And the best way to dis-

One of the Climax Molybdenum Company's advertisements in the late 1940s showcased its wartime Army-Navy Production Award.

courage further competition would be to hold the lowest possible price by increasing both volume and efficiency of mining and milling. But Climax had another marketing advantage. Unlike the copper companies that sold by-product generic molybdenum, the Climax Molybdenum Company sold *Climax* molybdenum, meaning Climax customers benefited from Climax research and technological support in their use of the metal.

The Climax Molybdenum Company continued to promote itself as the authority on molybdenum metallurgy. Post-World War II advertising focused on the proven reliability of Climax as a wartime supplier of molybdenum, on increasingly specialized molybdenum steels, and even on such new uses as molybdenum-based paint pigments. A typical 1948 advertisement depicted the Army-Navy "E" pennant waving over the Bartlett Mountain Glory Hole; prominent captions noted that "Climax Furnishes Authoritative Engineering Data on Molybdenum Applications."

Just as three copper companies now recovered by-product molybdenite, Climax turned toward by-product recovery of other minerals present in the Bartlett Mountain molybdenite ore. Wolframite, an iron-manganese tungstate, was a potential source of tungsten; cassiterite, a tin oxide, was a source of tin; and monazite, a complex, slightly radioactive cerium-thorium phosphate, was a potential source of the rare earth element cerium. The most abundant by-product mineral in Climax molybdenite ore was pyrite, a disulfide of iron that forms the familiar, glittering crystals of "fool's gold."

Climax metallurgists began separation studies in 1948 and engineers designed a pilot recovery plant the following year. The Climax molybdenite flotation process dropped the potential by-product minerals, which were considerably more dense than the quartz tailing grains. The first step in by-product recovery of the minerals was to classify the tailings into fines and sands. Fines went to the tailings pond, but a secondary mill system routed the sands through Humphrey spirals, a gravitational recovery system originally designed for gold recovery.

As the slurry of tailing sands flowed by gravity down spiral troughs, the lighter gangue minerals washed to the outer edge of the spirals. But the heavier minerals were trapped and removed through outlets on the inside of the spirals. This low-grade, by-product concentrate then passed through flotation tanks that separated and recovered the easily floatable pyrite. The remaining concentrate, containing the tin, tungsten, and monazite values, was cleaned and dried, then routed onto a belt for magnetic separation. A low-power magnetic separator first removed the tungsten values, then a high-power magnetic separator removed the monazite. The remaining material was basically a tin concentrate. Climax sold the pyrite to sulfuric acid manufacturers and shipped the tin and tungsten concentrate to refineries. The monazite, valuable for its cerium content, went to speciality refineries for eventual use in lantern mantles and lighter flints.

Climax experimented with limited open pit mining in 1947 to recover sections of high-grade ore that would have otherwise been lost, awarding a seven-year contract to C. Ryan & Son of Lakewood, Colorado. Working from "Ryan's Camp" near the old Upper Camp, Lee Ryan and his crew loaded ore from a steam shovel into ten-ton dump trucks, then dumped it down an ore pass to the Phillipson Level. Open pit work, impossible during the long winter, lasted only from June through September.

1948. C. Ryan & Son, contractors, make the first attempt at limited open pit mining at Climax. Ore that otherwise would have been lost was dropped down an ore pass to the Phillipson Level.

One of the biggest decisions facing the Climax Mine after World War II concerned future production. Arthur Storke did not believe the Phillipson Level alone could meet the production requirements of another national emergency or even the heavy demand that would be generated if the federal government began stockpiling molybdenum as a strategic metal. A new production level was clearly necessary. And with postwar inflation driving construction costs to record highs, the time to develop the new level was now.

Based on extensive core drill data, engineers designed the new production level 300 feet below the Phillipson Level, with the portal located at the southwest base of Ceresco Ridge at an elevation of 11,163 feet. Development crews began work on the 300 Level in fall 1948. Within one year, miners drove 2,900 feet of single-track, 13-by-15-foot haulage tunnel; 6,000 feet of hanging wall, footwall, and crosscut drifts; and 2,500 feet of main ventilation drifts. The rapid development pace reflected major advances in mining equipment and technology since Climax miners drove the Phillipson Tunnel in the early 1930s. But still facing large wartime stockpiles and a weak industrial market, Climax suspended further development of the 300 Level in fall 1949.

Meanwhile, the five-year-old Climax Molybdenum Workers Union ran into trouble when conservative political strength and public opinion in the United States joined together in a national crusade against communism. Communist-hunting conservatives targeted labor unions, such as the CIO-affiliated International Union of Mine, Mill, and Smelter Workers, which had locals at both Climax and Leadville. Possible communist infiltration of certain labor unions, political parties, and universities had been a heated political issue since 1948, when the Progressive Party, one of the prime suspects, backed Henry Wallace for president.

When ousted CIO general counsel and widely suspected communist sympathizer Lee Pressman visited Leadville in fall 1948 to drum up support for Wallace, many Lake County residents were convinced that the locals of the International Union of Mine, Mill, and Smelter Workers had been infiltrated. Public sentiment against "pinkos" and "commies" threatened to break both CIO-affiliated locals. Climax hang-up man Hugh Matlock realized that if the Climax local hoped to survive, it needed an immediate change of affiliation. Matlock pushed for an election, and the Climax union membership rejected CIO affiliation by a ten-to-one vote. The Climax union then became an independent local of the "not-infiltrated" American Federation of Labor, a move that kept unionism alive at Climax.

In the years following World War II, the flood of returning veterans created shortages of both jobs and housing. Climax was among the few large companies in Colorado that hired steadily during the national postwar adjustment and relocation period. Among the new faces drawn to Climax were those of Morgan and Eleanor Wadsworth and their five children, who came to Climax sight unseen, simply because the job included family housing. Safety Director Edwin Eisenach assigned Morgan Wadsworth a position in industrial hygiene. Eleanor raised the family and found life at Climax in the late 1940s to be both a challenge and an adventure that "only a certain kind of woman" could enjoy.

By trial and error, Eleanor learned the secrets of baking bread and cakes in a coal stove well over two miles above sea level. In winter, she strung clotheslines only from second-floor windows, as ground-floor clotheslines were buried under snow by Christmas. And she learned to cope with the Climax domestic water supply, which, during the long spring snow runoff, turned the color of tea. With no nearby alternative water supply, Eleanor melted icicles to obtain clear water for domestic use. Frequent spring snowfall, together with relatively warm days and cold nights, produced daily "crops" of huge, crystal-clear icicles. Housewives zealously guarded their crops from neighborhood "icicle thieves," sometimes by brandishing brooms. Not all women could adapt to life at Climax; some, Eleanor recalled, "took one look at the place, bowed their heads, and wept."

Like other Climax housewives, Eleanor Wadsworth shopped at the convenient, but somewhat expensive, Fremont Trading Post. The store was bigger and better than ever, and now even offered free home delivery. If anything, George Coulter proved adaptable to changing times. Gambling was now illegal, but George just moved the slot machines into a back room of the Slop Chute. During the postwar years of low production and no overtime pay, George knew money was tight. And that meant keeping a good stock of home brew supplies, along with rifles and hunting ammunition for the poachers who filled their "Okie iceboxes" with illegal elk and venison.

About the only publicity Climax received during the postwar years concerned a friendly argument over which U.S. Post Office was the highest in North America. The contenders, all in Colorado, included Climax; Summitville, a gold mining camp in the San Juan Mountains; and Trail Ridge in Rocky Mountain National Park. Neither Climax nor Summitville considered Trail Ridge an "honest" contender; although 477 feet higher than Climax, its post office catered only to summer tourists driving Trail Ridge Road.

But Summitville provided serious competition. When gold mining resumed at Summitville after the war, the post office moved to a shack several feet higher than the clapboard shed that housed the Climax Post Office. Postwar gold mining didn't last long; when the mines closed in 1947, Summitville moved its post office back to a desk in the general store located several feet lower than the post office at Climax. When newspapers in Denver and across the country ran the story that Climax had the undisputed highest post office on the North American continent, postmistress Mary Morrison was swamped with requests for special cancellations.

Climax had another claim to continental distinction: It provided some of the best skiing in North America. When Arthur Storke took over as president of the Climax Molybdenum Company, Jack and Zella Gorsuch, along with other members of the Continental Ski Club, knew the time was right to again ask the company for help in upgrading the local ski facilities. As expected, Storke, himself an expert skier familiar with the best slopes of Europe, offered full support. Climax provided materials and equipment, while the Continental Ski Club provided volunteer labor.

The Climax Ski Area opened for the season in November 1947 as the most modern and best-equipped ski area in the West. It offered a new 2,600-foot-long, all-steel, 300 skier-per-hour T-bar tow; an extended 720-foot vertical descent; and four runs fully lighted for night skiing. Climax employees paid $10.00 for a season pass and their dependents skied for free. After the new Climax Ski Area opened, Arthur Storke spent less time in New York. He visited Climax more frequently, and upper management at the mine quietly complained when Storke insisted on beginning company business before dawn—to assure time for his afternoon skiing.

Arthur Storke was enormously popular at Climax, but his tenure as president of the Climax Molybdenum Company was brief. He resigned his position in August 1949 to assume the presidency of the Kennecott Copper Corporation. One month later, Storke was killed in a commercial air crash near Quebec, Canada. Canadian police later determined that the aircraft had been sabotaged in order to kill a woman passenger whose husband wished to remarry. Storke's death marked the end of an era; he was the last active member of The American Metal Company group that established the Climax Mine in 1917.

8
The New Climax
1950-1957

◆

*Now the television is in, piped into Climax homes
by way of the highest television aerial in the
world. The housing program is complete, pay
checks are higher than any other place in the
country for similar work, and the turnover of
employees has slowed to a trickle.*

—Empire *magazine* (The Denver Post),
May 23, 1954

◆

Arthur H. Bunker, with a strong background in minerals and
finance and valuable experience in government, became the new
president of the Climax Molybdenum Company on July 1, 1949.
During World War II, Bunker held top positions in the Office of
War Production Management, then became chief of staff of the War
Production Board. From his years in Washington, Bunker knew
that federal cooperation could help shake the Climax Molybdenum
Company out of its postwar doldrums. In his first move as president,
he visited the Defense Materials Procurement Agency headquarters
in Washington.

Bunker saw two possible situations that could affect short-term
molybdenum demand. The first, which most economic analysts
confidently predicted, was an imminent industrial boom. The second, if military and political observers were right, was heightening
international tension between the United States and the "Eastern bloc"
nations led by the Soviet Union and China. Should both these situations develop simultaneously, Bunker anticipated molybdenum
demand would far exceed the current production capacity of the

Climax Mine. Furthermore, Bunker believed that Climax was less prepared to meet potential demands of the 1950s than it had been to meet the demands of World War II. Accordingly, Bunker proposed building a federal stockpile of molybdenum to best serve the interests of both Climax and the nation.

Bunker and the Defense Materials Procurement Agency formulated a program that charted the course of the Climax Molybdenum Company for the coming decade. The federal government would begin stockpiling molybdenum for strategic defense needs, purchasing fifty million pounds over the next five years at $1.24 per pound, considerably higher than the current $1.00 per pound market price. For its part, Climax would invest at least $10 million to double the capacity of the mine and mill to 30,000 tons per day. Bunker also assured the Defense Materials Procurement Agency that Climax would mine and mill seventeen million tons of low-grade ore that otherwise might be uneconomical to mine at all.

This so-called "low-grade contract" began on January 1, 1951, but immediately proved an operational nightmare. When low-grade ore was routed to a separate crusher, the low- and high-grade muck trains often blocked each other's access to their respective crushers, slowing the entire production process.

Beyond mine and mill expansion, Bunker also announced what he called "Moly's Design for Man," a $10 million program to expand and upgrade the Climax town into a model community that would, once and for all, solve the high labor turnover problem.

Climax emerged from its long postwar depression sooner than Bunker expected—in June 1950, when war broke out in Korea and American industry once again prepared for emergency production. Resident Superintendent Jack Abrahms ordered crews to begin immediate construction of a new 5,000-ton-per-day mill unit and an expanded by-products plant to triple recovery of tungsten, tin, and pyrite. Abrahms also resumed development of the partially completed 300 Level, now officially renamed the Storke Level.

Construction contractors began work on a huge new crusher at the Storke Level portal and on a 4,000-foot-long covered conveyor to transport crushed ore up the south side of Fremont Pass to the mill. Meanwhile, Climax stepped up production from 5,000 to 15,000 tons per day and put 120 new men on the payroll.

When Climax began mass hiring in 1951, it competed with booming nationwide industrial recruitment. The hiring program fell far short of fulfilling growing manpower needs because of the usual problems of alpine climate, altitude, isolation, and lack of sufficient modern housing. The Personnel Department countered with its "New Employee Bonus Plan," advertising it in the *Moly Mountain News*, a monthly employee newsletter that began publication in 1949. This was typical of the newsletter articles of 1951.

WANT TO EARN $15?

In the July issue of the Moly Mountain News, the Company announced it would gladly pay any Climax employee $15 for each new employee he could recruit. Since this announcement was made, quite a few employees have contacted the Personnel Office to obtain more information regarding the offer and to obtain application blanks and copies of the requirements and employee booklet to send to their friends and relatives.

To date twenty-five applicants for employment have been brot to the Personnel Office by employees. Some of them were unable to pass the physical examination but the rest are now working.

The Mine Department is still in need of about 150 men.

Only men between the ages of 21 and 35 are eligible. They will have to pass the usual screening by the Personnel Department and the regular physical examination. They must be willing to accept underground work, as very few surface jobs will be available. In order for the employee to receive the $15, the new man will have to work at least 30 days. The employee must bring the applicant to the Personnel Office personally or call and arrange for an interview for him. This will be sufficient proof of the employee's efforts in recruiting the new man.

Over a fourteen-month period, Climax employees tried to collect the $15.00 "bounty" on 280 applicants. But of the 212 actually hired, a mere 109 lasted the required one month in the underground. By then, the Mine Department already needed 200 new men. The Personnel Department discontinued the "New Employee Bonus Plan" and resumed advertising in newspapers in Kansas, Oklahoma, and Texas. Going one step further, the Personnel Department opened temporary recruitment offices as far away as Alabama and the West Virginia coal country, even chartering buses to bring prospective new employees to Climax.

When the Climax Mine embarked upon its grand expansion in the 1950s, Fremont Pass was no longer as remote and untraveled as it had been, and the privacy Climax once took for granted was disappearing. State Highway 91 was now paved and automobile tourism was growing. The nation was more informed and inquisitive; radio, newspapers, magazines, and the new medium of television competed for topics of unusual interest. And the Climax Mine, whether it liked it or not, was about to meet America face-to-face. But after twelve long years of company- or government-imposed seclusion and secrecy, Climax management wasn't quite prepared for the job.

The first hint of a serious public relations problem came in 1949, when the Voice of America asked to tape a program about Climax for a series on American industry to be broadcast in twenty-four languages. Jack Abrahms casually asked his mine and mill superintendents and foremen to cooperate. When it soon became apparent that they had no intention of wasting their time with "some radio people," Abrahms ordered them to cooperate.

Next to arrive were writers from *The Saturday Evening Post*, one of the most influential and widely circulated English-language magazines. Climax was completely unprepared to recognize a golden public relations opportunity that, if handled properly, could have greatly helped recruitment. But with little company interest, the *Post* writers took their own unguided tour of Climax, speaking with disgruntled housewives and veteran miners who, for a few beers in the Slop Chute, gladly recounted tales from the "hellhole" days. *The Saturday Evening Post* ran a feature article on Climax in February 1950.

WANT TO LIVE IN CLIMAX?
COOKING WOULD DRIVE YOU CRAZY
AND 3.2 BEER MIGHT KNOCK YOU FLAT!

A forewarned miner's wife, on moving to Leadville, Colorado, armed herself with a high-altitude cookbook that she had purchased from a women's magazine. After ruining several meals, she discovered that the cookbook's recipes were supposed to be prepared at 7,500 feet. She accordingly returned the book, requesting one that would be suitable for use at 11,000 feet. The magazine replied that no such cookbook existed because no one lived that high.

Climax, a company town surrounded by a wire fence, clings uncomfortably to the western slope of Bartlett Mountain. The elevation of Climax ranges from 11,320 feet at the gate to 11,465 feet at the entrance to the mine. Cooking at such altitudes, even with the help of accurate recipes, is seldom any fun. Water boils at 190 degrees instead of 212. It takes seven minutes, therefore, to boil a three-minute egg,

Extensive surface construction and a widening Glory Hole mark the Climax Mine in June 1953.

forty-five minutes to boil corn on the cob and an hour and a half to boil potatoes. . . .

The average mean temperature at Climax, which straddles Fremont Pass, the timber line and the Continental Divide, is twenty-eight degrees. The highest temperature ever recorded is seventy-two, the lowest thirty-seven below. Summer begins around the middle of June, when the snow melts . . . and winter takes up again around the end of August.

Life's complexities increase markedly above 10,000 feet. The only human beings who are entirely comfortable are the native-born children, whose hearts, lungs and blood cells have adapted to the altitude from birth. . . . Many adults find it impossible to get a good night's sleep at Climax because of the exaggerated huffing and puffing of their overtaxed lungs. Working in the Climax mine today is twice as dangerous as working in a cement plant, but only half as dangerous as working in the Merchant Marine.

Among the other effects of high altitude is its tendency to increase everyone's irritability. It frequently spoils good tempers and makes bad ones worse.

For all its natural beauty the town is still a mining camp, with an ugly glory hole in the side of Bartlett Mountain and an even uglier tailings pond which has flowed like lava over what used to be the town of Robinson. . . .

For many readers, the article painted a lurid picture of illegal gambling, round-the-clock drinking, communist-infiltrated unions, guns under every bunk, and shot-up road signs, all amid a stark setting

205

of jagged peaks and unmanageable snow. Climax recruiters weren't surprised when prospective employees abruptly stopped interviews and asked, "You mean this is the same place I read about in that magazine? Forget it, I don't need any job that bad." Yet, interestingly, the article also attracted a number of men.

The Saturday Evening Post article did serve a constructive purpose: It helped Climax recognize its own serious image problem and public relations ineptness. The image problem had begun with the austere, chain-link barbed-wire fence and somber-faced, armed guards from a Protection Department that employees cynically called "the Climax Gestapo." Former employees still referred to Climax as "the hellhole," "the slaughterhouse," or worse, especially when they returned to visit, only to be turned away by an unsmiling guard because they "had no business" there.

Tourists saw only a mountain being torn apart and a mountain valley filling with garish yellow tailings. They had no way to learn why, for Climax disseminated no information to the public. And while Climax said nothing, Otis Archie King was saying plenty, still giving interviews to the Denver newspapers about his gallant fight against "Metallgesellschaft" and "the Kaiser" on the slopes of Bartlett Mountain during World War I. If Climax was going to achieve its employment goals and realize Arthur Bunker's vision of a "new Climax," it would have to begin by rebuilding its own deplorable image.

Creation of the "new Climax" began with administrative reorganization in 1952. Climax restructured its Personnel Department into an Industrial Relations Department and a Community Relations Department. Industrial Relations handled hiring, training, and labor negotiations; Community Relations oversaw housing, recreation, and plant and community protection services.

Climax also created a Public Relations Department headed by Gordon Weller, whose job was to reverse the "anti-public relations" approach of the previous fourteen years and formulate an effective public relations program suitable for the 1950s. Weller wasted no time, beginning with internal company communications. He converted the monthly *Moly Mountain News* into a more readable bi-weekly publication with increased photo space and artwork. Weller also started publishing the *Hi Grade*, a twice-weekly bulletin that announced current news and activities.

1952. Construction of the visitor reception center was part of the "new Climax."

Weller ordered removal of the chain-link barbed-wire fence and construction of a modern gatehouse with a visitor reception center. Weller then filled the reception center's display room with mural-sized historic photographs, drawings of mine equipment and operations, and cutout drawings of Bartlett Mountain that revealed the mysteries of the Glory Hole, block cave mining, draw control, and underground haulage. To staff the reception center, the company trained and paid college-aged sons and daughters of employees to host the growing number of summer visitors. The guides handed out color brochures describing the "new Climax" and samples of molybdenite ore. And since Climax guards often met the public, Weller recommended that they familiarize themselves with all aspects of Climax operations so that they, too, could answer visitors' questions—with a smile.

In 1954, Weller hired Don Stephens as assistant director of public relations and initiated an invitational tour program "to reintroduce Colorado to its biggest mine and one of its biggest employers." Tour groups, as large as thirty-five people each, were composed of prominent Colorado political, industrial, educational, and community leaders. Tours lasted three days, and Climax paid for all food, lodging, and transportation. Visitors spent their entire second day touring

207

the mine and mill, concluding with a dinner and open "give-and-take" discussions with rotating management representatives.

To further enhance community relations, Climax established a scholarship program, providing two scholarships each year for full tuition, all normal fees, and a $500 annual stipend toward a baccalaureate degree in any field of study at a four-year university. Climax awarded the scholarships, one to a son or daughter of Climax employees, the other to any student of Lake, Summit, or Eagle County, on the basis of academic achievement, college entrance-examination scores, community and school activity records, and interviews conducted by the Climax Scholarship Committee, a group of three prominent Colorado residents not associated with the Climax Molybdenum Company.

In 1951, after twelve years as resident superintendent, Jack Abrahms moved to Denver to become the new manager of western operations of the Climax Molybdenum Company, overseeing exploration and acquisition of other mineral properties, notably uranium and thorium. Cautious diversification was new for the Climax Molybdenum Company, but neither Arthur Bunker nor Jack Abrahms lost sight of what had made the company such a huge business success—the Climax Mine, where a large part of the steady annual profits was always reinvested into expansion, modernization, and technical innovation.

Replacing Abrahms were Frank Coolbaugh and Robert Henderson, who became the two dominant Climax figures of the 1950s. Coolbaugh, a mining engineer from the Colorado School of Mines, arrived at Climax in 1933; Henderson, a graduate of the Massachusetts Institute of Technology, hired on in 1936.

Both had arrived as "school of mines punks." Henderson, with his slight stature and Boston accent, had greater difficulty winning acceptance among the Climax miners. But both blasted hang-ups and endured the powder headaches on the Phillipson Level. Henderson very nearly became a 1938 fatality when he broke a leg in a fall in a stope. And, in the years when Climax job security was a day-to-day issue, both young engineers had been fired.

Tex Romig had fired Coolbaugh over an argument about a conveyor belt. Bill Coulter fired Henderson for dutifully attempting to

March 1952. Crews worked through the winter preparing the foundation for the Storke Level crusher.

enforce company rules. Coulter, in a return visit to Climax in 1939, tried to enter the Phillipson Tunnel. Henderson, then a safety man, stopped him for not wearing the required hard hat. Coulter, irritated, ignored the warning and continued into the tunnel. But Henderson barred his way again. This time Coulter stopped, placed a firm hand on the young engineer's shoulder, and said in a low, menacing voice, "Son, I built this damned mine and nobody tells me what th' hell to wear when I'm in it." But Henderson told him one more time—and was looking for a job that same afternoon.

But both Frank Coolbaugh and Bob Henderson got back on the Climax payroll. In 1951, Coolbaugh replaced Jack Abrahms as resident superintendent. And in 1953, when Coolbaugh moved up to the new position of resident manager, Henderson became resident superintendent.

During the winter of 1951-52, major surface construction proceeded right through the coldest weather for the first time. Surface crews burned piles of scrap timber to thaw frozen ground for exca-

March 1952. Construction of the No. 3 Mill helped increase overall capacity to meet emergency production requirements for the Korean War.

vation and spent $15,000 just for snow removal. By spring, crews had poured foundations for the new mill addition and the Storke crusher.

Engineers, not about to repeat the original Phillipson Level ventilation problems, actually overventilated the new Storke Level with a nine-foot-diameter exhaust fan that moved 300,000 cubic feet of air per minute. Early in 1953, mine crews fired the big shot that initiated caving, and the first Storke Level production muck train—a nineteen-ton motor hauling twenty ten-ton muck cars—rumbled toward the world's largest crusher.

The huge Nordberg gyratory crusher at the Storke Level portal mounted a ninety-five-ton, sixty-inch-diameter, bell-shaped mantle inside a massive steel housing nearly four stories tall. A bank of powerful electric motors with very low, eccentric gearing simultaneously swung and rotated the mantle, which pulverized refrigerator-sized blocks of ore into minus-six-inch pieces. The capacity of the original Climax jaw crushers of 1918 was 250 tons per day; the Nordberg gyratory crusher handled 1,500 tons per hour.

Underground mining at Climax in the early 1950s saw many technological advances. The "jackleg" drill, a relatively light, powerful drill mounted on a pneumatic leg, made the old column drill mounts obsolete and greatly speeded the drilling process. Light, hexagonal drill steels tipped with carbide bits replaced the old heavy, square drill steels. Mobile, hydraulically controlled drill "jumbos" mounting two powerful drills speeded the development of large haulage drifts, and modern thirty-ton trolley locomotives joined the underground haulage fleet.

More of the "new Climax" emerged in 1953 with completion of community construction. The modern Climax community had 250 new living units, including 70 four-bedroom houses; 10 apartment buildings, each with 18 four-room apartments; and a new hotel annex with 68 units for single men. Construction crews expanded the hospital and the Max Schott School, adding a gymnasium-auditorium seating 800 for basketball games and 1,200 for stage performances. The baseball park was equipped with lights for night games, and a new youth center had a rink for ice skating and hockey. The Climax Ski Area had new jumps, improved base facilities, a two-story warming lodge, and a ski shop.

June 1953. Construction of a new apartment building nears completion.

March 1953. The full-service garage of the Fremont Trading Post.

Meanwhile, George Coulter transformed the Fremont Trading Post into a community shopping center, the most modern in central Colorado. Climax employees and families now had the convenience of a large, departmentalized grocery store; appliance, record, and apparel shops; beauty parlor; barber shop; soda shop and luncheonette; and a new, fully equipped service station. Climax employees still enjoyed drinks and credit at the Slop Chute, but the slot machines, tokens, and chits were gone.

A modern 700-telephone PBX system on an integral internal-external net replaced the antiquated telephone system installed in the early 1930s. But Climax residents weren't nearly as excited about telephones as they were about television. Denver had enjoyed three-channel television since 1949, but central Colorado had no immediate prospects for television, for the Rockies blocked line-of-sight transmission of the Denver signals. But Climax electrical foreman Bob Ver Steeg suspected that line-of-sight might exist between the Denver FM-TV transmitters and the nearby high peaks.

On May 17, 1953, Ver Steeg, along with Bill Barter, a surface maintenance foreman, and Burt Bauman, manager of the Fremont Trading Post garage, snowshoed to the 13,770-foot summit of Mt. McNamee, the high point of Ceresco Ridge. Using a makeshift antenna, a homemade variable-frequency FM receiver, and a field-strength meter, Ver Steeg detected and measured television signals transmitted from all three Denver channels. He reported his findings to Jack Abrahms in Denver, who made a deal: If Ver Steeg could prove that signals received atop Mt. McNamee had sufficient strength, the company would foot the bill to bring television to Climax.

Like Abrahms, Ver Steeg had reservations about the project's feasibility. The summit of Mt. McNamee was accessible only on foot by a steep, rocky, two-mile-long route with a vertical ascent of 1,200 feet. Erecting a large television antenna atop the peak was possible, but year-round maintenance in snow, ice, lightning, and hundred-mile-per-hour winds would be difficult. Nevertheless, Ver Steeg led volunteer weekend climbing expeditions to the summit to prepare for actual tests of television reception.

Amid rumors that television was coming to Climax, some families drove to Denver to purchase television sets. Weeks later, Motorola and RCA televisions with the new "big" seven-inch screens appeared on the appliance store shelves in the community shopping center. A cautious Ver Steeg attempted to temper the television excitement with a letter "To the People of Climax" in a June issue of the *Moly Mountain News*.

> Television has made many of us excited these past two weeks, so excited that some of us are going out and buying television sets.
>
> Much of this excitement can be attributed to reports of a trip a group of us made to the top of Mount McNamee where television signals were found, indicating there is a possibility of bringing television to Climax.
>
> As yet, I have not seen a picture from the top of this peak. Those of us working on TV plan to make a trip there with a TV receiver in the near future. Until this is accomplished, I do not know whether Climax will have television or not or whether it will be good enough reception to warrant spending a large amount of money to bring the signal into camp.
>
> The company has authorized me to go ahead with tests and make a full report on my findings. When this is done, we will know just how we stand on picture quality and how much it will cost to bring TV to Climax.
>
> Until this information is obtained, I suggest you do not rush and buy a TV set. . . .

Ver Steeg and a growing number of volunteers next "packed, cursed, and sweated" a half-ton of equipment—twenty gallons of gasoline, a portable AC generator, a small gasoline engine, sections

June 1953. Climax volunteers pack a half-ton of equipment to the summit of Mt. McNamee to erect the first television antenna in central Colorado.

of a thirty-foot-high antenna, guy wires, stakes, and a Motorola television set—to the top of Mt. McNamee. The climb was worth the effort for, on the afternoon of June 17, 1953, nineteen Climax men sat atop the 13,770-foot summit enjoying the first commercial television program ever seen in central Colorado.

When Jack Abrahms approved the project, Ver Steeg's volunteers trucked tons of material to a base camp in the high cirque separating Bartlett Mountain from Ceresco Ridge. From two-by-four lumber and 2,400 feet of guy wire, they constructed a miniature aerial tramway, then began tramming their materials to the summit. In August they built a wooden shack to house the signal amplifier and erected and tied down the big antenna with ten guy wires. Next, they laid 14,000 feet of coaxial cable from the summit of Mt. McNamee north along the crest of the cirque, down the face of Bartlett Mountain, into a vent raise leading to the Phillipson Level and, finally, out the portal of the Phillipson Tunnel.

June 1953. Crews install television antenna leads to individual homes, making Climax the first town in central Colorado to enjoy television.

Ver Steeg made the final hookups on October 3, when Arthur Bunker was personally hosting a special ninety-six-person tour group. At noon, the tour group joined several hundred Climax residents in front of ten television sets in the recreation hall. The first television program to be recreationally viewed in the Colorado Rockies came live from New York City—the third game of the 1953 World Series between the New York Yankees and Brooklyn Dodgers.

Weeks later, after Climax had strung antenna leads to individual residences, George Coulter couldn't keep television sets in stock. By that time, Bob Ver Steeg was a local hero, Climax had spent more than $80,000, and *Life* magazine ran an article on how television had come to North America's highest town. The glow from those little seven-inch screens made the Climax winter a bit shorter, and residents noted how friends from Leadville and Frisco seemed to visit much more frequently.

215

That winter, Climax hosted the world premiere of a major motion picture—*The Treasure of the Golden Condor*, a 20th Century Fox production starring Cornell Wilde and Constance Smith. Producers selected the Climax Fox Theater for the premiere for two reasons: The Climax Fox Theater was the world's highest motion-picture theater; and *The Treasure of the Golden Condor* and the Climax Mine shared a common theme—"wresting a treasure from the earth." That was about all they shared. When the adventure, filmed in steamy Guatemalan jungles, premiered at Climax, the temperature outside was two degrees below zero.

In two short years, the new Public Relations Department did more for the public image of the Climax Mine than had been done in the previous forty years. Its efforts were rewarded in 1954 when *Empire* magazine, the Sunday supplement to *The Denver Post*, printed a forty-page, special color edition titled, "A Salute to Climax Molybdenum." The cover, by noted Colorado artist Otto Kuhler, featured a stylistic watercolor painting depicting the Climax community and mill nestled beneath a towering, snowcapped Bartlett Mountain. Accompanying the lengthy text and profusion of photographs and artwork were dozens of advertisements from railroads, defense contractors, steel companies, automobile and appliance manufacturers, and power and communications companies—all of which used some form of Climax molybdenum.

The *Empire* magazine special edition emphasized the remarkable growth of the Climax Mine in the early 1950s, as well as its sheer size and economic impact.

> . . . Housing costs are 150 pct. of the Denver figure, but rental to employees is far below Denver prices. The company's bill for anti-freeze in this altitudinous climate is more than $7,000 per year, despite the fact it owns no automobiles, only trucks and tractors. It would top $100,000 a year if the operation were not powered electrically. The 70,000 horsepower installation makes it the second largest consumer of industrial power in the state and the biggest individual customer of the Public Service Company of Colorado. The company's winter heat bill runs up to $200,000 a year, $35,000 to heat its 10 apartment buildings alone. . . .
>
> Climax, they say, spends $1 million a year for dynamite; will meet an $8 million payroll this year; uses $700,000 of wooden barrels annually to ship out its concentrate; spends a like sum on steel balls to grind up the ore and, in all, will spend $17,500,000 in Colorado during 1954. . . .

Now the television is in, piped into Climax homes by way of the highest television aerial in the world. The housing program is complete, pay checks are higher than any other place in the country for similar work, and the turnover of employees has slowed to a trickle.

In 1954, the first full year of combined Phillipson and Storke Level production, Climax mined and milled 27,500 tons of ore per day to recover 42.5 million pounds of contained molybdenum, generating a record net income of $15 million. In another Climax success story, *Business Week*, noting that miners referred to molybdenum as "moly-be-damned," suggested another name to better fit the long string of hefty profits—"moly-be-praised."

A year after the end of the Korean War, the government scaled back its stockpiling program. The Climax Molybdenum Company immediately advertised that more molybdenum would be available to industry.

MOLY IS NOW FREE

The U.S. Government has just freed molybdenum from all domestic controls. . . .

A spectacular increase in production capacity at our mine at Climax, Colorado, has made this possible. This mine, one of the largest underground operations in the world, is the major producer of molybdenum. . . .

This expansion will enable us to satisfy more than adequately the foreseeable demands of both National Defense and our customers in the iron, steel, automotive, oil, chemical, electronics, and aircraft industries.

We thank all those who have waited so patiently for this moment.

Despite booming sales, Climax continued its research, advertising, and marketing efforts. Advertisements of the 1950s promoted not only standard alloys ("Send for our comprehensive 400-page book, free; *Molybdenum: Steels, Irons, Alloys*"), but also molybdenum-additive fertilizers and a growing line of special, high-temperature, "exotic" alloys ("Send for our free 72-page book, *Arc-Cast Molybdenum and Its Alloys*"). Climax also ran color advertisements, the most striking of which pictured a Ford Thunderbird in brilliant "Fiesta Red." Climax research chemists had used lead molybdate to intensify the basic lead chromate pigment in red automotive body paint.

Employment reached 1,100 in 1954. Climax became a magnet for single men with or without experience, who could hire on for $17.00 per day, pay only $2.40 per day for room and board in the

Many of the 1950s advertisements of the Climax Molybdenum Company emphasized the superior performance of molybdenum alloys at elevated temperatures.

hotel, and qualify for instant credit at the community shopping center and beer hall. Many single men drawn to Climax were taking sabbaticals of sorts from life or seeking experiences that might help put their lives in better perspective. One miner elaborated on that point in an interview with the *Summit County Journal*.

> "We are nearly all men with problems, that is, we single men at Climax or the ones without our families. . . .
>
> "I have a problem to figure out. It wouldn't seem important to you or anyone else, but it's vital to me. And all the other men I talk to seem to have a problem, too. Maybe it's the isolation that gives a man time to think things out straight. Some of the problems that bring men here are financial. Some are domestic, and some never talk about their problems, but they have them just the same. It may be the physical labor that helps purge one's soul. . . .
>
> "See this fellow on my left? He's a lawyer from Oklahoma working as a miner at Climax. With six years of legal education behind him, his problem must be worse than mine. . . ."

All Climax "new hires" spent their first week on the "cleanup crew," familiarizing themselves with underground procedures, equipment, and safety before beginning work as a miner's helper. After that, a Climax career could take any direction, as Ted Mullings learned. Mullings, a ranch hand, rodeo rider, and part-time art student, arrived at Climax "flat broke, with two pairs of Levi's and a bum ankle from a fall in the Fairplay rodeo." After a few weeks as a miner's helper, the Safety Department offered him work drawing weekly safety cartoons at $3.00 each. Soon Mullings was preparing cutout drawings of underground workings for use by safety and training instructors. When the Climax print shop, which opened in 1954, began producing, among other materials, training and safety manuals, it needed a steady supply of drawings and Mullings became a full-time industrial artist.

Assigned to an "art studio" in a corner of a Phillipson Level toolroom, Mullings set up his easel, pens, and inks beneath a 250-watt industrial light bulb. "When I started drawing down there I'd be working away and concentrating," Mullings recalled, "then some-

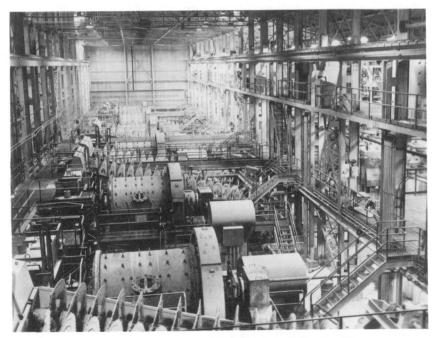

March 1954. Interior of the No. 3 and No. 4 mills.

219

body would shoot a hang-up right over my head. I'd jump so hard I'd wreck the easel and throw ink all over the place. But I got used to it. By the time they moved me to the surface a year later, I had the steadiest nerves in the state. Hell, you could light off a stick of dynamite alongside my foot and I wouldn't even blink."

Many people came to Climax simply for the pay, which was well above the western blue-collar average. For men who really wanted to make money quickly, the Mine Department started a bonus-incentive program to speed up development of drifts, stopes, and slusher workings on the Phillipson and Storke levels. Bonus pay was based on footage advance and installation of roof bolts and wire ground support. Contract miners earned at least the basic daily rate. But two experienced miners who worked well together and didn't stop for lunch and rest breaks could earn much more. In 1955, with the daily base pay rate at $18, a good contract miner could average $45 per day and occasionally earn more than $100 a day. A contract miner's annual income, therefore, could exceed $11,000—at a time when a new, fully-equipped Chevrolet cost only $1,800.

Introduction of the "jackleg" drill greatly speeded many mining processes and helped end the Climax bonus-incentive program in 1956.

The bonus program accelerated development, but proved very costly. The company employed the standard footage rates, but apparently underestimated how the "jackleg" drills, carbide bits, and other technological innovations speeded the mining process. In 1956, Climax proposed lowering the bonus rates. When the contract miners rejected the proposal in a union vote, the company exercised its option and dropped the bonus program entirely.

Big paychecks were reflected in the new cars that filled the Climax parking lots. At the visitor reception center, curious tourists sometimes asked guards just who owned all those new cars. Ken Reynolds, who later became chief guard, explained that miners owned most of them. "I could see from their faces that didn't fit their stereotypical idea of miners," Reynolds recalled. "Then they'd ask, 'Well, how much money do these miners make?' And I'd tell them, 'Some make more than a few lawyers I know.' They'd shake their heads and think long and hard about that one."

A few of the many Climax visitors warranted special attention from the Public Relations Department. One was Brainerd Phillipson's widow, who unexpectedly announced her imminent arrival for a brief memorial ceremony at her husband's grave site before removing his remains for reinterment in the East. Assistant Public Relations Director Don Stephens, assigned to coordinate the visit, quickly inspected the long-forgotten grave site above the Phillipson Tunnel portal. He was appalled to find it overgrown with weeds, the fence toppled over, and the stone obelisk leaning at a drunken angle. Worst of all, the engraved plaque had been torn off, probably as a souvenir for a Phillipson Level miner.

Stephens ordered emergency restoration of the grave site and a new plaque from a Denver engraver. Informed the plaque would take a week to engrave, Stephens replied he didn't have a week. The plaque better be ready in two days because he was sending a driver to pick it up. The driver returned to Climax in time for Stephens to glue the plaque onto the straightened obelisk just hours before the memorial service. As soon as Phillipson's widow had departed, Stephens pried the new plaque off the obelisk for safekeeping in his office.

Safety again became a problem at Climax, not in the mine or the mill, which continued to rack up national safety awards, but on State Highway 91, where miners going off shift were flooring those big, new cars. There was a rash of injury accidents, but after two Climax

1956. Mary Morrison, postmistress of the Climax Post Office, the highest U.S. Post Office in the United States.

employees died in 1954 and three more died in 1955, Governor Dan Thornton visited Climax to personally plead for caution on State Highway 91, which the state patrol rated as the most dangerous highway in Colorado.

Max Schott died on November 10, 1955, at age seventy-nine, his life a classic example of American opportunity fulfilled. He began his career as an office boy, but from that November day in 1916 when he and Ed Heckendorf snowshoed to the portal of the Leal Tunnel, his achievements made him a giant of American industry. He was wealthy and well respected by most of the men he had ever met, even, in the end, by his old rival Otis Archie King. Shortly after Schott's death, his wife Alice wrote this letter to Bob Henderson at Climax.

> All six of our children were here to help me through this ordeal. As you may well know, countless letters, messages and phone calls have come expressing sympathy.
>
> The fact which has comforted us most is that most have expressed their appreciation of him as a person who really loved his fellow man. So few people talk about the brotherhood of man and so few practice it.

1956. Resident Manager Bob Henderson at work in his office.

Those of you at Climax know how he loved that organization and how proud he was of it. Mr. Schott attended the last two board meetings and had his heart set on going to the next one. As you know, he had been ill since February. He had most of his meals in bed during the past nine months but was able to be up and out of doors frequently during the afternoons.

His trouble was a coronary occlusion. He had two minor strokes at the last and didn't have the strength to withstand them.

As a family, we read every word in the "Moly Mountain News" and so did Mr. Schott. It is wonderful to read about the things that are done for community life there. So many organizations think only about "how much we will make."

We have studied the faces of the adults and also the children. They all reflect what is called "good environment."

In my husband's name I send you all cordial greetings. Carry on!

The Climax Mine did carry on, setting new production records in December 1955. In a single shift, Warren Hatfield's muck crew moved a record 1,220 muck cars—61 trains—out the Phillipson Tunnel portal. Just five days later, Paul Grigg's muck crew set the Storke Level record with 1,280 cars. At 32,000 tons per day, Climax was now the largest underground mine in the United States and the second largest in the world.

In late 1955, Climax moved Frank Coolbaugh to Denver to become manager of western operations. Bob Henderson, a demanding manager who accepted only the best from employees, took over as resident manager of the Climax Mine. Henderson never forgot the men he worked with in the 1930s, some of whom had gotten rocked up or injured before the days of medical benefits and pensions. Against company policy, he sometimes authorized free hospitalization and medical assistance, or blatantly diverted company funds to help needy former employees. Always concerned about education, Henderson made time to personally advise sons and daughters of Climax employees about educational options and opportunities, providing them with introductory letters to influential personal contacts in universities and industry.

Bob Henderson liked nothing better than to don old diggers and a dirty hard hat and wander alone through the mine to see firsthand what was going on. In the headings, new hires would ask their lead man, "Who's the little guy?" "Keep workin'" was the likely answer. "That little guy is the big guy." Sometimes no one would recognize the resident manager—like the two miners he once met in an out-of-the-way heading on the Storke Level. "Howdy, Pard," one greeted him, "if you're killin' time, too, sit down and join us. We ain't done nothin' this shift and ain't startin' now. What'd you say your name was?"

Despite incidents like this, the overall Climax labor turnover, thanks to the availability of decent housing and community support facilities, dropped to 3.8 percent per month. Although it was the lowest Climax turnover rate ever, it still necessitated an aggressive hiring program. In 1956, Employment Manager Bud Weigang recorded a net increase of 256 employees, but to do it, his office had interviewed 3,450 individuals at Climax and temporary recruitment offices in Denver, Nebraska, and Oklahoma. By the end of 1956, Climax employment stood at a record 1,825, and the annual payroll at $12 million.

In 1957, when the Personnel Department transferred its records to microfilm for convenience and security, the Climax Mine had already employed more than 21,000 individuals. Some had worked thirty years; others had never finished their first shift. Still others had as many as three separate periods of employment, in keeping with the Climax reemployment policy limit of "three hires and three fires."

1956. Top Climax management (from left to right): Bob Henderson, Frank Windolph, George Pierce, John Petty, and Ed Eisenach.

The 1950s industrial boom also created a shortage of engineers. In 1956, Climax started a regular summer employment program for as many as 100 mining engineering undergraduates. General superintendent Ed Eisenach and mine superintendent John Petty staffed pregraduation recruitment booths at mining colleges and spoke to senior engineering classes, luring soon-to-be-engineers to Climax, but warning them that "breaking in" might not be what they expected.

Most mines hired new engineers as "trainees," and their degrees were tickets straight to the engineering office. But trainees had no earned authority and received respect neither from experienced line supervisors nor miners, who still considered them "school of mines punks" not worthy of sharing their camaraderie or invaluable practical knowledge. But at Climax, an engineering degree was a one-way ticket to the cleanup crew. To give new engineers "a better perspective on real life," Climax started them on the general payroll working alongside new miners. Then they moved on to regular production and development crews, learning about unions as union members, and learning how to give orders by taking orders.

If all went well after six months of "honest mining," the sweaty, grimy graduate moved into an engineering position. Not all lasted

Arthur Bunker (left), president of the Climax Molybdenum Company, and Bob Henderson, resident manager of the Climax Mine.

six months on the underground crews. John Petty, a 1942 Colorado School of Mines graduate, believed the program probably "scared off" half the Climax engineering applicants. But Petty also believed that after six months of pulling muck and blasting hang-ups, young graduates knew what they had in Climax, and Climax knew what it had in future engineers.

The full measure of success of the engineering recruitment program would not become apparent for a decade. But when later needs arose, Climax had an abundance of superb engineering, managerial, and executive talent, much of which was recruited in the early 1950s.

By 1957, the Climax community, with a population of 1,500, was arguably the best company town ever built in the American West. The Max Schott School sent more seniors on to four-year colleges than any other central Colorado high school. For their senior trips, Max Schott School students went to New York and Washington, where Arthur Bunker personally greeted them and paid the bill for rounds of tours, shows, and dinners that other high schools couldn't possi-

October 1957. Television crews filming another Climax feature.

bly afford. Athletics shared honors with academic achievement. In 1958, the Climax "Blue Devils" swept a state basketball championship. And young Dave Gorsuch, son of Scott and Zella Gorsuch and a recent Max Schott School graduate who trained at the Climax Ski Area, would represent the United States in the 1960 Winter Olympics at Squaw Mountain, California.

With low rents, virtually no crime, and 100 percent employment, the Climax community shared few of the problems common to most towns and cities. When television and print journalists wanted to report on life in a model company town, they came to Climax. *Life* magazine featured the Max Schott School's Boy Scout and Girl Scout troops; ABC-TV's *Mickey Mouse Club Show* filmed Climax youngsters in a segment on the Fremont Pass Station of the Harvard College Observatory; and NBC-TV's *Wide, Wide World* cited Climax for its solid industrial-community ties.

Wives arriving at Climax no longer "bowed their heads and wept," for they were welcomed by women's and church clubs and recreational and support groups that helped them adapt to life in the nation's highest town. The Climax print shop turned out cookbooks filled with "proven 11,000-foot-high recipes," and the Public Rela-

227

1956. Climax Elementary School students.

tions Department invited chefs from such corporations as Westinghouse and General Mills to present talks and workshops to Climax women.

Morgan Wadsworth was now Climax safety director. His wife, Eleanor, now with nine children to care for, still found time to poke a little fun at Climax cooking with "Hi Altitude Blues," a song she wrote to the tune of "Shortnin' Bread." With only slightly exaggerated humor, Eleanor remembered why Climax wives of the 1930s and '40s often cried when they looked in the ovens of their coal-fired stoves.

> *Roll out the biscuits, cut 'em out neat,*
> *Put 'em in the oven with plenty of heat,*
> *Call out the hoist, the bulldozer, too,*
> *Can't lift 'em out when they're through.*
>
> *Made some cookies the other noon,*
> *Hard and flat as a wrinkled prune.*
> *Tho' no one ate 'em, they gave us a laugh,*
> *They played real good on the phonograph.*

228

Climax youngsters dressed for Easter Sunday, 1957.

Sent Betty Crocker a lengthy note,
"Cut the ingredients!" is what she wrote,
"For each thousand feet, follow the book,"
When you get through cuttin', there's nothin' to cook.

Three little chiluns, a lyin' in bed,
Two are sick, the other 'most dead.
Spoke to the doctors, the doctors shout,
"Throw that Climax cookin' out!"

All of you ladies, wherever you be,
If you can't cook, just listen to me,
If hubby is naggin', don't take his abuse,
Come to Climax and have a perfect excuse!

Arthur Bunker's grand expansion of Climax during the 1950s was an unqualified success, as measured by both increased production capacity and upgraded quality of life in the Climax community. Business writers considered the "new Climax" a model corporation, for it had huge profits, remarkably smooth labor and community

229

relations, its lowest labor turnover rate ever, enormous ore reserves for the future, low production costs, and a market ready to buy every pound of molybdenum it could produce.

The expansion of the 1950s was symbolized by a landmark event in American mining history. On February 4, 1957, Governor Stephen McNichols and 100 other special guests gathered at Climax to witness a muck train rumbling out the portal of the Phillipson Tunnel. A white banner draped across the front of the grimy, twenty-seven-ton haulage motor announced:

THIS TRAIN CARRIES THE 100,000,000th TON OF ORE TO BE
MINED FROM THE CLIMAX MOLYBDENUM COMPANY MINE

The honorary motormen were Wayne Thompson and A. D. Graves, both of whom had started their Climax careers in 1933. After a brief ceremony at the portal, the train headed for the trestle loop and the crusher, while Governor McNichols and the guests moved to the mill for the ceremonial start-up of another new mill unit.

Just one month later, Climax production reached another record— 35,000 tons per day. In 1957, Climax mined and milled 10.6 million tons of ore, surpassing the annual production of the Kennecott Copper Corporation's Braden copper mine in Chile to become the largest underground mine in the world.

In a decade of remarkable statistics, perhaps the most significant was not one of production, but of ore reserves. At the end of 1957, engineers estimated the proven ore reserves of the Climax Mine at 417 million tons—four times more than the cumulative production of the past forty years. As one metal-market analyst wrote, the future of the Climax Mine seemed as strong as molybdenum steel itself.

On February 4, 1957, Climax mined its 100,000,000th ton of ore.

9
Some Very Rough Years
1958-1962

◆

*We all knew that the town's time had come, that it
stood in the way of progress and development.*

—Eleanor Wadsworth,
former Climax housewife,
recalling the closing of the company town

◆

When the directors of The American Metal Company proposed a corporate merger with the Climax Molybdenum Company in 1957, financial observers called it "a natural." The American Metal Company held large international interests in base- and precious-metal smelting, production, exploration, and marketing. The Climax Molybdenum Company owned the Climax Mine, which supplied 60 percent of the world's molybdenum; with huge reserves and its own market of loyal customers, Climax was enormously profitable. The Metal Company sought to supplement cash flow to pursue immediate diversification opportunities. Climax, of course, generated substantial cash flow and had itself recently dabbled in diversification. The Metal Company and Climax had a historic close relationship and, at least on paper, the strengths and assets of the companies complemented each other remarkably well with little overlapping.

Both boards of directors approved the merger proposal and submitted it to their respective shareholders for a vote on December, 30, 1957. Metal Company shareholders involved in the unsuccessful lawsuit of 1939-40 to take over the Climax Molybdenum Company

233

considered the proposal a long-overdue "remerger." Metal Company shareholders overwhelmingly approved the merger by a vote of thirty-eight to one. Climax Molybdenum Company shareholders were notably less enthusiastic. Nevertheless, they also approved the merger, but by only a four-to-one vote.

On January 1, 1958, the Climax Molybdenum Company became a division of American Metal Climax, Inc., one of the nation's largest integrated mineral resource companies, with assets exceeding $250 million. The directors of the new corporation elected Arthur Bunker as chairman and appointed Weston G. Thomas as president of the Climax Molybdenum Division.

Reaction to the merger varied at the Climax Mine. Some predicted that "getting tied to a big outfit like American Metal" might mean unlimited future growth and possibly a choice of worldwide job assignments. Most were indifferent, saying that "as long as paychecks don't bounce," the merger would have little personal effect. But some senior Climax employees, those who had endured the 1930s and war years, and who had worked on the expansion of the 1950s, voiced a more cautious assessment. "Climax got where it is just fine by itself," they reflected, "and it doesn't need any help now."

The first big postmerger project was development of a new shaft-accessed production level below the Storke Level. Climax had only three previous shafts. No. 1 Shaft was Carl Cunningham's declined ore pass, driven in 1931 to connect the old White Level with the Phillipson Level. Because of missing engineering records, No. 2 Shaft is a mystery, but it was probably the service raise above the Phillipson Level that accessed the coyote drifts used in the big caving shots of the 1930s. Miners sunk No. 3 Shaft from the Phillipson Level to access the exploration drifts of the old "500 Level," now the Storke Level.

The new No. 4 Shaft would be an internal shaft, collared from the Storke Level about one mile from the portal and serving two new levels 300 and 600 feet below. Engineers designated the new levels the 600 Level and the 900 Level, in reference to their distance below the Phillipson Level. No. 4 Shaft would measure 750 feet from its sump to the top of its internal headframe. It would be circular, lined with concrete, and have four compartments—two for counterbalanced ore skips, one for a service cage, and one for a manway ladder and compressed air, water, and sump service lines. Heavy steel construction would permit the service cage to lift and lower twenty-ton haulage motors. An underground electrical substation would provide power for the shaft and lower levels. The 69,000-pound shaft hoist-drum assembly, which included an 800-horsepower electric motor, could not be broken down; it fit through the mile-long Storke Level adit with only inches to spare.

As Climax engineers worked to develop the $1.4 million No. 4 Shaft on schedule, Climax Molybdenum Division executives concerned themselves with economic projections calling for an inevitable "adjustment" in the inflationary industrial boom of the 1950s. National economic growth began slowing in 1957; by January 1958 the economy was mired in a major recession and the domestic steel industry slowed to 50 percent of capacity. Although Climax researchers had created new uses for molybdenum and its compounds, 90 percent of molybdenum consumption remained tied to production of alloyed steels and cast irons.

On March 31, 1958, Weston Thomas ordered Resident Manager Bob Henderson to cut production. Henderson reduced the mine and

1960. Construction of No. 4 Shaft.

Many advertisements of the Climax Molybdenum Company in the 1960s promoted "Molysulfide" lubricants.

More cars than ever have to be greased with "Moly" Grease

Recently major car builders began turning out 1961 models lubricated with molybdenum disulfide grease . . . and, in some cases, advertised the point that these models will not have to be relubricated until 30,000 miles. Because of the established proof of the excellent lubricating qualities of Molysulfide®, it was a logical step for the car makers to take.

It makes this fact sure: FUTURE LUBE JOBS ON THESE CARS WILL HAVE TO BE DONE WITH A "MOLY" GREASE.

And, don't forget, the 61,500,000 older motor vehicles now on the roads will turn more and more to "Moly" Greases!

Experience in both controlled laboratory tests and in countless road tests—under the toughest driving conditions—has shown that cars greased with a 3% "Moly" Grease have definitely provided easier steering, more comfortable driving and quieter riding. Car owners who have had "Moly" Grease jobs have flatly stated they could *feel* the difference.

Ask your supplier about "Moly" Grease. Most major oil companies carry "Moly" Grease under their own brand names. They are *multi-purpose greases* that not only meet the demands of the new 1961 models—they have been proven superior lubricants for *all* cars new and old! CLIMAX MOLYBDENUM COMPANY, a division of American Metal Climax, Inc., 1270 Avenue of the Americas, New York 20, N. Y.

"MOLY" GREASE SUPPLIERS:

Amoco · Cities Service · Conoco · Crown · Frontier · Gulf · Jenney · Mobil · Pennzoil · Phillips · Shell · Sinclair · Skelly · Standard Oil Co. (Ind.) · Standard Oil Co. (Ky.) · Sunoco · Texaco

IN CANADA:

B-A · Canadian Oil Companies · Cities Service · Imperial Oil Limited · Shell · Texaco

mill six-day work week to five days. To avoid layoffs, Henderson terminated the seven-year-long hiring program, allowing the workforce to reduce by attrition. Employment dropped sharply, for many men were accustomed to "six-day paychecks." Don Stephens, now public relations director, received numerous expressions of public concern, including this from the editor of the *Chaffee County* (Buena Vista) *Republican*.

> There have been many unsubstantiated reports down here about the number of men who have left Climax since the five day work week became effective. The last remark, made by a man who is employed here, is to the effect that 102 quit their work last weekend. Would you please give me the dope on this? Also, I would appreciate it if you would advise what your total payroll is now, compared to last year at this time; advise if the company is yet hiring men; progress of the negotiations between the union and the company, etc.

Stephens replied that the recession had mandated a production cutback. Yes, more than 100 men had quit, but that had been antici-

236

pated, for many single men worked at Climax only because of the Saturday time-and-a-half pay.

Leadville was most vulnerable to a recession, because of its heavy economic reliance on the Climax Mine. After its frontier-era mining booms and busts, Leadville thrived on a World War I base-metal mining boom, then survived the lengthy busts of the 1920s and 1930s. With its economy already bolstered by the growing number of residents working at Climax, Leadville boomed again during World War II. Leadville managed yet another boom during the Korean War, but that was the old mining district's last hurrah.

Fortunately for Leadville, the final decline of its old mining district coincided closely with expansion at Climax in the 1950s. When the Resurrection Mining Company, one of Leadville's biggest employers, laid off half its workforce in 1953, the Climax hiring program took up the slack. Climax offered special health and age waivers, and even granted a half-day's pay to every former Resurrection man willing to interview. When the Resurrection Mining Company finally shut down for good in 1957, Climax was there again, hiring three-quarters of the laid-off Resurrection men.

By 1958, the Leadville mining district was a frontier relic with twenty square miles of collapsed headframes, flooded workings,

1958. Climax field geologists pose for a group photograph.

rotted timbers, and useless drainage tunnels. The three remaining active mines employed only sixty men between them. Yet, unlike other Colorado mining towns, which had become ghost towns, Leadville had actually grown. The sole reason, of course, was the Climax Mine, which now employed over half the Lake County workforce and accounted for three-quarters of the county property tax base. Leadville had shifted its economic base subtly, quietly, and very smoothly from its own mining district to the Climax Mine. Not everyone agreed, but some Leadville residents felt that Leadville, at least in the economic sense, had already become a de facto Climax company town.

When the Climax Molybdenum Workers Union Local 24410 (AFL-CIO) opened labor negotiations with the Climax Mine in April 1958, an air of uneasiness persisted over the issue of the five-day work week. The existing contract, valid through July 1960, included an automatic increase of eight cents to bring the base pay rate up to $2.50 per hour. But if the work week dropped below forty-eight hours, the union could renegotiate the base pay rate clause of the contract. Accordingly, the union exercised its option and asked for a 23 percent base wage increase.

But with sagging sales in the midst of the recession, the company refused. The union dropped its wage increase demand to 13 percent. But Climax refused again, claiming most major mines were already on a four-day work week, while it had already gone the extra mile by retaining a five-day week. Furthermore, with a big stockpile of molybdenite concentrate, the company was not interested in arbitration.

The union stuck to its demand of a 13 percent base wage increase and, in a meeting in Leadville's old Tabor Opera House on July 19, voted to strike. At 7:30 A.M. on July 21, 1958, pickets appeared at the main gate atop Fremont Pass and at the lower Storke Level entrance in the first labor strike in the forty-year history of the Climax Mine.

Most idle union members remained at Climax or Leadville through August, but when no settlement appeared imminent by September, they took the suitcases out of the closets. Enrollment at the Max Schott School fell from the previous year's 537 students to only 225, a decline of 58 percent. The six-week strike was finally settled on October 9, when the union voted 470-39 to accept a seven-cent-per-hour base wage raise, an increase of only about 3 percent, along with additional hospitalization, insurance, and retirement benefits.

Neither side won the strike. In return for modest gains, the union lost 250 members. Climax production plummeted 40 percent for the year, reducing both company profits and Lake County tax revenues. In Leadville, merchants estimated they would need a year to make up their business losses.

Union members who had a few dollars in the bank called it "a nice little strike," either finding other summer work or enjoying a pleasant vacation in the late summer and early fall. But the strike was never popular. Some thought the recession was a poor time for the union to push for a major wage increase, and that the union had struck not for the sake of its members but primarily to test the resolve of the "new" American Metal Climax.

The Climax expansion program of the early 1950s placed a premium on available space atop Fremont Pass. Plans for further mill expansion and development of the Ceresco Ridge ore body ruled out more community expansion, necessitating a new solution to the problem of employee housing.

1960. The Climax Ski Area. The lodge appears at the base of the run.

239

1960. A racer finishes a slalom run at the Climax Ski Area.

Climax realized that Leadville was the only logical site for large numbers of employees to reside. But Leadville was a collection of old houses, most of which had been built in the nineteenth century, with few existing vacancies. Furthermore, Leadville residents and businessmen had little interest in building more houses.

In 1957, Climax surprised Leadville by taking matters into its own hands. The company purchased a large subdivision just north of the Leadville city limits, then announced it had contracted with American Builders, Inc., of Security, Colorado, to construct 500 new homes within two years. Leadville residents were still talking about the purchase when crews began surveying streets and lots, clearing trees, and erecting the first model homes. Climax then announced that a major insurance company had contracted to guarantee mortgages for all nonmilitary Climax employees; the Federal Housing Authority and the Veterans Administration would guarantee mortgages for the many veterans on the Climax payroll.

Climax temporarily named its new development "Shangri-La," while conducting a "Name the Town" contest. Entries poured in: "Matchless," "Mountaindale," "Pine View," "Winterset," "Sky View." Climax miner Lloyd Smith won the first prize of $600 for the name "West Park." "I don't know what to say," Smith offered humbly. "I never won anything before except a wristwatch in a navy raffle and I'm sure happy about this."

But not everyone in Leadville was as happy as Lloyd Smith. Many Leadville residents saw the planned, spacious, ultramodern West Park community as a threat to their own faded, small, Victorian houses and crowded backyards. Merchants were especially concerned about the new shopping center that would be built one mile north of the Harrison Avenue business district. One voiced his personal fear in the *Herald Democrat* that "Climax is going to come right down off that hill and take this whole place over."

Seventy-three Climax employees quickly signed agreements to purchase new homes. But when construction began in June 1958, employees were less certain about becoming West Park home owners because of the economic uncertainties of the recession, the reduced five-day work week, and the pending strike. When the Climax union walked out in July, West Park suddenly seemed like an

January 1958. The flag-raising ceremony on Harrison Avenue after Leadville was named an "All-American City."

overplanned, half-built maze of unpaved streets and vacant new houses.

Meanwhile, the National Municipal League and *Look* magazine selected Leadville as an honorary "All-American City," citing its social and civic improvements of the 1950s. Climax Public Relations Director Don Stephens, along with Assistant Public Relations Director Terry Fitzsimmons, immediately congratulated Leadville in a glowing, three-page tribute in the *Moly Mountain News*.

Leadville, seeking to capitalize on the *Look* publicity, set about producing a new promotional brochure. Climax, a longtime member and big supporter of the Leadville Chamber of Commerce, eagerly offered to help and perhaps soothe some of the friction that had developed between Leadville and Climax. The Climax Public Relations Department generously laid out and printed the brochures in the company print shop, then donated the entire run, which was worth about $1,000, to the Leadville Chamber of Commerce. But that incurred the wrath of Robert Theobald, owner, publisher, and outspoken editor of the *Herald Democrat*. Theobald, who also operated a commercial print shop, dashed off a series of fiery editorials questioning "whether Climax is in the printing business or the mining business."

But the chamber of commerce, grateful for Climax support, defended itself and the company in its own editorial.

> The Leadville Chamber of Commerce, representing the merchants of the city, has always been, and still is, operating on a shoestring. . . .
>
> There was no desire to bring unfair trade practices to the city. The budget this year would not have permitted the purchase of so many brochures of high quality. Leadville would have lost a golden opportunity to advertise itself as an All-American City, in this, the Rush to the Rockies year.
>
> . . . We're positive that Don Stephens, Terry Fitzsimmons and Ted Mullings did not spend countless hours burning the midnight oil just to cut the Herald Democrat out of another source of revenue. No, they, Bob Henderson, and the powers that be in this powerful industrial giant, were humbly and magnanimously reaching out a helping hand to a friend in dire need.

But Theobald was not put off. In early 1959, he launched a vehement attack on Climax, criticizing everything from safety to the strike settlement terms. Another of Theobald's targets was the environment, especially since a riser pipe had recently broken in the

1959. Looking north along Leadville's Harrison Avenue. The new West Park development appears at upper left.

Robinson tailings pond, sending a torrent of muddy water surging down the Tenmile into the Blue River at Dillon. Even though Climax had mustered 200 men in a round-the-clock emergency repair job, Theobald implied that the mine should be shut down. Recalling that smaller mines had been shut down for less pollution, Theobald wrote that "it wasn't a matter of the amount of pollution, but who does the polluting."

Theobald's favorite and most vulnerable Climax target was West Park. In summer 1959, West Park was still unfinished, and only 28 of the 109 completed houses were occupied. Emphasizing that West Park had been built with nonunion labor, Theobald called the development "Scab Town" and described it as a "rapidly deteriorating comedy of errors" soon to become "the newest ghost town in the West."

Theobald's editorials, however, may have stirred up more pro-Climax sentiment, as typified by this editorial reply by West Park resident Luther Monberg on July 8, 1959.

. . . Do I note a tone of jealousy toward West Park, one of the few respectable districts in this town?

I am equally amazed at the editor's insistence on biting the hand that feeds it, namely the Climax Molybdenum Company. For whether you choose to acknowledge it or not, Leadville would be dead without Climax. It might not even be able to support (perish the thought) its local newspaper. . . .

So you may huddle in your unpainted shacks, muttering with indignation at non-union labor. I shall continue to live comfortably in the quiet, clean and lovely ghost town.

In June 1959, Weston Thomas moved Bob Henderson up to general manager of western operations at the new American Metal Climax regional headquarters in Golden. Edwin Eisenach, a 1939 graduate of the Colorado School of Mines who began his Climax career as a miner's helper in 1942, took over as resident manager of the Climax Mine. Eisenach, along with his assistant general superintendent, Frank Windolph, would guide the Climax Mine through some of its most transitional and turbulent years. One of their biggest challenges, and one with many social and economic implications, was deciding the fate of the Climax community.

Although off to a slow start, West Park clearly would provide future housing for Climax employees. The immediate problem at Fremont Pass was what to do with the Climax community. In 1959, the Climax community was at its peak of development with 1,800 residents, a new church, and a second Climax school, the two-year-old, modern Max Schott Elementary School.

With its low rental rates, the Climax company town had never made a profit. But now, because of record numbers of houses and streets and full municipal and protection services, maintenance and operation had grown increasingly expensive. Town management was a headache for the Community Relations Department, which was saddled with the unenviable task of deciding "who got which house and why." Constant repair and refurbishing was another costly problem. While some families scrupulously maintained their rented houses, others blatantly abused them, even knocking walls out for unauthorized "remodeling" and building fires directly atop the hardwood floors. And when a tenant painted the interior a bizarre color combination, Climax had to repaint it before new occupancy.

Since the 1930s, the town had served its basic purpose of providing housing to reduce the high labor turnover rate. But by the

1950s, greatly improved roads, road maintenance, and automobiles made commuting to Climax, even from towns as distant as Salida, fairly routine even in winter. When exploration of the Ceresco Ridge ore body began in 1958, Climax set up a diamond drilling station only 200 yards from an apartment building. By summer 1959, Bob Henderson and Ed Eisenach accepted the fact that the Climax community had outlived its usefulness and was standing squarely in the way of future mine and mill development.

Climax had few realistic community relocation alternatives. The nearest possible housing site was Kokomo, the old Tenmile camp that was now just a bar, restaurant, U.S. Post Office, and a few houses and apartments. But Kokomo's days were already numbered, for the old town sat directly in the way of future tailings-pond development. The town of Dillon, at the confluence of the Tenmile and Blue rivers, was also ruled out, for it would soon be relocated to make room for a reservoir project. The only logical alternative was Leadville, which offered both the partially completed West Park development and an existing community infrastructure capable of absorbing an influx of Climax residents.

The first rumors about the possible closure of the Climax company town reached Leadville in fall 1959, eliciting among residents both the worst fears and the brightest hopes. In December, the *Leadville Leader*, a new maverick weekly, warned about being taken over by "Big Brother."

> MUST WE SELL OUR SOULS TO AMERICAN METALS
> AND BECOME JUST ANOTHER COMPANY TOWN?
> For several weeks now everyone has been excited about the proposed move of Climax personnel to Leadville. Many people with whom we have talked think this will be the greatest thing that has happened to Leadville in recent years.
> Granted that any increase in population will help boost the economy of the city, BUT, should we grovel on our knees and in effect sell our very souls to this corporation? Let's look at a few facts. If reports are indicative of the truth, they will have to move present housing to make way for mining operations. The question is where else can they go?
> We have seen these operations before in Arizona and other areas. The corporation will invest in housing, news media, etc. They pay the workmen and then the workmen pay them in return, for housing, and in some cases for the very food they eat. . . .
> The next move is usually to start taking over the shops, to start loan companies and banks, and to gain complete control over the populace.

If a citizen doesn't like this he can leave. Many of these things are in the works now, some have already taken place. Of course, "Big Brother" must control politics also, he can't have some official passing a law or bill that is not favorable to the interests of the corporation. . . .

Although some initial reaction to the move rumors was negative, most Leadville residents took the more realistic stand that Climax represented the future of Leadville. In December, a group of forty Leadville business, civic, political, religious, and educational leaders drove up the hill to meet personally with Ed Eisenach. Their message was straightforward: They would do everything possible to welcome Climax residents into their community and to help make Leadville the living and trading center for all Climax employees.

Eisenach made the formal announcement in February 1960. Although expected, many were shocked by its suddenness and the schedule of Eisenach's plan. Climax had already sold nearly all the Climax community structures, including West Park, to the John W. Galbreath Company, an Ohio-based national real estate firm and company town mover. When the deal closed on February 11, the Galbreath Company announced it would move all Climax housing to Leadville within two and a half years. To facilitate the move and encourage home ownership, Climax offered the housing at bargain basement prices, and Galbreath financed sales at a low 4.5 percent interest on twenty-five-year mortgages. Home ownership would be possible for as little as $200 down, with monthly payments even lower than the rock-bottom Climax rental rates. Furthermore, costs of moving the houses to Leadville could be conveniently incorporated into the purchase price. Climax gave its current tenants first right to purchase the houses they occupied. Nontenant employees were next in line, and the general public could purchase any houses that remained.

Galbreath moved the first Climax house on August 10, 1960. With all household belongings in place, crews jacked up a one-story duplex, then lowered it gently onto a flatbed truck that had backed under it. At 8:30 A.M., the truck moved out onto State Highway 91. Two hours later, the duplex arrived at West Park. Crews lowered it onto a waiting foundation, then quickly hooked up the utility and sewer connections, making the house ready for occupancy the next day.

By fall, Galbreath crews had moved thirty-three houses to West Park, then turned their attention to the first of the big, three-story, eighteen-unit apartment buildings. They cut the building into thirds, jacked each section up, placed it on long steel girders, then slid it onto three tandem flatbed trucks. Each 125-ton section rode on the combined forty-eight wheels of the side-by-side tractor-trailers, which, of course, took up the entire highway. Several hundred curious spectators watched as the huge load crept slowly down the steep Fremont Pass grade with two heavy bulldozers cabled to the rear to prevent a disastrous runaway. The thirteen-mile trip to Leadville, with numerous stops while state patrol officers directed traffic, took eight hours.

The transition in education began in 1959 when the newly formed Lake County School District incorporated the Max Schott School. At the start of the school year in September 1960, Climax bused Max Schott School seniors to Leadville High School. Climax moved its elementary grades into the vacated Max Schott School, and immediately converted the Max Schott Elementary School building into mine administrative offices. Climax also donated parcels of West Park land to Lake County as sites for construction of two new county elementary schools.

1961. Start of development of the Ceresco Tunnel. The Ceresco portal appears in the center of the photograph, very near the edge of the Climax community.

March 1961. In countless thousands of muck train runs, an occasional bit of trouble was not to be unexpected.

Although moving the Climax community did not interfere with mine production, anticipating molybdenite demand had become increasingly difficult. The recession had weakened the molybdenum market, but the 1958 Climax strike, along with a prolonged copper-industry strike that curtailed by-product molybdenum recovery, reduced overall supply to tighten the market. The result was several years of erratic production. After the record 1957 Climax production of forty-two million pounds of contained molybdenum, output dropped to twenty-five million pounds in 1958, bounced back to thirty-three million pounds in 1959, then reached a new record of nearly fifty million pounds in 1960.

Employment had by then recovered to 1,800, and Climax began two new development projects. Crews started construction of a collar and headframe and excavation of No. 5 Shaft, the first external shaft at Climax. Located near the Storke Level portal, No. 5 Shaft would access the 600 and 900 levels from the west, thus permitting simultaneous development of the two new lower levels from different directions.

As the molybdenum market strengthened, Climax began development of Ceresco Ridge through a portal located at an elevation of 11,435 feet. The Ceresco Level would be quick and inexpensive to develop; although it would have only a seven-year life, production would begin within four years. Portal blasting began in summer 1960 and rattled the windows of the not-yet-vacated nearby apartment buildings. Within one year, crews completed the quarter-mile-long Ceresco Tunnel and began level development.

In 1961, Climax employment topped 2,000 for the first time. But in Leadville, employment in the old district's mines, mills, and smelters had virtually ceased. Leadville's last smelter, ASARCO's Arkansas Valley Plant, shut down, putting its last fifty men out of work. Within one week, Climax invoked special age and health waivers to hire every smelter man who wanted a job.

The closing of the Arkansas Valley smelter was a significant point in Leadville's history. Leadville was still a mining town, but had now completely shifted its economic dependence from the old mining district to the Climax Mine.

On June 1, 1962, classes at the Max Schott School adjourned for the final time. Seven faculty members and 100 students attended a subdued closing ceremony, which effectively marked the end of the Climax community. A few weeks later, a *Moly Mountain News* columnist wrote a touching farewell to the old town of Climax.

> Forty years from now, God willing, I will return to our old homestead in Climax with our grandchildren and listen to their grandfather tell them about the days when a regular little city occupied this site.
>
> I'll hear him tell about the days when Bartlett Mountain reached clear to the sky, before the "Glory Hole" reduced it to that "puny" little mountain. I'll hear him tell how food and housing cost too much and pay was always too little, how an ancient steam locomotive used to whistle about the property with food and mail, and how there was even a church and school here, about the recreation hall where he won all the trophies for being the best bowler and pool shooter in the state.
>
> He will tell the starry-eyed youngsters about working a full eight hours every day and working a full eight hours meant a full eight hours then, about the car pools and how they bucked the snow drifts fighting to get to work every day.
>
> He'll ask me to confirm that womenfolk hardly ever left the house for fear of getting lost in a blizzard or running into a mountain lion, how finally they moved the entire town because it was such a fearful place to live.
>
> And later when the youngsters leave us alone and run to play along what was once Ninth or Tenth Street, he'll turn to me with just the hint of a tear in his eye and say, "Those were the good old days, weren't they?"

Despite a twenty-three-inch snowfall on Labor Day, 1962, the Galbreath crews finished moving apartment sections to Leadville the next week. The only community buildings left behind were the hotel for single men, the U.S. Post Office, and the Fremont Trading Post, now owned and operated by Kenneth Leighton. With the town gone, resident manager Ed Eisenach's title was changed to general manager.

Some Climax residents were glad to see the town go, for they felt they never really left the job. Even after quitting time, they saw the same faces and discussed the same company business. The incessant rumble of muck trains put them to sleep and woke them again in the morning.

But for many others, the Climax town had been a special place and saying good-bye was a sad, emotional experience. "When we came here in 'forty-six, there wasn't much and living was rough," Eleanor Wadsworth recalled. "But everyone worked together and we built our own little town, and we built a good one. We had the best of everything. I couldn't have found a better place in this country to raise nine kids.

"We all knew that the town's time had come, that it stood in the way of progress and development," Eleanor continued. "But a lot of us felt that the company had somehow betrayed us, that it was taking away something that we had worked so hard to build, and that we were really proud of."

Shortly after the unpopular strike of 1958, union leaders again changed their affiliation, and the Climax Molybdenum Workers Union Local 24410 (AFL-CIO) became Local 2-24410 of the Oil, Chemical and Atomic Workers Union (OCAW). The new affiliation, however, did little to smooth labor relations. By spring 1962, negotiations toward a new two-year contract stalled on issues of basic wages, contractual work rules, management subcontracting rights, and arbitration procedures.

Local 2-24410 and Local 1823 of the International Brotherhood of Electrical Workers both approved a preliminary strike vote on June 22. Three more weeks of continuous negotiations proved fruitless, and on July 16 both unions rejected a final company offer. Two days later, when the graveyard shift started at 11:30 P.M., pickets appeared at the main gate and the Storke Level entrance, and the Climax Mine

1963-64. Management-labor (IBEW) negotiating committee. Standing: Rusty Moyer (IBEW, on left), George Sanders (IBEW). Seated, from left to right: Les Stout (IBEW), Bill Distler (Climax), Dennis Thuis (IBEW), Urban Coucher (Climax), Lou Cantrell (IBEW), Ed Eisenach (Climax general manager), George Mitchell (Climax).

faced its second strike in four years. The following morning, the *Herald Democrat* carried the headline that Leadville dreaded:

CLIMAX MOLYBDENUM COMPANY CLOSED BY STRIKE LAST NIGHT

Ed Eisenach warned that the strike represented a "no-win" situation for both sides. Hugh Matlock, the former union activist who led the move to break with the CIO fifteen years earlier, now sat on the other side of the table as the Climax Director of Industrial Relations. Matlock cited grievance, overtime, and subcontracting policies as areas where compromise seemed unlikely.

Leadville, home to 1,600 of the 2,087 Climax employees, reeled under the strike's economic effects. On August 13, with both sides growing further apart, the *Herald Democrat* headline pleaded:

LET'S GO BACK TO WORK NOW!

But the unions stood firm, and the company reminded them that it was sitting comfortably on an eight-month stockpile of molybdenite concentrate. Climax also mounted a public-opinion campaign, printing full-page "Strike Facts" in the *Herald Democrat* noting that its wages were the highest of any major western metal mine, and those wages gave Lake County the highest per-capita income of any rural Colorado county. Nevertheless, the unions, confident of victory, flatly rejected the next Climax offer.

251

Inside the cab of steamer No. 641 as it makes one of its last runs in 1962.

The Climax Mine remained shut down through September 1962, a month that marked the end of another era in Colorado mountain railroading. Steam locomotives had been a familiar sight on Fremont pass for eighty-one years. Many Climax men remembered when the Colorado & Southern abandoned its right-of-way east of Climax after a decade of lawsuits in 1937, and how the old narrow-gauge line had been converted to standard gauge in 1943. Since then, the Colorado & Southern Railroad had been absorbed by the Chicago, Burlington & Quincy Railroad, which in turn became the big Burlington Northern system. But many Climax miners and Leadville railroaders still called the Burlington Northern's isolated Leadville-Climax spur the "C&S" or simply the "Climax Line." A few old-timers even called it the "High Line."

Since 1943, the locomotive that faithfully maintained five-day-per-week, all-season freight service between Leadville and Climax was old C&S No. 641, a big 2-8-0 B-4-R Consolidation-class steamer built in 1906 by the American Locomotive Company. Rail buffs, historians, photographers, and old railroaders often journeyed to Climax to watch No. 641 thundering up the steep mountain grades under a full head of steam hauling loads of steel, timber, cement, fuel, mining equipment, and mill reagents. On its afternoon return trips, No. 641 hauled molybdenite concentrate, a half-million tons since 1943 alone. No. 641 represented classic mountain railroading at its exciting best, with black smoke belching from the straight stack, whistle shrieking, and wheel flanges squealing on the tight, hairpin curves. Rail buffs came from as far away as Europe, because the Leadville-Climax line had achieved a measure of railroad fame: It was the last and highest steam-operated, regularly scheduled, standard-gauge, common-revenue carrier left in the United States.

In 1961, the old steamer needed a major boiler overhaul, but parts and skilled labor to handle the job were no longer available. A year later, Burlington Northern made the inevitable announcement: No. 641 would make its final run in September 1962 and would be replaced by a modern, diesel-electric locomotive. Rail buffs and photographers visited Climax more frequently, for the last runs were historic events that would never be repeated. Author David Digerness, in volume two of his railroading classic *The Mineral Belt*, recounted one of those last runs.

> The 641's whistle filled the silence with beautiful railroad crossing signals—a sound the people of Leadville were accustomed to—as the engine's drivers glided along the frosty rails and squealed to a stop to couple the caboose. The crew received their train orders for the day, and the hostler handed the engine over to them. . . .
>
> The 641 started making up the train of cars brought in by the connecting D&RGW, all having the common destination of Climax. With eight cars and caboose, the train started the ascent toward Fremont Pass. We moved out of town, past the old C&S freighthouse. Along the way we noticed many small boys perched high atop the snowbanks at road crossings. Obviously, they were on their way to school and stopped to watch the locomotive go by. Waving to them, I thought of all the times I used to walk down the tracks just to see the trains. It was all steam then. . . .
>
> It was just after noon when we arrived at Climax, and time for a lunch break. We stayed aboard and ate our sack lunch with the crew in the caboose, and they talked about railroading and some of their exciting experiences. After lunch, the job of switching was performed, with the cars being shunted to different locations. Some went up the switchback, which was higher in elevation than the pass, while others went alongside and into the concentration mill, where we picked up loaded cars of molybdenite concentrate for the return trip. The locomotive was turned on the wye and ready for the trip back to Leadville.

Artist Otto Kuhler recorded his impression of steam railroading at Climax in this watercolor painting.

Before continuing, the crew stopped at the trading post to pick up some of their grocery supplies and to mail a couple of letters at the Climax Post Office, the highest post office in the United States.

Digerness was also present for No. 641's final run. After the old steamer had dropped off its six cars of molybdenite concentrate and its boiler had cooled down, its replacement, No. 828, an SD-9 diesel-electric locomotive in the green-and-white Burlington Northern colors, moved No. 641 slowly to its final stop alongside the old Leadville passenger depot. Digerness wrote:

> Having ridden with the crew and experienced steam railroading on this line—having smelled the wonderful aroma of coal smoke, watched the cinders fly—having heard the sounds of the locomotive echo through the Upper Arkansas River Valley—bouncing off 14,142-foot Mt. Democrat, to re-echo again and again . . . I find it hard to believe that dieselization is real progress. It was like watching the death of an old friend to see the diesel push No. 641 to her final resting place.

But, for the time being, the new diesel-electric locomotive had little work, for Climax remained shut down by what became known as "the '62 strike." The strike made clear the degree of Leadville's economic dependence on the Climax Mine. By October 1962 nearly

200 Climax employees, unable to make ends meet on picket pay, left to seek work elsewhere. School enrollment in Lake County dropped 18 percent, four businesses closed their doors, and state wildlife officials reported a sharp increase in poaching.

The interruption in molybdenum supply came at a critical juncture in international relations. The October 1962 Cuban missile crisis compounded tensions already heightened by a recent confrontation with East Germany in Berlin. Citing the possibility of war, the Department of Defense cancelled plans to release part of its strategic molybdenum stockpile. On October 19, after urging by the Department of Labor, Climax and the unions agreed to move their negotiations to Denver—where both unions immediately rejected the next company offer.

A new worry arose with the first cold winter weather. If Climax allowed the mill to "deep freeze," production would be impossible until spring, and then only after costly repairs. The company-union rift widened abruptly on October 26, when Climax, citing the cold weather and a possible national defense emergency, announced it would resume production immediately.

The news media reported the story nationally when 400 Climax management hands started up the mine and mill with a production

No. 828, the Burlington Northern diesel-electric locomotive that replaced steam power on the Leadville-Climax line in 1962.

plan reminiscent of the wartime system. Climax would defer all development and major maintenance work, concentrating on drawing, hauling, and milling selected high-grade ores. Management hands who had previously only "operated desks" had an experience they would never forget.

The start-up did not go smoothly. When operations began, Leo Bartell, a mechanic crew shift boss working in the mine, suffered a severe head injury. Bartell died in a Denver hospital two days later, becoming the fifty-fourth fatality in the history of the Climax Mine. Nevertheless, within a week management had production up to 15,000 tons per day. Because of high-grade ore, molybdenum recovery reached 75 percent of normal.

The National Labor Relations Board intervened on November 2, citing the strike's severe economic effects on Leadville and the need for molybdenum for defense requirements in "tense times." The Federal Mediation and Conciliation Service ordered both sides to Washington for closed talks. When the unions expressed interest in a new company proposal on November 9, Leadville businessmen and clergy pleaded to company and union leaders for a quick settlement, only to be disappointed. Settlement hopes rose again with rumors that Secretary of Labor Willard Wirtz might personally intervene to end the strike by Thanksgiving. But that hope, too, faded when Secretary Wirtz announced he would consider doing so "only as a last resort."

By Christmas, with the strike in its sixth month, bitterness and uncertainty reached levels that Climax employees had not imagined. The strike even divided families; while some collected management checks, brothers, fathers, and sons in the unions struggled to hang on through the long, bleak winter. Nevertheless, working management hands chipped in to buy holiday turkeys and trimmings for striking union families.

Finally, the unions tentatively agreed to another company proposal on January 2, 1963. On January 8, to the great relief of everyone in Leadville, the unions ratified the agreement. In settling the strike, the unions gained a ten-cent-per-hour basic wage increase, twelve cents per hour in fringe benefits, improved accident and health benefits, and a favorable provision for weekend premium pay. The original strike vote in July 1962 had been 1,100 to 165; the ratification vote that ended the strike was 668 to 65. More than 500 Climax employees couldn't hold out and had left to find jobs elsewhere. On January 9, 1963, as Leadville churches rang bells in citywide services of thanks, the *Herald Democrat* headlined its best news in a long time.

STRIKE IS OVER
CLIMAX WORKERS RETURN TO JOBS

In 1963, both Leadville and Climax were still reeling from the effects of five turbulent years of corporate, social, and industrial change. The comfortable myth that Climax was somehow immune to labor trouble had crumbled. And when the Climax town was dismantled and moved, it took with it a certain element of warmth, togetherness, and trust. The frequent off-shift social contact between management and union members was replaced by a more impersonal, adversarial "us and them" relationship. Climax was now home to no one; all employees commuted, put in their shifts, then drove home to Leadville or more distant towns. Public Relations Director Don Stephens would later remember the 1958-63 period as "some very rough years." Most Climax men and women, both management and union, would later agree that "things weren't the same after they moved the town and the 'sixty-two strike."

By summer 1963, with Climax employment above 2,000, Leadville was the biggest "pure" mining town left in the West. Climax paid $18 million in annual wages and 77 percent of Lake County property taxes. As long as the Climax Mine operated, business along Harrison Avenue boomed.

Aware of the sweeping social and economic changes that accompanied the moving of the Climax town, the Leadville-Lake County Regional Planning Commission had asked the Denver Research Institute of the University of Denver to conduct an economic study of Lake County. Interestingly, the 1962 study found that both residents and tourists considered Leadville a "historic" mining community, with its history, traditions, and architecture bound to the frontier era. Yet, paradoxically, residents also believed that Leadville, because of its close association with American Metal Climax, Inc., a broadly diversified, multinational corporation, was no longer a "boom-bust mining town," but a "typical American community."

The Denver Research Institute, however, concluded otherwise, reporting that Leadville had become Colorado's most economically specialized town. Mining was now of far greater economic signifi-

257

cance than at any time in Leadville's history, including its fabled 1880s silver boom. Not only did a record percentage of the Leadville-Lake County workforce rely on the mining industry, it now relied on a single mine—Climax. Furthermore, Leadville was deluding itself to think it was an "All-American City" in a balanced economic sense. In reality, Leadville was more dependent upon exports and the market strength of one commodity than any other town in Colorado.

Concluding that such total reliance on an "extraordinarily narrow" economic base was "precarious," the Denver Research Institute recommended that Leadville immediately expand its economy into tourism and diversified manufacturing.

With tourism booming in the Colorado Rockies, former mining towns like Aspen, Central City, Georgetown, and Breckenridge already actively competed for a share of the growing tourism and mountain recreation market. But beyond chamber of commerce brochures, Leadville felt no need to compete for tourism dollars, nor did it feel compelled to attract diversified manufacturing. The sole reason, of course, was that the Climax Mine "sent down" payroll checks totaling $1.2 million every month.

Leadville was indeed Colorado's last "pure" mining town, and the Climax Mine would perpetuate its mining economy, traditions, and attitudes. Wherever the Climax Mine was going in the future, Leadville was content to go with it.

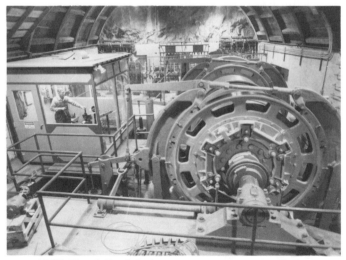

1962. No. 4 Shaft hoist room nearing completion.

258

10
The Cash Cow
1963-1969

No one has thought of moly without thinking of Climax for the past 50 years . . . And won't for the next 50 years or longer.

*—Climax Molybdenum Company
advertisement in the late 1960s*

Following the Korean War, the United States embarked upon an unprecedented, prolonged period of industrial growth and economic prosperity interrupted only briefly by the recession of 1958. In just ten years, annual world consumption of elemental molybdenum had doubled. Of the seventy-seven million pounds used by industry in 1963, the Climax Mine supplied forty-seven million pounds, or 61 percent of the world market.

The price of a pound of molybdenum stood at $1.20, representing the lowest relative price increase of any industrial metal over the past forty years. That reflected the success of the traditional Climax policy of "holding the line" on prices to discourage competition. During those forty years, the cost to mine and mill one pound of contained molybdenum at the Climax Mine had risen from fifteen cents to only sixty-four cents. Even with postwar inflation and sharply increased labor and materials costs, Climax continued to minimize production costs by emphasizing high volume and operational efficiency. The remaining profit margin—an impressive fifty-six cents per pound—was enough to generate a net annual 1963 operating profit at the Climax Mine of $26 million.

259

As world molybdenum consumption rose at 5 percent, or nearly four million pounds, per year, a tighter market forced the Climax Molybdenum Division for the first time to allocate molybdenum to its steady customers. The continued success of the Climax Molybdenum Division, and in large part the success of American Metal Climax, depended upon high production at the Climax Mine. And increased mine production was the only way to achieve a number of vital goals: holding the line on molybdenum prices, retaining the largest possible market share, meeting future projected demand, and providing flexibility for unexpected future market fluctuations and possible labor problems.

Climax continued its research and technical assistance programs. Alloyed steels and cast irons still accounted for most molybdenum use, but during the 1960s researchers found new uses in "Molysulfide" and "Moly Grease" lubricants, special corrosion- and abrasion-resistant alloys, and high-temperature alloys for rocket engine parts for the space program. One of the most effective advertisements of this period stated simply:

NO ONE HAS THOUGHT OF MOLY
WITHOUT THINKING OF CLIMAX
FOR THE PAST 50 YEARS . . . AND WON'T
FOR THE NEXT 50 YEARS OR LONGER

No one has thought of moly without thinking of Climax for the past 50 years

	Yearly Production Rate	Reserves* (1967)
The Climax Mine 1918—	58,100,000 lb Mo in 1967	1,764,000,000 lb Mo
The Urad Mine 1967—	7,000,000 lb Mo	52,980,000 lb Mo
The Henderson Mine 197x—	~50,000,000 lb Mo	1,781,640,000 lb Mo

And won't for the next 50 years or longer

CLIMAX MOLYBDENUM COMPANY
An AMAX Division

*Proven and probable, in place, without allowance for mining dilution.

This Climax Molybdenum Company advertisement from the late 1960s emphasized the fact that the names Climax and molybdenum had long been synonymous, and that huge ore reserves would be sufficient for future demand.

260

The Climax Mine sat atop 450 million tons of proven ore reserves. To exploit those reserves faster, Climax formulated a $40 million, five-year program to complete the Ceresco and 600 levels, continue Storke Level development, and expand the mill. But engineers first had to direct their immediate attention to the Phillipson Level, which was entering its thirty-second year of continuous production.

Since 1961, engineers had noted increasing rock pressures along the 260-280 haulage drifts in the deepest part of the Phillipson Level, a condition reflecting the surprisingly delicate nature of the massive block cave mining system. About 1,000 feet of overhead rock had begun caving prematurely and beyond the intended limits. The rock bore down upon properly caved ore and on the underlying workings in the competent rock of the Phillipson Level.

Drawing the tightly compacted broken ore became difficult, then impossible. Finally, the seriousness of the problem became clear when workings began to collapse. The enormous weight shattered foot-thick timbers and compressed others to three inches in thickness. In some workings, miners and engineers crawled on their stomachs to reach places where muck trains once rolled. If the weight was not relieved, the imbalance would threaten larger sections of the Phillipson Level and could prevent access to twenty million tons of higher-grade ore worth $80 million.

The problem was apparently caused by a miscalculation of the mining sequence and inattention to proper draw-control practice. The solution, ironically, came as a result of the 1962 strike. When production mining stopped, the entire area "quieted down," allowing management crews under Joffre Johnson and Warren Shriver to replace much crushed concrete and timber.

After the strike was settled, mine repair crews replaced damaged timber sets in the 260-280 haulage drifts with yieldable steel arches on two-foot centers, then remined and heavily concreted the overhead slusher drifts and fingers. But controlled caving could not be reinitiated by conventional undercutting of stope pillars. Instead, miners drove narrow coyote drifts through the tightly compacted, previously caved ore above the fingers. Next, they drilled 350 twenty-foot-deep longholes, loading them with 16,000 pounds of powder. After four months of preparation, the crews detonated the coyote drifts and longholes—with no apparent effect whatever on the caving balance.

1964. The 260 haulage drift on the Phillipson Level, where increasing rock pressures have crushed the overhead steel arches.

When no caving was detected, miners tried their last alternative—blasting high in the fingers. Finally, there was a very subtle, almost undetectable, yet massive, shifting of weight within Bartlett Mountain. Miners crossed their fingers as the shifting weight crushed the remaining overhead pillars and bent many of the new steel arches. But the internal weight of the mountain had equalized, and normal caving resumed. As soon as ore could be drawn through the fingers, production muck crews returned to "260-280 country." Interestingly, the balance "adjustment" placed greater weight on sections of the Storke and 600 levels, testimony to the delicate nature of the block cave mining system.

In May 1964, a planned caving shot attracted the attention of every mining publication in the country. "Big shots" had been routine at Climax since 1933, when miners detonated 110,000 pounds of powder to initiate caving above the Phillipson Level. Another notable shot consumed 78,000 pounds of powder in 1936, and miners detonated 81,000 pounds of powder to crumble a "stubborn" arch above the Phillipson Level in 1956.

But the coming shot would be much larger, dislodging 1.5 million tons of ore from the side of Bartlett Mountain and dropping it into the Glory Hole, where it could be mined through the Storke Level. The shot would require 417,000 pounds—208 tons—of powder, making it the largest underground detonation in mining history. The energy released would be the equivalent of one-fifth of a kiloton of TNT, a measure usually associated with the energy levels of tactical nuclear weapons.

Preparations took two months and the full-time attention of Assistant Mine Superintendent Dale Johnson and General Mine Foreman Bill Nelson. Forrest "Flash" Gordon, the direct operational supervisor, coordinated the combined crews of shift bosses Paul Grigg, Don Green, Dwain Johnson, and Bill Powell.

Crews accessed the shot area through what was left of old No. 1 Shaft, then drove a 200-foot-long inclined raise and, finally, four 60-foot-long coyote drifts. Miners loaded the workings with eleven semitrailer truckloads of explosives, including 1,050 fifty-pound cans of Nitramon, a water-resistant chemical explosive, and 5,550 fifty-pound sacks of ANFO, an ammonium nitrate fuel-oil blasting agent.

General Mine Foreman Bill Nelson and Repair Crew Foreman Forrest "Flash" Gordon prepare to throw the switch for the "Big Shot" of May 23, 1964, the largest underground detonation of conventional explosives in history.

DuPont de Nemours, Inc., which provided most of the explosives, sent engineers to help plan and load the shot, and to record the detonation with high-speed motion-picture cameras. Miners primed the shot with 2,100 pounds of primer sticks and 4,000 feet of detonating cord. After carefully checking hundreds of connections between the electric blasting caps and detonating cord, crews stemmed the coyote drifts with 6,000 fifty-pound sacks of tailings.

Because of its size and location, the shot offered a unique opportunity for seismic study. The United States Geological Survey alerted all North American seismic stations and set up twelve special recording stations along a 150-mile-long line from Climax north into Wyoming. The National Bureau of Standards sent a team to record the precise time of detonation to atomic clock standards of .001 second.

Climax scheduled the detonation for 2:45 P.M. on May 23, 1964. Shortly after the formal countdown began at 1:00 P.M., foremen evacuated all underground levels and surface facilities, with the exception of twelve men needed to keep vital mill equipment operating. Day shift was dismissed early, while swing shift was held at the gates.

State patrol officers closed State Highway 91 to all traffic at Fremont Pass. Two shifts of Climax men and women, most in sunglasses and shirtsleeves on an unusually warm spring day, lined the shoulder of the highway, eyes on Bartlett Mountain. And at dozens of seismic stations across the continent, seismologists watched the needles of their instruments.

Crews had made fifty-five separate, final safety checks by 2:30 P.M., when Dale Johnson and Flash Gordon stepped to the master switch just inside the Phillipson Tunnel portal. After a verbal count, Gordon threw the switch. The National Bureau of Standards later reported that electrical initiation of detonation occurred at 2:44:59.124. Detonation of the 208 tons of explosives was complete just two-tenths of a second later.

After a moment of delay that seemed like an eternity, the entire back of the Glory Hole—a section a quarter-mile wide and 1,000 feet high—swelled out from Bartlett Mountain, hung momentarily as if suspended, then plunged slowly downward. The sound—a dull, heavy thud followed by a low, deep rumble—echoed across Fremont Pass several seconds later. As a column of dust and smoke rose 1,500 feet into the sky over Climax, seismic tremors radiated outward through

May 23, 1964. The "Big Shot" collapses a 1,000-foot-high, quarter-mile-wide section of the back of the Glory Hole.

the Earth's crust. At the Colorado School of Mines in Golden, seventy miles northeast, the shock registered 2.9 on the Richter scale. Two minutes later the shock waves registered on a seismograph at Pasadena, California; six minutes and thirty-seven seconds later, the shock waves had traveled 3,500 miles to move seismic needles at Yellowknife, in Canada's Northwest Territories.

The United States Geological Survey correlated the recorded data from eighteen stations to develop the first seismic profile of a 220-mile-long section along the backbone of the southern Rocky Mountains. Contrary to existing theory, the seismic data proved that there was no proportional thickening of the Earth's crust beneath major mountain systems. The data also enabled geologists to infer the nature of the crustal structure below the southern Rockies. Fifteen miles of granitic rock lay atop fifteen miles of basaltic rock; that, in turn, capped the Mohorovic Discontinuity—the actual transition between the Earth's crust and mantle.

So closely had engineers balanced the explosive energy with the rock mass that no surface buildings sustained damage. As expected, however, the shot knocked out underground power and slightly damaged some arches on the Phillipson Level. But electricians quickly restored underground power and, just three hours later, Storke Level muck crews began drawing the newly caved ore. That single shot displaced roughly the same amount of ore that had been mined during the first eight years of operation at Climax.

Soon after the "big shot," Climax set another production record of 38,000 tons per day, but the increase in tonnage was accompanied by a marked decrease in safety. In March 1964, a 600 Level miner was crushed to death between two muck cars. Just two months later, a Phillipson Level miner died in a raise climber accident.

Then, on July 8, Climax suffered another fatality in a bizarre accident that nearly became a major human disaster. Fire broke out at 9:00 A.M. in a surface building enclosing the collar of a Storke Level ventilation intake raise. A half hour later, Storke Level miners noticed smoke and began evacuating the level. But the location of the fire was not discovered on the surface until 9:55 A.M. By then, flames had ruptured a compressed-air pipeline and burned through a 13,800-volt power cable, cutting all underground electrical power and stopping the intake fan at the bottom of the raise.

The inoperative fan stopped airflow in the raise, allowing explosive gases to accumulate at the bottom. The gases exploded just as five miners were investigating the source of smoke at the bottom of the vent raise, blowing out the intake fan and heavy timber bulkhead and killing one man instantly. Another suffered a broken arm and three others were overcome by smoke. Even with firefighters from Leadville and the New Jersey Zinc Company Mine at Gilman assisting Climax teams, the stubborn fire smoldered for eight hours. Without electrical power or compressed air, the Mine Department shut down both the Storke and 600 levels.

As the heated ground at the heavily damaged collar began "sloughing," losing the entire raise became a real possibility. As soon as the fire was extinguished, emergency crews lowered a steel caisson into the collar and poured 1,400 cubic yards of cement around it to try to save the raise. Climax cancelled all production shifts indefinitely and scrambled to find replacement materials. Engineers located 5,000 feet of replacement power cable in Philadelphia, had it flown by chartered aircraft to Denver, then trucked immediately to Climax. They tracked down compressed-air pipeline sections in Tulsa, but the pipes required modification before they could be shipped. Production finally resumed eight days later; the downtime, while minimal considering the extent of the damage, seriously disrupted the tight production schedule.

However, the vent raise was lost and miners immediately began driving a parallel raise to replace it. Although there had been one fatality, every man in the underground at the time of the fire had been exceedingly fortunate. Had the power cable not burned through to stop the intake fan, heavy smoke and lethal levels of carbon monoxide would have vented through the underground levels, possibly causing a human disaster.

Of all the duties at the Climax Mine, few were more diversified than those of the guards. The twenty-two guards, headed by Chief Guard Tom McAuliffe, came in contact with virtually every aspect of the Climax operation. Much of their work involved routine plant security, logging truck traffic in and out of the mine property, issuing and filing employee car permits, greeting the public, and registering the endless stream of business visitors. But the guards also assisted with accidents and first aid both on company property and on State Highway 91. When occasional snowbound winter travelers abandoned their vehicles and walked to the Climax gate, the guards provided hot coffee and a warm place to wait out a Fremont Pass blizzard.

In 1960, the guards assumed a new public responsibility. The mountains blocked radio communications between dispatchers and mobile police units in many parts of Lake, Summit, Eagle, Chaffee, and Park counties. In an agreement with the state patrol and the five counties, Climax volunteered to act as a radio communications link for regional law enforcement agencies. At the main gate, Climax installed a powerful 100-watt transmitter and a seventy-five-foot-high antenna with a 125-mile transmission range. By relaying through Climax, police and emergency radio communication became possible almost anywhere in the five-county area.

Guards used the equipment to transmit on company frequencies, greatly improving communications with the growing Climax fleet of radio-equipped vehicles. They also monitored all civil defense messages and, in the event of a serious emergency at Climax, were assured of immediate contact with county law enforcement and emergency agencies, even if telephone service was interrupted.

By fall 1964, the radio net actively involved Climax guards in public law enforcement operations. In one incident, three armed men shot up a Georgetown bar, wounding a patron before fleeing west over Loveland Pass. A state patrol officer took up pursuit in Summit County, where the trio turned south on State Highway 91 heading for Climax. Climax guards William Adamich and Billy Adkins had monitored the Summit County chase transmissions. When they recognized the car speeding over Fremont Pass, they radioed Leadville requesting a police roadblock, then took off in pursuit in a Climax vehicle. With nowhere to go, the three suspects surrendered seven miles from Fremont Pass. When police made the arrest, they also found in the stolen car three revolvers, four high-powered rifles, a large quantity of ammunition, and "enough booze to open a liquor store."

A few months later, the guards were back in action when they monitored the state patrol pursuit of a vehicle headed north from Leadville on State Highway 91. This time they rolled out the Climax fire truck for a roadblock atop Fremont Pass. The suspects roared to the top of the pass, only to see the fire truck and two armed, uniformed Climax guards. They turned back and state patrol officers made the arrest minutes later. The two armed suspects were wanted on Texas bank-robbery warrants.

During the Cold War years, marked by the threat of Soviet nuclear attack, the Colorado Civil Defense Agency not only appointed and trained Climax guards as civil defense wardens, but quietly turned an unused section of the Phillipson Level into one of the West's biggest and most secure nuclear bomb shelters. The U.S. Army shipped in truckloads of surplus field rations, five-gallon water cans, blankets, cots, toilet paper, and bathing and medical supplies. Civil defense workers set up an underground shelter capable of accommodating 12,000 Lake and Summit County residents for one week. Climax engineers helped solve the big problem of waste disposal, at least in theory. Accustomed to meeting the demand for "high production," they designed a sturdy "ten holer" out of mine timbers and lagging, securing it over an old ore pass connecting to the lower Storke Level.

While Climax did some unusual things with law enforcement and civil defense, it did far more in the fields of scientific, industrial, and military research. Since 1941, when the Harvard College Observatory established its Fremont Pass Station, Climax had earned a reputation as a generous supporter of worthy research.

After World War II, operation of the Fremont Pass Station observatory passed from Harvard to the University Corporation for Atmospheric Research (UCAR), a Colorado-based association of fourteen member universities. In 1951, UCAR moved the observatory from its original site at the base of Ceresco Ridge to the north slope of Chalk Mountain, away from the lights and dust of the growing mill and community. UCAR spent $250,000 to build a new dome and install a 16.25-inch coronagraph, the world's largest and most sophisticated. Other new instruments included a spectrograph to analyze light from the solar corona, a magnetograph to detect and record solar magnetic features, and an automatic "patrol" monitoring device to help predict solar flare activity.

Now known as the High Altitude Observatory, the research facility still enjoyed free use of Climax land, utilities, and support services. During the 1960s, its most important function was advising the National Aeronautics and Space Administration of the prob-

1967. The High Altitude Observatory on the north side of Chalk Mountain was a continuation of the Climax tradition of supporting scientific research.

ability of solar flare activity as a consideration in scheduling manned space flights.

Climax had also supported important dental research. During World War II, chemists had regulated the fluoride content of domestic water tapped from diamond drill holes in Bartlett Mountain to one part per million. Climax thus became one of the world's first "fluoride-regulated" communities. Beginning in 1946, Max Schott School students had participated in a three-year-long comparative dental survey performed jointly by the Colorado Department of Health and the University of Colorado. Data obtained at Climax on the enzyme-inhibiting action of fluoride to reduce tooth decay helped establish today's widely accepted practice of adding controlled levels of fluoride to drinking water and toothpaste.

Considering elevation, company cooperation, and availability of services, Climax made a superb high-altitude research base. In 1949, Climax had supported a secret cosmic ray study, hosting six physicists from the Office of Naval Research, the Atomic Energy Commission, and University of Washington Physics Department. For three years, physicists operated from a small field laboratory building near the Robinson Reservoir pump house, using cloud chambers, electromagnets, and special cameras to study the interaction of solar gamma radiation within controlled electromagnetic fields.

In 1960, Climax permitted Colorado State University scientists to set up a camp atop Chalk Mountain to study the potential of cloud seeding to increase mountain snowfall. Backed by a National Science Foundation grant, the scientists installed a radar unit to track weather balloons and upper-level, moisture-bearing winds, and to study the dynamics of snow-crystal formation in clouds. They stationed four large silver-iodide generators upwind from Chalk Mountain and set up an elaborate system of snowfall-measuring devices on Climax property. Climax supported the six-year project with funding contributions, materials, utilities, and even housing for researchers. Most miners were amused by the project; noting the natural 320-inch seasonal snowfall of 1962-63, some suggested that "making a little less snow" might be a more logical goal.

In the early 1960s, General Motors Corporation's Electro-Motive Division considered building a controlled-environment facility in Illinois to simulate thin, cold air to "mountain test" new diesel-electric locomotives. But cost studies showed that bringing the locomotives to Climax on the nation's highest standard-gauge railroad and then monitoring engine performance for months at a time would be far cheaper.

When aerospace contractors developing specialized compression systems for military and space applications had to study compression dynamics at high altitude, they, too, came to Climax. Their "laboratory" was the main compressed-air system serving the underground levels.

In May 1964, Climax aided the U.S. Army in conducting "human performance" research studies to better determine relationships between altitude, diet, and exercise. The tests involved twenty doctors and nutritionists, twelve volunteer soldiers, twelve dogs, and several dozen white rats. The joint study, conducted by the U.S. Army's Research Institute of Environmental Medicine and its Medical Research and Nutrition Laboratory, compared data recorded at Climax with that obtained from similar tests conducted simultaneously in Denver and Boston. For a full month, the troops marched around the Climax property, observed closely by researchers with stopwatches and clipboards. Amid many jokes, one miner quite familiar with the relationship of altitude, diet, and exercise suggested, "Hell, just put 'em on drills up in the Phillipson stopes and count how many baloney sandwiches they eat."

In fall 1964, mine crews initiated caving in Ceresco Ridge after a four-year, $10 million development program. With the Ceresco Level on line, overall mine production rose to a record 42,000 tons per day. Because of the shallow ground above the Ceresco Level, a small surface subsidence, named the "baby glory hole," appeared in just six weeks.

To boost production even higher, Climax engineers also worked on a more innovative approach—recovery of the oxide portion of the Bartlett Mountain ores. When Bartlett Mountain was mineralized, the molybdenum had originally been emplaced in the form of molybdenite, or molybdenum disulfide. But thirty million years of erosion and faulting with subsequent exposure to air and water had chemically altered, or oxidized, the shallow molybdenite into molybdite, or molybdenum trioxide. The near-surface "cap rock" was almost completely oxidized. Several hundred feet below the cap rock, oxides and sulfides combined in a mixed ore zone. Below that rested

271

the sulfide ore, which historically had provided most of the molybdenum production of the Climax Mine.

Millions of pounds of elemental molybdenum were present as molybdite, which was not amenable to flotation separation. Over the decades, Climax had mined enormous quantities of molybdite, only to drop it in flotation and discard it with the tailings. Climax consulting metallurgists had conducted the first oxide recovery experiments in 1919 in a rented laboratory at the Colorado School of Mines. Several chemical recovery methods seemed promising, but, at the time, molybdenum prices discouraged further work. But with the tighter markets, technological advancements, and pressing need for more molybdenum in the 1960s, oxide recovery seemed a logical and expedient way to boost production and profits.

In 1961, thirty Climax metallurgists, chemists, and engineers, working with independent research laboratories, started a $2 million, four-year research program to design a 5,000-ton-per-day plant to treat selected mixed ores from the Ceresco and Phillipson levels. The $20 million plant would recover three million pounds of contained molybdenum per year, both increasing production and maximizing conservation of the Bartlett Mountain molybdenum resource.

1964. Construction of the $20 million moly oxide plant is near completion.

Unlike the relatively simple, physical flotation separation process, oxide recovery involved a complex chemical treatment of mixed ore tailings that had already passed through sulfide flotation. After basic classification of the mixed-ore mill tailings, a preconcentration step separated the thickened fines by particle size, then pumped them as a pulp to the chemical recovery plant. There tanks heated the incoming pulp, agitating it with sulfur dioxide and sulfuric acid to dissolve the molybdite particles. The mixture then went to desorption tanks, which drove off the sulfur dioxide, recovering it for reuse. Next, injection of compressed air slightly reoxidized the dissolved molybdenum so that an adsorption process using activated charcoal filters could attract and "capture" the molybdenum. Finally, the molybdenum-containing charcoal filters went to stripping columns, where a mixture of air and ammonia produced a recoverable, high-grade solution of ammonium molybdate. After purification, heat evaporation crystallized the ammonium molybdate. A roasting process then converted it to commercial molybdic oxide, while recovering the ammonia for reuse.

Because of its complexity, engineers considered the "moly oxide" plant a technological risk from the beginning. Pilot plant testing showed that the process required precise control of temperatures, pressures, and volumes, as well as large quantities of toxic, corrosive chemicals. When Bob Henderson, who was now vice president of western operations of American Metal Climax, announced construction of the moly oxide plant, he emphasized the high level of technological risk in a public statement.

> Speaking generally, expansion programs frequently create a surface impression of being "cut and dried" from the standpoint of investment and expectations.
>
> In view of this, I think it is only fair that some other considerations of this expansion program be pointed out.
>
> First of all, there was a definite risk in the investment of some two million dollars in the research program which might easily have proven fruitless. Let me emphasize the importance of research in this and all such projects. Research is costly and often speculative. Yet, without the ability to invest substantial amounts into research, the future of molybdenum, as well as most other minerals, would not be especially bright.

273

Ten contracting firms and several hundred workers began constructing the big moly oxide plant in summer 1964. Crews anchored the foundation on steel pilings driven through thirty feet of compacted early tailings and into glacial gravel beds. The huge plant superstructure utilized 1,500 tons of structural steel. When fully enclosed in May 1965, the moly oxide plant was the largest building ever erected in the central Colorado Rockies. Unlike new underground mine levels, which weren't apparent to the public, the prominent moly oxide plant was a highly visible statement of how big the Climax Mine had grown.

Considering the size and cost of the moly oxide plant, some Leadville merchants complained to Bob Henderson that they might not be sharing as fully as possible in the Climax prosperity. Henderson was well respected in Leadville, ever since his days as resident manager at Climax, when he generously committed company support to Lake County public education and Leadville's St. Vincent Hospital project. When Henderson offered to address merchants' concerns at a public chamber of commerce function in early June 1965, more than 200 Leadville residents were in the audience.

Henderson's tone, as always, was serious, and his "discussion" was really a lecture. To confirm rumors, Henderson revealed that the Climax Mine did indeed purchase over $1 million in supplies every month. While Climax would not "hand" anything to anyone, any Leadville businessman could become a Climax supplier, but only by taking the initiative himself. "Our warehouse department is more than willing to work with any of you who have enough initiative to try to obtain this business for Leadville," Henderson said. "Leadville people, if they will, can get this business, but we are not going to furnish the money, the capital, or anything else it takes do business with Climax." Citing the moly oxide plant, Henderson went on to emphasize that seeking rewards always involved some risk. Bob Henderson was one of the very few people who could have delivered that lecture in Leadville and walked away from the podium with a sincere round of applause.

Just three weeks later, Leadville, the Climax Mine, and the mining industry were shocked to learn that Bob Henderson, at age fifty-seven, had succumbed to cancer. As was his style, Henderson had worked full-time until just four days before his death. American Metal

Climax President Frank Coolbaugh, who had worked with Henderson at the Climax Mine in the 1930s, penned this tribute:

> . . . To many people who did not know him well, Bob represented a tough, penetrating and unsympathetic exterior, and indeed he could be just as cold and tough as the situation demanded. Actually, Bob had a heart as big as all outdoors, and yet he could not tolerate anyone who was lazy and would not perform honestly within his inherent capabilities. His unsolicited generosity to veritable scores of individuals and families, and unlimited time he took to counsel and steer a confused boy or girl into a logical course of training, education or solution to a personal problem, were undoubtedly not appreciated even by many of his closest friends.
>
> I do not expect that I will ever know a man with the dedication to his company, the job or his fellow workers as that of Bob Henderson. We all know of the long hours that he devoted to his work in reading, planning and directing operations. He established and guided his life by the highest principles. In his many supervisory capacities he never asked a man to do a job he could do himself or show the man how to do it better, whether that job were to blast a hangup, set a staging for a buzzy in a stope, rerail a string of muck cars, or any other.

In July 1965, the Climax Molybdenum Division ordered Ed Eisenach to replace Bob Henderson as vice president of western operations. Frank Windolph, a chemical engineering graduate of the University of Colorado who had started his Climax career in the mill in 1937, took over as general manager of the Climax Mine.

On January 27, 1966, Windolph presided over ceremonies commemorating another Climax production landmark—the mining of the 200 millionth ton of ore. Windolph presented symbolic gifts to the employees with the greatest and the least company seniority. The senior employee, Dunbar Arnold, had hired on in 1933 and held work number 0006 on the employee numbering system that had been reorganized in 1957. Dan Delay was a new hire with work number 7005. Climax mailed mementos, bronze trays with a ceramic emblem bearing the Climax "C" and the date the 200 millionth ton of ore was mined, to all 2,575 employees. The event underscored the dramatic expansion of production at the Climax Mine: Mining the first 100 million tons of ore had taken forty years; mining the second 100 million tons took just eight years.

Mine crews working toward each other from opposite sides of the 600 Level "holed through" on May 11, 1966, then began developing an underground crusher room in one of the largest underground chambers ever excavated. Measuring 180 feet long, 48 feet wide, and 54 feet high, the crusher room would house a sixty-inch gyratory crusher and two standard seven-foot crushers with a combined capacity of 30,000 tons per day. A thirty-six-inch-wide conveyor belt operating through a 3,300-foot-long inclined tunnel would transport crushed ore to the mill.

Another step toward higher production came in July 1966, when the moly oxide plant came on line. The huge, enormously complex plant had 14.5 miles of pipe, 130 miles of electrical wiring, 22,500 square feet of steel floor grating, 3,000 valves, and 100 pumps and compressors. To prepare the plant for operation, paint crews applied 160 fifty-five-gallon drums of a specially formulated resistant paint to protect interior metal surfaces from the corrosive effects of the chemicals used in the recovery process.

Colorado Governor John A. Love, Representative Wayne Aspinall, and 175 special guests dedicated the plant on November 26, 1966. Also present were Frank Coolbaugh, the new board chairman of American Metal Climax, and Ian MacGregor, the new corporate president.

The moly oxide plant met its production expectations, treating 5,000 tons of selected mixed ore tailings per day and recovering 1.5 pounds of molybdenum per ton. With the subsequent major increase in overall tax valuation of the Climax Mine, the Climax share of the Lake County property tax base reached 85.5 percent, making possible an across-the-board 5 percent cut in Lake County personal property taxes.

The combined production of the Phillipson, Storke, and Ceresco levels now stood at 43,500 tons per day—another new record. The moly oxide plant boosted the 1966 molybdenum recovery total to a remarkable 56.3 million pounds, or 28,000 tons, of elemental molybdenum. And that led to two more records for 1966: The annual net operating profit of the Climax Mine topped $25 million, while the 1966 annual net earnings of the Climax Molybdenum Division of American Metal Climax, Inc., reached $65 million. The Climax Mine and the Climax Molybdenum Division were clearly the cash cows of American Metal Climax.

After the Climax community closed in the early 1960s, Climax became closely involved in the affairs of Leadville and Lake County.

One particularly ambitious example came in 1964, when Colorado Mountain College, based 100 miles away in Glenwood Springs, contemplated forming a multicounty tax district to facilitate regional expansion. Although skiing, tourism, and mountain recreation were steadily growing in economic importance, the Climax Mine remained by far the region's largest tax revenue source, and its workforce of more than 2,500 represented a sizable potential student population. If Colorado Mountain College was going to expand, the new tax district would need a suitably high assessed valuation—higher than Pitkin, Eagle, Garfield, and Summit counties could provide together. It also needed the participation of Lake County and the Climax Mine.

From the Climax standpoint, a local college campus would be a big asset, making Leadville a more attractive place to live and providing educational facilities to train employees in mining-related skills. Colorado Mountain College presented its expansion plans to Climax in 1964 and found immediate interest and support from Ed Eisenach and Don Stephens, both working from the corporate offices at Golden, and from governmental affairs representative Harold Ballard and budget director Patrick Harvey at the Climax Mine. Twenty-five additional Climax men and women quickly volunteered to work on committees to help bring a college campus to Leadville. The joint college-Climax committees established the required tax district and formulated plans for a campus. The final obstacle standing in the way of construction was the uncertainty of raising $2 million through a general-obligation bond issue. That hurdle fell when Climax alone picked up 96 percent of the bond issue.

The groundbreaking ceremony for the Timberline Campus of Colorado Mountain College was held in April 1967, on a hill overlooking Leadville's historic California Gulch. When classes commenced in September 1968, the initial enrollment included eighty-one Climax men and women. The new campus offered two-year liberal arts and other preprofessional programs leading to associate degrees or, upon transfer to four-year colleges or universities, credit toward baccalaureate degrees. The Timberline Campus offered a broad occupational career training program along with the West's biggest nondegree mining safety and technical skills program.

As the Timberline Campus opened in Leadville, the last reminders of the old Climax community finally disappeared. Climax closed the hotel, the last active residence, and Ken Leighton moved the old

277

In hundreds of cartoons, industrial artist Ted Mullings poked fun at many aspects of Climax life.

Fremont Trading Post building to Leadville to serve as a showroom for an automobile dealership.

Not all of the Climax influence on Leadville was positive. Climax attracted many young, single men, and the combination of big paychecks and restless energy created the inevitable boomtown consequences of drinking, rowdyism, gambling, prostitution, and fighting, much of which took place along "Two Street," the heart of the old frontier-era red-light district. The Leadville police and Lake County sheriff's officers had their hands full, and the *Herald Democrat* noted that many fights and even some shootings went unreported. The Leadville City Council annually debated renewing liquor licenses for bars where trouble was frequent. But the licenses were always renewed, and on payday weekends the bars were "standing room only." And on Sunday mornings, so was the Lake County Jail.

In its first year of operation, the moly oxide plant recovered 2.6 million pounds of molybdenum, while revealing an array of serious problems that began with general operating cost overruns. Some oxide plant workers developed nasal and respiratory ailments obviously attributable to chemicals used in the recovery process. Even the moly oxide plant tailings, which were highly acidic because of residual sulfuric acid, were causing trouble, just as some planners had predicted. Those tailings were piped into a temporary disposal site—a small, separate tailings pond just west of the big Robinson Tailings Pond. But chemicals failed to neutralize the acidic tailings. By 1968, just as federal environmental regulation was about to heavily impact the mining industry, the highly acidic oxide tailings pond promised to become a major environmental headache.

But the biggest and most immediate concern was that moly oxide plant operations were compromising the efficiency of the primary sulfide milling system. The special effort needed to mine, crush, and mill 5,000 tons of selected mixed and high-oxide ores every day on a separate circuit was disrupting the smooth daily flow of 39,000 tons of regular sulfide ore. And any disruption of standard mill operation, which was vital to production, could not be tolerated.

Executives and top engineers debated the fate of the moly oxide plant for months. By summer 1968, a slight weakening in the molybdenum market reduced the importance of the moly oxide plant's production, and that was the final nail in its coffin. After only two years of operation, the $20 million moly oxide plant closed in September 1968. Closing the plant was not a temporary decision; within months, crews stripped most of the pipes, pumps, and motors for use elsewhere. With a full write-down, the moly oxide plant was not a financial catastrophe, but, as the first major operational failure in Climax history, it did shake the confidence of many Climax executives, planners, and engineers.

Development of the Urad Mine at Red Mountain, near Empire, Colorado, helped compensate for the production loss. The Primos Chemical Company had first mined the Urad deposit briefly during World War I. Seeking ways to supplement its Climax production, American Metal Climax took options on the property in 1961, then purchased it two years later when exploration revealed a twelve-million-ton low-grade deposit. To speed development of the mine, some top engineering and management talent moved from Climax to Urad. Climax mill superintendent Fred Hoff became Urad's general manager, and mine foremen Harold Wright and Bob Kendrick became successive Urad mine superintendents.

279

The Urad Mine, which utilized a block cave system similar to that of the Ceresco Level, began production at 5,000 tons per day in 1967. Similar to the Ceresco Level in size and short projected life, Urad was intended to supplement molybdenum supply in a tight market. Urad was also the first American Metal Climax molybdenite mine at a site other than Bartlett Mountain.

American Metal Climax purchased the property not only to develop the Urad Mine, but because certain geologists inferred the existence of a much larger molybdenite body at depth. Bob Henderson had been their biggest supporter and pushed hard to fund an extensive drilling program. Core analysis eventually revealed and delineated a huge ore body 3,000 feet below the Urad Mine in Red Mountain.

In 1968, American Metal Climax announced it would exploit the new deep deposit with a major 30,000-ton-per-day mine and mill. Named the Henderson Project, the new mine would incorporate many of the ideas and methods proven at Climax, but would utilize the latest in computer concepts of design and engineering. Costing $500 million, the Henderson Project would be a model of cost efficiency and environmental compliance.

The Climax Mine, which still had more than 400 million tons of ore reserves and the big, new 600 Level nearing completion, would provide most of the experience, the money, and, most important, the people needed to complete the Henderson Project. William F. "Bill" Distler, who was on track to become Climax general manager, was assigned overall responsibility for development of the Henderson Project. The core of the Henderson Mine's operating management also came from Climax and included Joffre Johnson, Flash Gordon, Warren Shriver, Art Vincent, and Jack Trevethon.

As the 1960s came to a close, the Climax Mine remained the cash cow of American Metal Climax, but it was no longer the corporate "crown jewel." American Metal Climax had quietly passed that distinction on to the Henderson Project.

11
The Giant on the Hill
The 1970s

◆

The essential ingredients of our business are . . .
people, ore reserves in the ground, and money.

—Ian MacGregor,
AMAX chairman and CEO, 1970

◆

In 1970, American Metal Climax, Inc., with headquarters in Greenwich, Connecticut, was better known by its popular and soon-to-be formally adopted corporate acronym AMAX. Asked by industry analysts to define the basic elements of AMAX, chairman and chief executive officer Ian MacGregor, a former mining engineer noted for his aggressive and confident management style, replied, "The essential ingredients of our business are . . . people, ore reserves in the ground, and money." MacGregor also announced his goal to make AMAX "the world's largest integrated and diversified natural resources and industrial materials company."

MacGregor had all three of his "ingredients" to spare at the Climax Mine: 2,100 employees; 400 million tons of proven ore reserves that extended mine life well into the twenty-first century; and annual mine earnings of $60 million, nearly half of which of was profit.

The Climax Mine accounted for 40 percent of total AMAX annual earnings, yet it was a single operation within a multinational corporation embarking on an ambitious $2 billion expansion program into such diverse fields as coal, nickel, and aluminum. In 1969, the Climax Molybdenum Division became a part of the AMAX Molybdenum and Specialty Metals Group headed by president Pierre Gousseland. With degrees in both law and mining engineering, the French-born Gousseland had joined the sales force of the Climax Molybdenum Company in 1948. His aggressive promotion of molybdenum among European steel manufacturers was an important factor in the strong growth of Climax during the 1950s and 1960s.

During the 1960s, the AMAX share of the world molybdenum market dropped from 61 percent to 48 percent. The decline reflected increasing industrial consumption, but, more important, growing competition from a number of small, primary molybdenum mines and the by-product production of copper mining. With molybdenum consumption projected to increase by 7 percent annually through the 1970s, Gousseland's basic strategy adhered to the traditional Climax philosophy: Match both production and future production capacity as closely as possible to projected consumption, while holding prices low to discourage further competition and retain the greatest market share possible.

The Climax Mine produced a record fifty-nine million pounds of molybdenum in 1970, and Gousseland's plan seemed well on course.

Climax Molybdenum Company advertisements of the 1970s continued to present Climax as the world authority on molybdenum uses.

The new 600 Level would soon replace the rapidly exhausting Phillipson and Ceresco levels; when the Henderson Mine began production in the mid-1970s, the total production capacity of the Climax Molybdenum Division would double to 100 million pounds of molybdenum per year. Molybdenum prices had reached $1.70 per pound, but Climax Mine production costs had risen to only seventy cents per pound, leaving a substantial profit margin. And labor relations had been smooth since the 1962 strike.

Research and advertising continued to play important roles in marketing. The "Add Moly—Call Climax" series, aimed at steelmakers and taking a subtle shot at the molybdenum by-production of copper mining, was typical of the advertisements of the 1970s.

ADD MOLY
AND SAVE MONEY FOR YOUR CUSTOMERS

When your customer needs metal that is stronger or tougher . . . more corrosion resistant or more wear resistant . . . chances are that the addition of molybdenum, alone or in combination with other alloying elements, will give it to him at the most economical cost.

CALL CLIMAX
AND SAVE MONEY FOR YOUR OWN COMPANY

When it comes to alloying with molybdenum, no company can help you as much as Climax with its:

VAST ORE RESERVES, comprising the largest molybdenum deposits known and assuring you of continuing supply independent of the demand for any other metal byproduct or coproduct.

WORLD-WIDE DEVELOPMENT STAFF ready to give you on-the-spot assistance in your office or plant.

RESEARCH LABORATORY with over 35 years experience in solving knotty alloying problems and probing future applications of molybdenum.

TECHNICAL LITERATURE that covers every use of molybdenum known and is supplemented by a comprehensive Information Retrieval System for quick answers to your specific questions.

When a minor economic recession in November 1970 created a temporarily oversupplied market, Climax cut production back to 37,500 tons per day. Within six months, attrition reduced employment by 350, leaving a total of 1,750. The Climax mine and mill achieved maximum efficiency when operating at capacity level. Although orders to adjust production levels may have appeared simple

I SURE HOPE SUMMER COMES ON SUNDAY THIS YEAR — LAST YEAR IT CAME ON A TUESDAY AN' I HAD TO WORK —

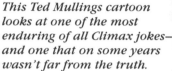

This Ted Mullings cartoon looks at one of the most enduring of all Climax jokes— and one that on some years wasn't far from the truth.

on paper, engineers and supervisors found them difficult to implement. Production adjustment demanded reestablishment of the delicate operational balance that affected everything from mine draw control and mill head feed grades to general manpower and material requirements. Adjusting daily production from 42,000 tons per day to 37,500 tons, while retuning the overall operation for maximum efficiency, could easily take six months.

Industrial artist Ted Mullings used production adjustments as the subject of a popular, albeit unauthorized, cartoon. Mullings drew a telephone resting atop the summit of Bartlett Mountain. From the side of the Glory Hole protruded a huge spigot that spewed forth a stream of hundred-dollar bills. The cartoon was a fanciful illustration of how many engineers and supervisors thought AMAX executives in Greenwich viewed the Climax Mine. Whenever an executive wanted more or less molybdenum—usually it was more—they could just telephone Climax and someone would walk out and adjust the spigot valve accordingly.

Passage of the federal Clean Air Act and Clean Water Act in the early 1970s ushered in an era of environmental regulation and compliance that profoundly impacted the American mining industry. The new environmental regulations effectively separated mines into two groups: new mines designed for compliance with the new regulations, and old mines, which were environmental liabilities. In its Climax Molybdenum Division, AMAX had one of each.

AMAX heralded its new Henderson Mine as the nation's first environmental "showcase" mine, for designers and engineers were devoting great attention and expense to minimizing environmental impact, facilitating eventual reclamation, and using contours and colors to blend surface facilities unobtrusively into the natural surroundings. The Henderson Mine also had another major environmental advantage: It was located in a secluded mountain valley far from the public eye.

But the Climax Mine, originally designed and built in 1917, was the environmental antithesis of the Henderson Mine. The Henderson Mine was a single, integral unit, whereas Climax had grown to its present size through a half-century of "tack-on" expansion. Surface structures of every conceivable size, type, and age sprawled across the top and down both sides of Fremont Pass.

The slowly enlarging Glory Hole was the dominant feature of Bartlett Mountain, but the tailings ponds drew the greatest public criticism. Until 1936, Climax disposed of tailings in the original pond just north of the mill and east of State Highway 91. Then Climax built the Robinson Tailings Pond three miles from the mill atop the old town site of Robinson in the upper Tenmile Canyon west of State Highway 91. Based on late 1930s production levels, engineers believed the big Robinson Pond, several hundred feet deep at its deepest point and covering a full square mile, would last indefinitely. But after government-mandated emergency wartime production and the subsequent high production to satisfy government stockpiling requirements in the 1950s, the Robinson Pond had filled to capacity and Climax began constructing the lower, slightly larger, Tenmile Pond in 1957.

Whereas Henderson enjoyed seclusion, the Climax Mine was eminently visible, for State Highway 91 passed through the length of the mine property skirting the growing tailings ponds in upper Tenmile Canyon. Puzzled by the flat, dusty, barren expanse of sand filling a mountain valley, confused tourists sometimes thought they had reached Great Sand Dunes National Monument. In winter, when a glistening, white sheet of snow covered the ponds, some travelers vowed to return in summer to view the "magnificent high lakes" that must lie beneath the ice. Others, noting the tops of 100-foot-tall spruce trees protruding from the pond surfaces, were shocked to realize just how massive the volume of tailings had become.

Mining had severely polluted Tenmile Creek fifty years before Climax ever existed. In the early 1860s, placer miners worked many upper Tenmile tributaries, disturbing streambeds and stirring up huge loads of silt. Pollution worsened in the 1880s when silver and lead mining boomed in the Tenmile District. The uncontrolled drainage from hundreds of prospect holes, shafts, tunnels, and miles of underground workings, together with a stream of acidic and heavy-metal pollution generated by mill and smelter wastes, wiped out most aquatic life in the Tenmile from Kokomo all the way to its confluence with the Blue River.

Prior to 1936, the original, free-draining Climax tailings pond also polluted Tenmile Creek. But to retain and recycle industrial water, Climax engineers had designed the Robinson Tailings Pond and all subsequent ponds as closed systems, which reduced, but did not stop, the pollution. Containing the high volume of water during the peak spring runoff period was physically impossible; a broken riser pipe had once released torrents of muddy water that discolored the Tenmile for twenty miles downstream.

The last major accidental discharge of Climax tailings material occurred in 1958. Minimizing pollution became a priority at Climax in 1962, when the Denver Water Board constructed the Dillon Dam to impound the flows of Tenmile Creek and the Blue River to create Dillon Reservoir, a source of municipal water for Denver.

At a production level of 40,000 tons per day, engineers projected the life of the Tenmile Tailings Pond at less than eighteen years. In 1964, Climax had begun acquiring land in lower Tenmile Canyon for future tailings disposal. AMAX attorneys A. J. "Jack" Laing and H. Stanley Dempsey sorted out the complex ownership of Tenmile land, which over a century had been claimed, bought, sold, leased, traded, passed on to heirs, and sold for taxes. It included both patented and unpatented lode and placer mining claims, U.S. Forest Service land, and town sites.

One legal concern involved the municipal lands of the old mining towns of Kokomo and Recen. The original Kokomo site was a ghost town, but Recen—now known as Kokomo—still had a bar, restaurant, a post office, and a dozen residents. A state court granted the original Kokomo, the ghost town, a judicial declaration of abandonment. But Recen, still active, had to vote its own disincorporation. In a special, single-issue election in November 1965, the nine registered Recen voters approved disincorporation. The Summit County commissioners then approved disinterment of remains from the old cemetery for reburial in Breckenridge. Laing and Dempsey next arranged for land exchanges between the U.S. Forest Service and Climax. The legal process took six years, but by 1970 land consolidation and acquisition in Tenmile Canyon was complete: The contiguous property of the Climax Mine now included 11,320 acres, or about eighteen square miles.

Climax originally limited its environmental work to tailings impoundment and stabilization and recycling of industrial water. But in 1963, the company and Colorado State University began a joint study on mine-tailings revegetation. Two years later, Climax started its own research program to devise methods to reduce wind erosion and dust pollution from the tailings ponds, to reclaim old access roads, and to recontour and reseed mine- and road-impacted land. In 1970, Climax retained a water resources company to survey and study aquatic biology in watershed streams where they entered and left the mine property.

Climax published a master reclamation plan in February 1971. The *Comprehensive Plan for Land Reclamation and Stabilization at the Climax Mine* focused on three major areas: reclamation of tailings disposal areas, maintenance and improvement of water quality in natural drainage areas, and reclamation of mining-impacted lands. Environmental engineers compiled a computerized inventory of all 11,320 acres, subdivided them into ten-acre plots, and categorized each plot by ten different classifications: ecological life zone; current reclamation status; past and current use; cover vegetation type; reclamation plan; reclamation method; soil treatment; revegetation method; revegetation species; and miscellaneous considerations, such as specialized wildlife habitat.

The master plan also specified reclamation plans for the hundreds of old Tenmile District workings and two town sites, to include development of reservoirs and roadside parks, prevention of outfall water pollution, construction of dust-collection systems, restriction of dump burning to reduce air pollution, and salvage of recyclable materials.

Complying with the array of new environmental regulations would be difficult and costly for a fifty-year-old mine that had already accumulated more than 200 million tons of tailings. Anyone expecting a sweeping reclamation program in the 1970s, however, was disappointed: Since Climax was still a working mine with a projected production life of forty years, the master plan was designed to be implemented over an eighty-year period.

Although the era of environmental concern was just dawning, two points were already clear. First, Climax would not become a showcase of mined land reclamation, at least not in the short term, but neither would it become an environmental disaster. The second point, which would have great immediate consequence, was that environmental compliance would help drive the mine's operational costs much higher.

By 1970, Jim Ludwig had replaced Frank Windolph as general manager of the Climax Mine. Ludwig, a mining engineering graduate of the Wisconsin Institute of Technology, began his Climax career as a miner's helper in 1950, then worked his way through the ranks to become mine superintendent in 1963. When he took over as general manager, the Climax Mine was about to embark on another production-boosting innovation—large-scale open pit mining.

Although Climax had conducted seasonal, small-scale open pit mining from 1947 to 1953, elevation and climate had ruled out large-scale, year-round open pit mining. In the late 1950s, Climax rejected open pitting as an alternative to development of the Ceresco Level. Although some engineers continued to toy with the idea in the 1960s, the Henderson Project discouraged serious interest.

But by 1970, with underground mining costs increasing sharply, open pit mining began looking much more attractive. Advanced open pit haulage and drilling equipment had made surface mining safer, cheaper, and less manpower-intensive. Climax needed two years to train a good underground miner, but with the labor turnover only one new miner in ten lasted two years. Furthermore, an open pit could be developed much faster and less expensively than a new underground level, and could economically exploit lower-grade ores.

But the primary reason to develop an open pit at Climax was the pressing need to get more molybdenum to market. As subsidized foreign copper mines turned out more by-product molybdenum, the Climax market share continued to decline. Furthermore, AMAX was incurring very high costs in both corporate expansion and development of the Henderson Project. AMAX desperately needed more molybdenum, and a Climax open pit mine was the quickest way to get it.

After an open pit feasibility study, Climax decided to proceed with development in February 1972. A diamond drilling program defined ore grades and boundaries, and engineers used core drill data to construct a computerized model of three-quarters of a square mile of Bartlett Mountain and Ceresco Ridge, subdividing it into 100-by-100-by-40-foot sections based on average ore grade. Rock mechanics studies determined competent slope gradients for both in-place and broken rock. With the cutoff grade pegged at 0.13 percent, the lowest ore grade Climax had ever considered mining, engineers calculated the open pit reserves at 230 million tons. Because pit reserves overlapped with underground reserves, total ore reserves increased by only 80 million tons.

The huge open pit would eventually cover 400 acres, or two-thirds of a square mile, stretching nearly from the summit of Bartlett Mountain and around the west side of the half-mile-wide Glory Hole to an elevation of 12,800 feet on Ceresco Ridge. At its deepest point, the open pit would in time expose Storke Level workings at an elevation of 11,163 feet.

Removal of overburden and construction of access and haulage roads began in June 1972. Because of the overburden-ore stripping ratio of 1.6 to 1, more overburden than ore would actually be moved. Destination and use of the overburden was computer controlled. Soil and subsoil were stockpiled for later use in reclamation. Some waste rock went immediately to reclaim and stabilize the pre-1936 tailings, which had eroded into an eyesore, and to prepare a new roadbed to relocate a half-mile section of State Highway 91 near Buffehr's Lake.

As the open pit took shape, mine crews brought the 600 Level on line, initiating caving in September 1972. Within months, expansion of the caving limits in Bartlett Mountain separated an enormous

On January 22, 1973, Climax mined its 300,000,000th ton of ore.

section of rock 400 feet thick, 1,000 feet wide, and some 1,500 feet tall. A deep, 100-foot-wide crevice opened just below the summit of Bartlett Mountain; imperceptibly slowly, the huge section of rock began to panel and subside into the Glory Hole.

On January 22, 1973, Climax mined its 300 millionth ton of ore, a production milestone that was overshadowed by the rapid pace of open pit and underground development activity.

High-tonnage milling accelerated the accumulation of tailings. The Tenmile Tailings Pond, which opened in 1958 with a projected life of eighteen years, was nearing capacity ahead of schedule. In 1972, Climax began work on the new Mayflower Tailings Pond, located 5.5 miles from the mill, 1,000 vertical feet lower, and well beyond the recently acquired Kokomo and Recen town sites.

Construction of the Mayflower Tailings Pond was very costly, for it required moving 4.4 miles of State Highway 91. At its own expense, Climax had already moved other sections of the highway at least four times. In 1935, Climax moved the highway clear of encroaching tailings in the original pond. It moved relocated highway sections twice in the 1950s, then again in 1972 with construction of a $1.4 million overpass to allow heavy truck traffic between the

290

mill and Tenmile tailings ponds. The latest project would replace a highway section that stood in the way of pond development with a $20 million modern highway high on the east side of Tenmile Canyon.

With expansion of the tailings area down Tenmile Canyon, maintenance of water quality became a formidable problem. Since expanded tailings areas greatly increased the volume of inflowing natural drainage water from both sides of Tenmile Canyon, several thousand acre-feet of spring runoff water would now have to be released directly into Tenmile Creek. The Mayflower Tailings Pond dam was downstream from the mine, mill, and smelter wastes of the old Tenmile Mining District that polluted Tenmile Creek. Climax, therefore, also assumed responsibility for the Tenmile District pollution. On the bottom line, the Mayflower Tailings Pond dam would be the biggest improvement to water quality in Tenmile Creek in over a century.

As the Mayflower Tailings Pond dam began to fill in 1973, Climax started work on an elaborate, continuous-discharge water system. Engineers performed a detailed, natural drainage survey within thirty square miles of Tenmile Canyon, then constructed eight miles of interceptor canals to collect all the natural drainage water possible before it entered the tailings impoundment areas, and to divert it directly into lower Tenmile Creek. Next, engineers designed a modern water treatment plant to treat all outfall water from the Climax tailing impoundments and the old Tenmile District before it entered lower Tenmile Creek.

In July 1972, Jim Ludwig became vice president of western operations and Don Achttien, an engineering graduate of the University of North Dakota who began his Climax career on the cleanup crews in 1953, took over as general manager of the Climax Mine. Achttien's first job was bringing the open pit into production on an accelerated schedule.

Through the 1950s, there had been no question as to who ran the Climax Mine. Bob Henderson had gained great respect from his subordinates by making that point clear to Climax executives in New York. "You run things in New York," Henderson said simply, "but I run things at Climax." That "home rule" policy began shifting in the 1960s; just how far it had shifted became clear during open pit development.

291

1976. Blasting a single shot in the open pit could consume 25 tons of blasting agent and break 75,000 tons of rock.

After the open pit feasibility study, Climax engineers presented a methodical, long-range development plan leading to production in three years. But, given the need to sell every pound of molybdenum possible, AMAX didn't have three years to wait. AMAX ordered the open pit development plan accelerated to begin production not only as soon as possible, but with the highest grades of ore available. Climax planning engineers, whose reactions ranged from disbelief to disgust, wryly referred to the modified open pit as the "panic pit." Nevertheless, open pit production of 4,000 tons per day began in November 1973 after just eighteen months of hurried development.

When Climax declared both the Phillipson Level and the Ceresco Level closed in January 1974, crews stripped those levels of all salvageable materials and abandoned the workings. At the time it was closed, the Phillipson Level was the oldest continuously producing mine level in the United States. Over forty-one years, muck trains had hauled 150 million tons of ore out the familiar concrete portal, ore that had paid for the level many, many times over and made the Climax Mine a huge success. But the Ceresco Level, over its short, nine-year production life, had been at best a break-even venture.

AMAX also closed the Urad Mine at Red Mountain in January 1974. In terms of environmental regulation, Urad had been a transitional mine. Designed and developed in the "pre-environmental" early 1960s, the mine was now subject to mandatory full reclamation when it closed. Every penny of profit Urad ever made during its seven-year life went right back into environmental reclamation and land restoration.

By 1975, Climax open pit production topped 10,000 tons per day. Track-mounted drill rigs drilled forty-foot-deep, ten-inch-diameter down holes in just nine minutes. For a standard round, drills patterned fifty holes within a 6,500-square-foot bench section. Every round required twenty-five tons of ANFO, with a half-ton loaded into each hole. To supply the huge amount of blasting agent required, a contractor set up an on-site plant to prepare and truck ANFO to the open pit. Detonation of each standard open pit round broke 75,000 tons of rock, which huge electric shovels mounting fifteen-cubic-yard buckets quickly loaded into 120-ton diesel-electric haulage trucks.

During 1975, the combined daily production from the Storke Level, the 600 Level, and the open pit reached a record 46,000 tons

No. 4 Shovel, an electric shovel with a fifteen-cubic-yard bucket, after topping out on Ceresco Ridge, elevation 12,300 feet.

293

per day. Annual molybdenum recovery also hit a new high of 59.8 million pounds.

By the mid-1970s, the traditional stability of the molybdenum market had eroded. The 1973-74 crude-oil embargo ordered by the Organization of Petroleum Exporting Countries (OPEC) was first to disrupt molybdenum demand projections. Although inflationary, soaring oil prices generally slowed the world economy, they also spurred a worldwide drilling-exploration boom creating unprecedented demand for oil-field steel. Top quality oil-field steels contained a bit more than 1 percent molybdenum, which imparted not only strength and durability, but resistance to the highly corrosive effects of "sour" hydrocarbon gases common to most deep wells. The net result of the OPEC embargo on the molybdenum market was a sharp increase in demand and price.

Demand increased further in 1975, when the federal government finally depleted the molybdenum stockpile it had amassed in the 1950s, terminating sales to industry. That effective reduction in molybdenum supply, coupled with the booming demand for high-molybdenum oil-field steel, boosted molybdenum prices to $3.25 per pound.

Sharply rising production costs compounded growing market instability. During the 1960s, the cost to mine and mill a pound of molybdenum at Climax had remained relatively steady at about seventy-five cents. But higher labor and materials costs, inflation, and substantial environmental compliance costs drove production costs to $1.00 per pound in 1974, then to $1.40 per pound in 1975—the greatest short-term production cost increase in Climax history.

The fifty-year market pattern of ample supply, low production costs, and flat prices that Climax had steadfastly maintained was in transition. Nevertheless, with prices keeping well ahead of rising production costs, the Climax Mine remained a huge moneymaker.

Business journals, meanwhile, regularly cited AMAX as an example of what a "confident, aggressive management style" could accomplish. On August 2, 1976, *Business Week* described AMAX as "bucking a pessimistic trend in mining." Big mining companies, the magazine noted, faced with limited capital, skyrocketing development and operating costs, and increasing nationalization of properties in politically unstable nations, were pulling back. But AMAX, fueled by big molybdenum profits, plowed ahead with diversification and expansion. AMAX was now the third largest steam coal and the fourth largest potash producer in the United States. Increasingly involved in iron ore, lead, aluminum, nickel, and zinc, AMAX was moving into gas and oil and even into forest products with acquisition of southeastern pinelands.

But not even molybdenum profits could stay ahead of the cash costs of the ambitious AMAX diversification and expansion program. In 1974, strapped for cash, AMAX sold 20 percent of its stock to Standard Oil of California for $334.4 million, and later took on a Japanese partner in its aluminum subsidiary for another $134 million.

When Ian MacGregor retired as the head of AMAX in 1977, he had very nearly achieved his announced goal of making AMAX "the world's largest integrated and diversified natural resources and industrial materials company." But when his handpicked successor, Pierre Gousseland, took over as president and chief executive officer of AMAX, Gousseland also took over management of a billion-dollar debt with an annual interest burden of nearly $200 million.

In autumn 1976, Bob Kendrick replaced Don Achttien as general manager of the Climax Mine. Kendrick, an engineering graduate of the Colorado School of Mines, started at Climax as a miner's helper in 1953, and later spent ten years at the Urad Mine and the Henderson Project.

As Kendrick took charge at Climax, the Henderson Mine, the AMAX corporate crown jewel, began production at 10,000 tons per day. But the Henderson Mine would need three years to work up to its capacity production level of 30,000 tons per day. In the meantime, maximizing production at Climax, the corporate cash cow, would be more important than ever. In 1976, the Climax Mine set its all-time record for annual production—nearly sixty-one million pounds, or 30,500 tons, of elemental molybdenum. The Climax Mine would never break that record, for its best ores, including those mined in the "panic pit," were gone. In 1977, the average grade of ore mined and milled at Climax dropped below 0.3 percent for the first time. The only remaining way to recover more molybdenum was through more tonnage. And the only way to get more tonnage seemed to be through more people.

In 1976, Climax employment reached a record 2,650, far above the 1,850 employees of 1972. Behind the 800-employee net increase stood a monumental effort by the Personnel, Medical, Training, and Safety Departments to attract, interview, evaluate, examine, hire, test, and train 3,500 "new hires," half of whom never lasted one month. Even excellent pay and benefits could not negate the high labor turnover, caused primarily by the rigors of underground work at high elevations. For a while, Climax thought the answer was to recruit experienced southeastern coal miners. But after one January blizzard and the subzero cold that followed, most caught the first Greyhound right back to Kentucky.

In 1972, the federal Equal Employment Opportunity Commission investigated the mass hiring practices. After learning that Caucasians and Hispanics filled virtually all the jobs at Climax, the Equal Employment Opportunity Commission directed Harry Ashby, manager of industrial relations, to increase minority hiring. Ashby set up recruiting offices in the black neighborhoods of Denver and on the Ute and Navajo reservations in the Four Corners region. Climax lured many minority recruits, only to learn that underground mining was foreign to their cultural backgrounds. Shift bosses reported to Ashby that the underground "scared the daylights out of some of these people." But Ashby found the real problem to be lack of a friendly ethnic community. "After a shift," Ashby recalled, "they went to Leadville, where there wasn't a thing for them to do but sit in their rooms and stare at the walls."

In its most controversial directive, the Equal Employment Opportunity Commission also ruled that Climax hire women for underground work. Since 1918, when Jack White invited the Summit County War Bond Committee ladies into the White Level, losing several infuriated miners in the process, women, with the exception of special tours in the 1950s and 1960s, had rarely entered the Climax underground. In 1972, Climax management remained unreceptive to the idea of women miners and, on recommendation of company attorneys, prepared to fight the federal directive.

But Ashby sensed the determination of the Equal Employment Opportunity Commission's attorneys. Because Climax was central Colorado's biggest private employer, federal attorneys were fully prepared—Ashby thought even eager—to make an example out of the case. "I reported to management that the commission was dead

296

serious," Ashby said. "I recommended that Climax hire women for the underground immediately. I'll always remember the silence. I thought they were going to fire me."

Climax abided by the directive. By the end of 1973, six women worked on underground mine and muck crews. Patti Wood, the fourth woman hired for underground work, found the initial harassment much more difficult than the work. "Single mothers couldn't raise kids on a clerk's pay," Wood remembers. "When mine jobs opened to women, we had to take them. Some of the older hands were still superstitious about women being 'bad for the rock' and all that bull, but our real problem was the younger men. Maybe we threatened their *machismo* or something. I wasn't there two weeks before they tied me to a timber. Once, they even set my clothes afire. They tried their best to intimidate us all shift. Do you know how we survived? By being just as damned tough and ornery as they were."

By 1974, forty-one women worked as regular underground miners. Perhaps the ultimate statement of underground equality came on the morning of September 16, 1976, in a Storke Level slusher dash. Miner Charlene Salazar, with two years of underground experience, was helping a hang-up man place a bomb in a finger when the muck "came down." Salazar, in an accident categorized as "run of ore," became the first female fatality at Climax, and the seventy-third since operations began.

Climax set its all-time daily tonnage record on February 1, 1976—51,133 tons, more than half the tonnage mined during the entire year of 1918. High tonnages required especially close coordination between the mine and the mill. At the start of every shift, open pit and underground muck crews collected "grab samples" from benches and draw points. Lab workers separated the sulfide and oxide values, flamed the sulfides in an atomic absorption spectrophotometer, then analyzed the spectrum to quickly and accurately determine ore grade, sending computerized grade reports to the Mine Department, which scheduled that shift's draw control to assure consistency of mill head feed grade. When the mill added a fifth-stage flotation step in the regrind plant, the molybdenite concentrate grade topped 95 percent.

High tonnage also boosted by-product recoveries. Engineers replaced the thirty-year-old Humphrey spirals with more compact Reichert cones, which increased gravitational separation efficiency.

Although Bartlett Mountain ore contained just 0.03 percent wolframite, or iron-manganese tungstate, high-tonnage milling recovered 2.5 million pounds of elemental tungsten annually, making Climax the second largest American tungsten producer and accounting for one-third of all domestic production.

Open pit production reached 17,000 tons daily by 1977, but miners now removed nearly two tons of waste rock for every ton of ore trucked to the crusher. New open pit equipment included 170-ton diesel-electric haulage trucks and a 75-ton bulldozer, one of the world's largest, mounting a 10-ton blade seven feet high and seventeen feet wide.

In open pit blasting operations, a single shot now included more than 300 holes containing 300,000 pounds—150 tons—of ANFO blasting agent, enough to break a half-million tons of rock. For safety, the biggest open pit shots were preceded by underground and surface evacuations. To determine exactly how much energy could be released in each electrical delay of a big shot without damaging sur-

1978. In the open pit, track-mounted drill rigs drilled forty-foot-deep, ten-inch-diameter down holes in just nine minutes.
—Stephen M. Voynick

face facilities, open pit engineers installed a seismograph to measure ground vibrations on horizontal, vertical, and transverse planes.

Since weather was critical to open pit operations, especially in winter, engineers installed an automated, remote weather-monitoring station high on Ceresco Ridge. The station continuously reported general meteorological conditions, determined when temperature levels and fluctuations would necessitate special lubricating oils in certain equipment, and warned when strong winds might interfere with the high-towered drill rigs working on the upper-pit benches.

The 1970s brought dramatic alteration of the topography of Bartlett Mountain. Enlargement of the Glory Hole exposed a protruding "core"—the hard, durable, barren rock of the central section of the Upper Ore Body. Open pit miners cut Ceresco Ridge into benches resembling a huge staircase and hauled and dumped millions of tons of waste rock into the high cirque at elevations above 12,000 feet. To reach a half-million tons of otherwise inaccessible ore, miners bladed a road from the open pit around the cirque to move equipment to the top of the Glory Hole core. Most impressive was the sheer vertical extent of the open pit. Moving a big electric shovel to the highest benches at elevations above 12,130 feet took

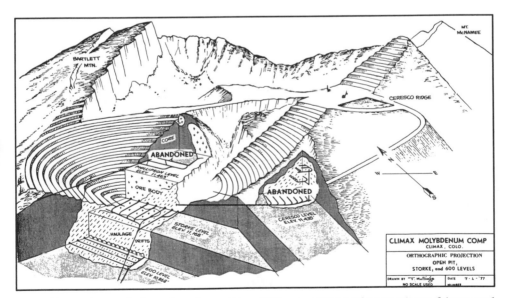

1977. This schematic drawing shows the relative positions of open pit workings and underground levels in Bartlett Mountain and Ceresco Ridge. –drawing by Ted Mullings

six weeks. One thousand feet lower, the deepening pit had already "daylighted" drifts along the west hanging wall of the Storke Level.

By 1978, the new Mayflower Tailings Pond, only five years old, already contained eighty million tons of tailings. A new state-of-the-art plant at the base of the Mayflower dam treated outfall water. Designed jointly by the Climax Mill Department, the AMAX Extractive Research Group, and the AMAX Environmental Services Group, the $10 million facility treated 2,000 gallons of water per hour in a complex process of ion exchange, electrocoagulation, electroflotation, and chemical pH adjustment. But the plant could not handle the huge seasonal volume from the melting winter snowpack. State and federal agencies granted Climax a permit to discharge untreated or minimally treated outfall water directly into Tenmile Creek for a sixty-day period each spring, with an extension provision for periods of unusually heavy runoff. Peak runoff periods, of course, provided large amounts of natural dilution to minimize unavoidable pollution. Tenmile Creek water quality was not pristine, but it was so improved that trout reestablished themselves in the river for the first time in a century.

The relocated $20 million, 4.4-mile section of State Highway 91 on the east side of Tenmile Canyon was among the region's finest stretches of state highway. Environmental Department crews contoured and seeded highway slopes and cuts with 36,000 pine, fir, and spruce seedlings. They also completed work on Clinton Reservoir, opening the beautiful, subalpine roadside lake for public fishing and recreational use.

But environmental costs had become a major factor in the Climax Mine budget. In just over a decade, Climax spent more than $100 million on work directly related to environmental compliance, protection, and improvement.

By 1979, many mineral-commodity analysts expressed fear about growing molybdenum-market instability. At Climax, inflation and heavy spending had dramatically increased the cost to mine and mill one pound of elemental molybdenum from seventy-five cents in 1970 to $3.25 by 1979. But the price of molybdenum, in a decade-long bull market, had risen from $1.40 per pound in 1970 to $7.00 per pound in 1979, and even higher on an emerging short-term spot market. With the hefty profit margin still there, the Climax Mine remained the AMAX cash cow, producing fifty million pounds of molybdenum each year.

Employment topped 3,000 in 1979. But the record employment and tonnage figures overshadowed a substantial decline in overall production efficiency as measured in tons per man-shift. Although tonnage had increased 25 percent during the 1970s, employment had increased 80 percent. Nevertheless, as measured in the all-important pounds of recovered molybdenum, production had actually begun to decrease because of declining ore grades.

More Climax employees than ever were assigned to jobs with little connection to mining or milling molybdenite ore. Mining was highly regulated; by 1979, no less than twenty state or federal agencies affected Climax operations. Among state agencies were the Division of Mines, Labor and Industrial Commission, and Department of Health; federal agencies included the Mine Enforcement Safety Administration, Occupational Safety and Health Administration, Environmental Protection Agency, National Labor Relations Board, U.S. Forest Service, Bureau of Land Management, Federal Energy Agency, Federal Communications Commission, and the Equal Employment Opportunity Commission. Some Climax employees worked full-time fulfilling the requirements of governmental agencies by writing reports, hosting inspections, ordering remedial actions to correct compliance deficiencies, and then reporting on the success of the remedial actions.

There seemed no end to growing costs. One example of new costs over which Climax had no control was the Colorado mineral severance tax imposed in 1977. Intended to recoup wealth lost from the mining of nonrenewable mineral resources, the state earmarked severance tax revenues for various public projects and as a trust fund to aid mining-impacted communities. The state imposed a fifteen-cent tax on every ton of molybdenum ore. With Climax mining an average of 46,000 tons of ore per day, the annual severance tax assessment amounted to $2.4 million.

The rising cost of doing business was not the only problem, for others arose in the areas of morale, safety, employee experience level, and labor relations. When employment was climbing steadily toward 3,000, not all the older hands liked it. Of the 2,000 new employees Climax hired each year, only one in six lasted a year; that turnover, coupled with normal attrition, reduced annual net employment gain

301

to just 100. But the changes went beyond numbers. In 1979, the average Climax employee was only twenty-eight years of age with less than four years seniority. And as work experience declined, so did loyalty, authority, and discipline. Underground crews became so large that shift bosses, themselves younger and more inexperienced than ever, had difficulty providing close supervision and instruction.

The basic hiring process was somewhat self-defeating, for Climax still had a reputation for "always hiring and never firing." Although the Personnel Department did its best to screen applicants, every week brought a certain number of transients and freeloaders who intended to do nothing more than sit through a week of training and safety classes, collect a check, then quit.

Labor friction arose over the union-management grievance system. Union members filed grievances literally by the hundreds; although many were trivial, they kept joint grievance committees working full-time. Any manager seen picking up a small part in the warehouse for an urgent replacement in the mill risked a grievance. Underground, a shift boss could no longer fire a sleeping miner on the spot. Now, the boss had two options: He could wake the miner immediately to see if he was injured or hurt, or he could search for a union shop steward to witness the awakening and later testify at what was always a lengthy and frequently unproductive termination procedure.

The decline in experience and morale was accompanied by a decline in safety. From 1973 to 1979, Climax recorded fifteen fatalities, five in 1979 alone, including a double fatality that occurred when a three-case hang-up shot detonated prematurely, killing miners Mary Bradley and Porter Sims and injuring five others.

Meanwhile, the visitor reception center was busier than ever. During an average summer month, 3,000 visitors viewed the exhibits and historic photographs and took home a ton of golf ball-sized molybdenite ore samples. Each year, more than 1,500 visitors took free guided mill tours.

Invited groups, often composed of mining professionals or political figures, received special tours of the open pit and sometimes of the underground. Jim Ludwig recalled leading a group of engineers from the People's Republic of China through the Storke Level. "They were all feeling the altitude," Ludwig recounted. "Their faces

1979. The huge 120-ton open pit haulage trucks were a favorite with visitors.
—Stephen M. Voynick

were pale green and they stumbled around on the verge of collapse. I told them to sit down, put their heads between their knees for a while, and they'd feel a lot better. Sick as they were, they absolutely refused. It occurred to me later that bowing their heads might have been an Oriental gesture of subservience. So they wobbled around like drunks for the whole tour."

When U.S. Senator Gary Hart visited Climax in 1978, he was especially impressed by the 170-ton open pit haulage trucks, with their nine-foot-diameter tires and thirteen-rung ladders leading up to the high cabs. Hart, like many prominent political figures who knew the value of a good public relations photograph, insisted on wearing a Climax hard hat and having his picture taken waving from the cab of a big haulage truck. Hart, a youngish man in good condition, had little difficulty climbing up to the cab, but that wasn't true for everyone.

1979. The deepest part of the open pit exposed some Storke Level underground workings.
—Stephen M. Voynick

"The altitude already made some of the older politicians woozy," recalled open pit foreman Paul Latchaw. "We'd practically have to push them up the ladders, then hold them steady while they grinned and waved. I was convinced that sooner or later somebody would fall off a truck and break his neck."

In November 1978, Climax hosted a visitor from its own past—a 1926 Wills Sainte Claire Grey Goose Traveler that was displayed around the plant for a week. The old Goose was fully restored with gleaming paint, leather upholstery, and its original Wills straight-six overhead cam engine. Virtually every steel part in the vintage automobile had been manufactured from Brainerd Phillipson's "mo-*lyb*-den-um steel."

In 1979, Climax hosted troops of the 82nd Airborne Division and 5th Special Forces Group. Both units were conducting mountain war games, and officers thought Climax would be an ideal industrial facility to add realism to defense and infiltration exercises. When Climax agreed to the officers' request to use the mill, the war was on. As Special Forces commandos parachuted into nearby Camp Hale, 82nd Airborne Division troopers, dressed in full combat gear, set up a defense perimeter around the mill buildings.

Had the M-16 rifles been loaded, the Climax mill hands would have suffered the heaviest losses. The Special Forces men, disguised

304

as mill mechanics, "killed" five airborne troopers and seven mill hands in their first assault. The military evaluation of that assault noted "the valiant but unsuccessful efforts of the crane operator in dodging mock machine-gun fire." To the great amusement of the mill hands, the Special Forces men staged another successful assault by infiltrating a visitors' tour group. But the Climax Mine's first effort to support military exercises was also its last; mill supervisors, concerned with molybdenite flotation and not military infiltration, finally ordered a premature end to "this damned circus."

In January 1979, the mining of the 400 millionth ton of ore at the Climax Mine passed almost without notice. Muck trains had hauled 94 percent of that total tonnage from the underground in two million runs covering two million miles. Underground haulage had been the lifeblood of the Climax Mine since miners hand-trammed the first half-ton ore cars on the Leal Level in 1918. Mules had hauled muck on the old White Level until "electric mules" took over in 1925 to haul muck on the Phillipson, Storke, Ceresco, and 600 levels in the following decades.

At one time or another, thousands of Climax miners had served as motormen, operating the big twenty-ton, twenty-seven-ton, and thirty-ton "locies" that hauled the endless succession of muck cars from the underground drawholes to the crushers and back again. In 1977, Storke Level shift boss Gerald Luoma recalled his days as a motorman in a poem titled "The Tally of No. 8." In rhyme rich in the vernacular of the Climax underground, the poem tells of pulling ropes to throw rail switches, of enduring the drawhole spray that kept the dust down, of dumping cars at the big Storke crusher under the eye of a television monitor, and of "tallying out," or making the last run of a long shift, which Luoma used as a metaphor for life itself.

> When my motoring days are over
> And I've pulled my share of ropes,
> Wash my body off with mine water
> That runs down from the stopes.
>
> Make my casket out of flume boards,
> Place my pie-can 'neath my head,
> Don't forget to turn my brass in,
> There's no overtime for being dead.

Gently place me in a muck car
And don't worry 'bout my fate,
Cover me slow with fine gray dirt
So my casket won't take weight.

Oh say, turn off your drawhole spray,
'Cause there's a hole in my left boot,
And when you sound the hi-ball
Give me a sixteen-case salute.

Send me to the Happy Dumping Grounds
And pour me in the hole,
And give the woodpicker a coffee break,
'Cause there's pure moly in my soul.

Tell the gyratory operator
To watch the screen for me,
It really isn't all that bad,
But it's my first time on TV.

You've probably heard it all before
That "Old Motormen Never Die,"
They ride those golden rails up yonder
To the Great Dispatcher in the sky.

I've written my own epitaph,
Here's what it's all about:
Put my marker on the tailings pond
Worded: "No. 8 has tallied out."

When employment at the Climax Mine reached 3,000 in 1979, the annual payroll topped $67 million. Leadville and Lake County, where 1,800 Climax employees resided, rode its biggest sustained economic boom ever. With the average Climax employee earning $21,000 annually, Lake County had by far the highest per capita income of any rural Colorado county. Every other week, Climax workers took home—after taxes—$1.1 million. Climax accounted for 86 percent of Lake County property taxes: Each year Climax paid $2.7 million to the Lake County School District, $800,000 to Lake County, and $425,000 to the college tax district. And regular Climax contributions helped support community groups from the chamber of commerce to the Little League and the Boy and Girl Scouts.

The Climax Mine had particular impact on education in Leadville and Lake County. Since 1954, Climax had awarded nearly $1 million for fifty-two full, four-year university scholarships to qualifying regional high school seniors. In 1979, the Lake County School District had 2,100 students, 128 faculty members, and five schools, including a $5 million intermediate school that was one of the newest and best-equipped in Colorado. Climax hosted an annual dinner and happy hour every September to welcome back veteran teachers, introduce new teachers, and confirm its support of local education. When teachers and administrators needed aids and assistance not available through normal channels, they often turned to Climax for professional speakers, specialized research information, displays and exhibits, films, audio-visual equipment, transportation for a sports team to a distant county, or a special tour of the mill and the open pit for an entire class.

Ralph Schuster, principal of the Lake County High School, came to Leadville in 1966. "I came here specifically to work in a district where industry fully supported education," Schuster said. "And Climax certainly did that. Climax knew that by helping the local schools and the local kids, it was really helping itself."

High-paying summer jobs at Climax shaped career goals for many high school and college students. If a high school senior didn't aspire to further education, a lucrative mine job was waiting on the day he or she graduated. But Climax motivated many students toward higher education, for its payroll included hundreds of well-paid professionals who were examples of the value of higher education. They included accountants; doctors; nurses; a dozen different kinds of engineers; computer specialists; geologists; laboratory, environmental, and medical technicians; specialists in training, safety, communications, personnel, and public relations; and an upper echelon of top-level management. Such career role models, along with the strong financial positions of parents who earned Climax paychecks, helped send 45 percent of Lake County High School seniors on to four-year colleges and universities, tops among all rural Colorado counties.

Climax also helped sustain the traditions and culture of western hardrock mining in Leadville. Ever since Jack White, the first Climax superintendent, staged his Fourth of July celebration in 1918, Climax had sponsored or supported mine-drilling contests. Drilling

307

1978. Traditional annual mine-drilling contests in Leadville were presented largely through the sponsorship of the Climax Mine. –Stephen M. Voynick

contests originated as competitive tests of hand-steeling ability among frontier-era miners. By the 1950s and 1960s, competing miners employed both the traditional hammer and steel as well as modern pneumatic "jackleg" drills. In the early 1970s, Climax and two other local mines, ASARCO's Leadville Unit (Black Cloud Mine) and the Hecla Mining Company's Sherman Mine, continued to support the contests. Many local miners participated in the contests, which were rowdy and often involved more drinking than drilling.

In 1975, Charlie Marshall, manager of industrial education at Climax, along with shift bosses Sam Wild and Chuck Smythe, upgraded the contests with standardized rules, better equipment, an atmosphere suitable for tourists and families, and more company support for bigger cash prizes. When Marshall began announcing the events and explaining their historical significance to visitors, the increasingly popular contests developed into a regular circuit that included other Colorado mining towns. Drilling contests are a regular part of Leadville's annual "Boom Days" summer festival, attracting top competitors from across the West to test their drilling skills against a ten-ton boulder of molybdenite hauled to town from the Climax open pit.

Leadville was the biggest and perhaps the last pure mining town left in the West. Shopping, traffic, business in the bars and restaurants, and, to some extent, the pace of life of itself moved in rhythm with the changing of the Climax shifts and the mailing of Climax payroll checks. In places like the Golden Burro restaurant and the Pastime and Silver Dollar saloons, the conversations more often than not focused on mining, and usually on the Climax Mine. Even time was routinely defined by Climax shift schedules: "I saw him before he went up on days last Tuesday," or "We all had breakfast together when they came down off graveyard."

While Leadville thrived as a traditional mining town, content with its colorful mining culture and booming mining economy, much had changed in other central Colorado towns. Tourism emerged as a major regional economic force in the 1970s, and Aspen, Vail, and Breckenridge established themselves as world-class, year-round resorts. Copper Mountain, Colorado's newest resort, sprang up along Tenmile Creek, just five miles north of the base of the Mayflower Tailings Pond dam. The economies of most central Colorado towns, with or without major resorts, shifted steadily away from traditional agriculture and mining toward tourism and outdoor recreation.

But Leadville had not changed and had no reason to change. It had everything it needed and wanted in the Climax Mine—the giant on the hill.

12
Shutdown
The 1980s

During the 1970s, the molybdenum market changed more rapidly than at any time since the erratic years of World War I. The Climax Mine share of the world market dropped from 48 percent to only 25 percent. But with production from the Henderson Mine, AMAX still supplied half of the booming market. By 1980, Climax Mine production costs had risen to $3.60 per pound of molybdenum, but the market price had surged above $8.00. Even though Climax continued to sell molybdenum to its preferred customers at 20 percent below market price, the margin still added up to record earnings and big profits.

In 1980, business analysts warned of an imminent national economic recession, but at Climax, where employment was at a record 3,080, everything was business as usual. With an annual payroll of $80 million, the mine was busy producing 52.1 million pounds of molybdenum and a clear annual profit of another $100 million.

In February 1980, as American industry braced for a serious recession, *Forbes* ran a glowing article about AMAX, molybdenum, and the confidence of Pierre Gousseland.

THE SHEIKH OF CLIMAX MOUNTAIN
IN THE HALL OF THE MOLYBDENUM SHEIKH—AMAX—
THINGS COULDN'T BE BETTER THESE DAYS, THANK YOU.
HE'S TAKING STEPS TO KEEP IT THAT WAY

"No matter how fast and aggressively we try to diversify away from molybdenum, it grows too fast for us to succeed." Pierre Gousseland, CEO and chairman of AMAX, is sitting in the company headquarters in Greenwich, Conn., and smiling gleefully.

This, mind you, is not going to be one of those stories about a company that wishes to heaven it had never diversified away from its familiar old business. Still, the reason Gousseland is gloating is that his original business does even better than his diversification—and that's saying plenty.

. . . Yet molybdenum and AMAX's role as the Saudi Arabia of the molybdenum business are still the real heart of Gousseland's giant company, based upon the mountain of moly at Climax, Colo.

AMAX produces nearly half of the noncommunist world's moly supply (the Reds are serious net importers of the stuff), and that gives AMAX enough market weight to have a heavy influence on events. . . . Last year [1979], AMAX sold all the moly it could currently produce—about 90 million pounds—for some $600 million, netting something like $180 million, or nearly 30% after tax.

. . . Ah, molybdenum! How the money rolls lushly in. It's not merely because important end markets will probably skip the recession, but also because AMAX has long arranged its affairs to keep things going that way for itself. Right now, for example, other U.S. producers charge about $9.50 per pound to their (mostly long term) customers. The spot market . . . shot up as high as $28 per pound last year and is currently around $14. Through all this, AMAX charged its regular U.S. customers just $5.50 to $7.00. You can see why Shorr [Bear, Stearns metal-market analyst] doesn't think a recession will nick AMAX's moly profits; if competitors cut their prices by 20% or more AMAX would still be underselling them.

. . . "Moly has a historical growth rate of 6% to 7%," says Gousseland, explaining his price, "and we have to protect that growth rate. If we raise the price too high, our customers will reconstitute alloys with competing metals. . . . Once they make a shift away from molybdenum, they won't want to shift back. It is essential that we guarantee them reliable supplies at relatively reliable prices."

Many financial observers agreed with Pierre Gousseland's confidence in AMAX and its molybdenum profits. Economic trouble surely lay ahead, but AMAX, with its market control, low prices, and two big molybdenum mines, didn't seem vulnerable.

Analysts had warned of a developing oversupply situation in the molybdenum market as early as 1978, but few, if any, gauged the full

312

extent of market instability. Trouble in the molybdenum market had been eight years in the making, and the developing problems, complex, interactive, and cumulative in nature, had often been masked by confusing and contradictory market events.

The trouble began when the 1973-74 OPEC oil embargo spurred demand for high-molybdenum oil-field steel, disrupting the projected market growth patterns. The market tightened further in 1975 when the federal government terminated its molybdenum stockpile disposal sales, driving $1.70-per-pound molybdenum to $3.25.

Higher prices attracted the attention of competition, namely copper mining companies, which could recover by-product or co-product molybdenum. When prices remained below $2.50 per pound, relatively few copper mills bothered to construct molybdenum recovery circuits in return for, at best, a marginal profit. But at $3.25 per pound, cost studies of molybdenum by-product recovery produced attractive results. When molybdenum hit $5.00 per pound in 1977, every copper mining company from British Columbia to Chile was operating or building by-product or coproduct molybdenum recovery circuits.

The Japanese steel industry also contributed to market instability in the late 1970s. Unlike American and European steel producers, the Japanese favored short-term buying on a very high-priced, volatile spot market. In turn, those high prices created the erroneous impression that molybdenum demand was outstripping supply. When the spot market price rose above $10.00 per pound in late 1977, several standard alloy manufacturers quietly cancelled molybdenum contracts, turning instead to vanadium and other cheaper alloying elements.

When high prices encouraged at least five oil and mining companies to begin evaluating or developing primary molybdenum deposits, some analysts, seeing molybdenum clearly headed for production overcapacity, advised slowing development.

But the opinions of the market analysts and AMAX differed. And AMAX, the leading industry bellwether of molybdenum mining and marketing, was not slowing down; the Climax Mine was at maximum production and the new Henderson Mine was nearing design capacity. Furthermore, with an eye toward quick development, AMAX was already evaluating a major primary molybdenum deposit at Mt. Emmons near Crested Butte, Colorado, and two other primary

313

the climax   by Ted Mullings

"I've been working like a horse so I figured I might as well eat like one."

One of Ted Mullings's last cartoons before the shutdown of the Climax Mine.

deposits in Washington and British Columbia. There was no reason to question what the Climax advertisements had proclaimed for decades: "No One Knows More About Molybdenum Than Climax." And if AMAX was confident enough to plow ahead developing additional production capacity, so, too, was everyone else in the suddenly crowded molybdenum mining industry.

Two ironically timed events in the 1970s masked the developing oversupply situation. First, a prolonged strike at a primary molybdenum mine at Endako, British Columbia, restricted exports to Japan. The temporary, noncritical shortage exerted maximum leverage on the sensitive Japanese spot market, pushing short-term prices to $28.00 per pound. The second event had even greater effect. The Iranian Revolution restricted international oil supply, creating another energy crisis, which in turn generated immediate demand for high-molybdenum oil-field steel.

314

By the late 1970s, emergence of a global market structure further complicated the metal-market picture. American mining, burdened by lower-grade ores, escalating environmental restrictions and costs, and high labor costs, was hard-pressed to compete with higher-grade ores and cheap labor of foreign mines. Of particular concern were the expropriated mines of Third World nations. The governments that subsidized the mines were, in turn, supported by World Bank loans. Under enormous debt and desperate for hard currency, such nations maximized mine production and dumped "cheap" metals on the world market. In South America, booming subsidized copper production resulted in growing supplies of subsidized by-product molybdenum.

Analysts could no longer accurately project long-term supply and demand, as speculation and "panic" buying steadily inflated prices. And as prices offered no prospect of flattening, more molybdenum consumers turned to alternative alloying metals. By 1980, despite Pierre Gousseland's confidence, the molybdenum market was effectively out of control.

In August 1980, Ralph Barnett, a mining engineering graduate of the University of Texas at El Paso, took over Bob Kendrick's position of general manager. Barnett was the sixteenth individual to hold the top management position of the Climax Mine.

Seemingly unaffected by the deepening national recession, Climax pushed ahead with development of the 900 Level, construction of an open pit road almost to the summit of Bartlett Mountain, and installation of a new open pit crusher. Even as American copper, lead, zinc, and uranium mining began to falter, Climax continued at maximum production on a seven-day work schedule.

The only sign that the Climax Mine was not immune from effects of the recession was its growing stockpile of molybdenite concentrate. By November 1980, eighty million pounds of molybdenum contained in 85,000 tons of concentrate—the equivalent of eighteen months of production—filled the Climax warehouse. No one was really surprised or unduly concerned in December 1980 when Climax abruptly terminated its eight-year-long hiring program. Those who felt 3,080 employees were a few too many were, in fact, pleased. By April 1981, attrition reduced employment to 2,800, and business continued as usual.

An ABC-TV production crew visited Climax to shoot a feature on Bonnie Thurman, one of several Climax women miners who were now shift bosses. When the segment aired on *Real People* several months later, millions watched Thurman drilling, operating a load-haul-dump vehicle, talking about explosives and underground mining operations, and supervising her eleven-man crew.

The depth of the worsening recession became fully apparent in summer 1981. The inflationary, soaring oil prices of 1980 began collapsing, killing the drilling boom along with demand for high-molybdenum oil-field steel. Automotive and general manufacturing slowed dramatically; U.S. steel companies, operating at half-capacity, laid off thousands of workers. The U.S. Bureau of Mines' monthly metal-market report noted that, for the first time in a decade, industrial consumption of molybdenum declined for the third consecutive month.

The molybdenum mining industry, and AMAX in particular, suddenly faced the worst possible scenario: Burdened with record stockpiles and a huge overproduction capacity, the molybdenum market began falling apart.

Disconcerting rumors that "something," perhaps even a layoff, was inevitable swept through Climax and Leadville. On August 26, 1981, the *Herald Democrat*, which had reported Climax news for sixty-five years, acknowledged and attempted to quell the rumors in a front-page article.

NO LAYOFFS PLANNED AT CLIMAX

Rumors have been rampant on the Climax property and in Leadville concerning the future of operations at Climax, of contemplated layoffs, cutbacks, etc. . . . . These rumors are not true. . . .

Days later, the *Hard Rock News,* the newsletter of Local 2-22410 of the Oil, Chemical, and Atomic Workers Union, also discounted the rumors.

A rumor is an idea that has no fact to make it happen. Rumors usually are about bad events that may happen in the future. The effects rumors have on the worker are not pleasant. Some rumors make us worry about our jobs. Walking around worrying makes us harder to get along with both on the job and at home.

Rumors about layoffs are one thing that is bothering our Union brothers and sisters now. Here are some facts about why being laid off is only a rumor.

316

First, the Company cannot lay off while a subcontractor is working on the 900 Level access. . . . Also, since operations started in 1924,
there has been only one layoff. At that time, fifty Union hands laid off
for a period of 28 days. . . .

There are no plans whatever for any layoffs. It is expected that
new employment goals will be set that can be implemented through
attrition. . . . At mid-August the employment level was 2,774 with the
reduction being accomplished through those quitting or retiring. . . .

But few Climax employees believed the reassurances. In a sud-
den rush of "bumping," employees used seniority and experience to
"bid up" into what they hoped were more secure job positions. When
the fall semester began at the Timberline Campus of Colorado
Mountain College, Climax employees enrolled in record numbers in
trade and technical courses to gain a competitive edge if and when
layoffs began.

Ralph Barnett announced plans to adjust production in October
1981. He suspended the temporary summer job program, reduced
tonnage 10 percent to 42,000 tons per day, halted seven-day production and all Saturday shifts, and ordered two of the big, $1.3 million
open pit shovels mothballed. Furthermore, Barnett announced that
he would shut down the mine and mill for one month, but not until
July 1982—nine months later.

Barnett's announcement brought a collective sigh of relief at
Climax and Leadville. Climax had avoided layoffs and would simply
continue stockpiling concentrate until the economy turned around.
Climax had weathered other storms since 1924, and it would weather
this one, too.

But the economic prospects continued to grow darker. In November 1981, the U.S. Bureau of Mines announced that monthly
molybdenum consumption, compared with the previous year, had
declined 25 percent, while production had increased 10 percent.

With the gap between production and demand widening at a
frightening pace, Climax prepared a series of production-employ-
ment contingency plans to cover all possible market developments.
"They included everything from full market recovery to a worst-case
scenario of market collapse and a layoff of six hundred people,"
Barnett recalled. "But we really didn't expect layoffs. We continued
production, hoping—praying—that the market would pick up."

But continued market deterioration, coupled with a leak of confidential company information, heightened speculation that real

trouble was inevitable. On December 7, 1981, the *Herald Democrat* reported:

> Homes and business places in Lake and Chaffee County were buzzing this weekend as the result of stories in several mountain area newspapers either speculating or purporting to know for a fact that Climax was planning to lay off a large number of employees early next year.
>
> This speculation has included the possibility of 600 employees at Climax, 300 from Henderson and 100 at the Golden Western Operations Headquarters.
>
> If all this were to be true it would be quite a blow to the economy of the affected areas. However, fortunately for now, this speculation remains exactly that—pure speculation.
>
> Climax has taken a number of cost-cutting measures in recent months, including the hiring freeze, the elimination of two crews from open pit operations, the elimination of the road building program to the summit of Bartlett Mountain, and the mothballing of new equipment as it arrives.
>
> The most recent move has been the elimination of 30 jobs in the mill with the employment being shuffled to other jobs of a lesser category. . . .
>
> So there seems to be no question that some kind of cutbacks in production and possibly employment will be taking place in the next several months, but no one seems to know what the form will be. . . .

Herald Democrat readers and Climax employees didn't have to wait long to find out. On Friday, December 11, 1981, Ralph Barnett received a telephone call from Manager of Western Operations Jim Ludwig in Golden. "I couldn't believe it," Barnett remembered. "It was the worst-case scenario. Jim ordered me to lay off six hundred within one month. He didn't have much else to say. He wished me 'good luck,' and that was that."

Barnett immediately summoned his top managers to decide when to make the announcement. There were two points to consider. Some favored delaying the announcement for two weeks so employees could enjoy the holidays. Others insisted that Barnett announce the layoff immediately, so employees could plan their holiday activities—and holiday spending—accordingly.

On Monday morning, December 14, Barnett notified the unions, then ordered the announcement posted on all plant bulletin boards. For the Climax Mine, the simple, terse announcement was the beginning of the end of an era.

Ralph Barnett announced today that due to continued deterioration of the molybdenum market, production and manpower at the Climax Mine will be reduced.

Approximately 550 OCAW employees, 35 IBEW employees, and approximately 10 OPEIU [Office Professional Employees International Union] employees will be placed on lay off in accordance with their respective bargaining agreements. Reductions in manpower levels will occur in early January, 1982.

Barnett stresses that if there is not a positive upswing in the molybdenum market that further reductions will be necessary in early summer.

Leadville's holidays were the quietest since the 1962 strike. On January 6, 1982, with the full attention of Denver television news crews and reporters from *The Denver Post* and *Rocky Mountain News*, 595 Climax employees worked their last shifts. The Colorado Job Service quickly opened its first branch office ever in Leadville. Laid-off Climax miners knew it better as the "unemployment office." As they waited in long lines to file for unemployment benefits, most voiced the sincere belief that the layoff would be temporary.

Through late winter and early spring of 1982, 1,900 Climax employees mined and milled only 33,000 tons per day, about 60 percent of capacity. Remaining employees and laid-off miners searched the financial pages of newspapers for encouraging economic news, but the market reports for February and March told only of declining molybdenum consumption and prices, while production held steady. In April, Climax posted a second layoff notice.

NOTICE TO EMPLOYEES
April 12, 1982

Ralph Barnett announced today to the leadership of the three bargaining units that further reduction in molybdenum production is necessary because of a continued decline in molybdenum consumption and sales.

In detailing this reduction, Barnett announced that 269 production and maintenance, 20 electrical, and 5 clerical workers would be placed on layoff status to bring molybdenum production in line with molybdenum consumption. A reduction in management and staff is also planned. With this reduction, the Climax mine will be operating at approximately 40 percent of capacity.

These layoffs will be in effect until market conditions warrant a recall.

Barnett scheduled the new round of layoffs for April 29 and cut production to 20,000 tons per day. The layoff reduced employment to 1,450, less than half the level of December 1980. As scheduled, Climax shut down completely during the month of July. When work resumed on August 2, early retirements further reduced employment to 1,200. Then, just one week later, Barnett announced a plantwide shutdown, effective September 17, that would last "at least two months."

Financial concerns went beyond the immediate loss of jobs and paychecks; over the years, Climax men and women had purchased tens of thousands of shares of AMAX stock through payroll-deduction plans. In 1981, when AMAX stock traded at $70.00 per share, Pierre Gousseland, still confident about the future of AMAX, had rejected a $78.50-per-share buyout bid by Standard Oil of California. But by summer 1982, AMAX stock had plummeted below $20.00 per share.

By then AMAX and the molybdenum mining industry were bona fide business disasters. On October 18, 1982, *Business Week* reported:

> For more than a decade, AMAX, Inc., under the aegis of a dynamic entrepreneur, flouted the conventional wisdom of its industry. Instead of cautiously mining its traditional ores, AMAX diversified its mineral base widely; added new ore bodies; researched new uses for its primary metal, molybdenum; and aggressively developed new mines. Its defiance paid off. By the end of the 1970s, with a new chief executive [Pierre Gousseland] in place AMAX operations covered nearly every major mineral, and its earnings had grown 900% in just ten years. Cocksure that its winning streak would last forever, it swaggered into the 1980s, intent upon pursuing the same strategy that had brought it such vast success.
>
> Today, the swagger is out of AMAX. Most of the company's businesses, which include the ore that underpinned AMAX's extraordinary growth, molybdenum, have hit the floor. Total sales are flagging and, instead of profits, the company is projecting a loss for 1982 that could top $350 million. Sweeping plans are underway to cut the executive staff by 25%, which is demoralizing in itself. Worst of all, AMAX is shouldering a staggering debt of $1.7 billion, on which about $300 million in interest will be paid this year.
>
> . . . Moreover, AMAX's current prodigious debt, much of it run up by [Ian] MacGregor, already shackles him [Gousseland]. Then, too, MacGregor had molybdenum. As a strengthener of steel used in space vehicles, drilling equipment, pipelines and even as an oil additive, it was a cash cow and particularly valuable when OPEC refired U.S. oil

operations. The moly business today is drastically different. Not only are more companies producing it, but the prime customers are recession-struck. AMAX, like other moly producers, is stuck with huge inventories.

AMAX, though, is still left with an array of resources, and most face a bleak future. Most serious of all, molybdenum is particularly hard hit, and oversupplies "stretch as far as the eye can see," says one analyst from Smith Barney. "Its future is dreadful."

Climax employees and Leadville residents would always remember 1982 as "the year of the shutdown." Emotions ran the gauntlet from sadness and disbelief to puzzlement and bitterness, the latter common among many senior employees who drew the inevitable "what if" comparisons with the "old Climax." Many adamantly believed that the "premerger Climax," the original Climax Molybdenum Company, would never have racked up such an enormous debt to finance grand plans of expansion and diversification. It would have taken care of things "at home," continuing to methodically develop the Climax and Henderson mines for the long term, and keeping production in step with increasing molybdenum demand. There would have been no "panic pits," nor an inefficient army of 3,000 people trying to squeeze every pound of molybdenum possible out of Bartlett Mountain.

Many Climax veterans felt certain that, during the critical mid-1970s, the "old Climax," which would have been free of debt that demanded cash flow, could have held the line on molybdenum prices, undercutting the market to whatever degree was needed to starve the competition. Those seeking a scapegoat readily found one in Pierre Gousseland. In fairness, Gousseland had inherited many of the policies and much of the staggering debt of Ian MacGregor. But the ship had gone down on Gousseland's watch, and in Leadville's long unemployment lines, Pierre Gousseland's name was mentioned often and usually accompanied by a string of epithets.

But there was more sadness than bitterness, much of it over the mass retirements of senior employees who were the heart and soul of Climax. Ralph Barnett had offered the first early retirements in fall 1981, to accelerate employment attrition. Twenty- and thirty-year Climax men and women beat a steady path to the Personnel Department to negotiate their early retirements. Climax honored each at the traditional retirement coffee on their last Friday. The retirements

321

became so numerous and frequent that, as one departing man commented, "they can't make the coffee fast enough." Week after week, the *Hi Grade* carried retirement notices, usually a photograph and brief synopsis of another long Climax career coming to a premature end. In May 1982, the *Hi Grade* printed a ten-page special issue devoted solely to retirements.

Climax always seemed to have a muck-crew poet who could express feelings in rough meter and simple rhyme. One anonymous scribe captured the feelings of helplessness and frustration over the collapse of molybdenum and the uphill battle that threatened domestic mining, while remembering the pride with which most Climax men and women prepared to leave their careers and friends.

> *Even though we know that the end is near*
> *Those fellas in Greenwich have nothing to fear,*
> *For as we take our very last ride*
> *We'll always be men with a whole lot of pride.*
> *We'll shoot and load and send trains out,*
> *After all, that's what muck's all about.*
> *We all remember the years that we had,*
> *Some years were good, others were bad;*
> *We'll be leaving much sooner than we should,*
> *But we all know we did the best that we could.*
> *Now we all know what shape this country is in,*
> *We're fighting a battle impossible to win;*
> *It seems that the foreigners rule the roost*
> *And we in America can get no boost;*
> *And as we put up with all their tactics,*
> *This whole damned world will be made of plastic.*

In September 1982, Climax held a special dinner at the Leadville Elk's Lodge to honor 150 retirees. The dinner commemorated the end of an era and marked an irreplaceable loss, for the collective Climax experience and service of that group alone exceeded 3,000 years. Some of the dinner conversation inevitably drifted back to "what might've been" if the "old Climax" were still running the show, but most focused on the trophy trout and the big elk that would no longer get away, or about "building something nice" on that little piece of land back in Oklahoma. While many would remain in Leadville, others were heading for warmer climes. One retiree, remembering the Fremont Pass blizzards, was headed for southern Spain, "where it doesn't snow—ever!"

The retirees generally agreed that Climax had treated them well, and that if they had a choice, they'd "do it all over again." Among them was T. K. Bolin, who retired as supervisor of the 600 Level "locie" repair shop. Jobs were hard to find in Alabama in 1951 when Bolin received his army discharge, but some outfit called the Climax Molybdenum Company had set up a recruiting office. Bolin signed on and found himself on a bus headed for Climax, Colorado. Half the men quit before they even reached Colorado; eight years later, Bolin was the only one left of the entire busload. Arriving in September, he looked at the early snow and doubted he'd last until the first paycheck. But he surprised himself and stayed, met his wife Lucille, and together they raised six children, who reaped perhaps the greatest rewards of Bolin's thirty-year Climax career. "Three of our boys have graduated from college as electrical engineers," Bolin said at the retirement dinner, "and I know none of that would have happened if I hadn't stayed on that first year."

Years later, General Manager Ralph Barnett remembered the mass retirements of 1982. "When I watched all those people take their retirements, I thought of all their years of experience, service, and loyalty," Barnett said, "and I could see then that everything was falling apart."

Things were falling apart in Leadville, too. In eighteen months, Lake County's population fell from 13,500 to 8,500. School enrollment and faculty numbers were halved. Lake County quickly revised personal property tax rates upward. At the Commercial Bank of Leadville, the total number of accounts dropped from 10,000 to 4,000. In Leadville, where realtors had never listed more than thirty houses at one time, "For Sale" signs appeared in droves. In 1980, a typical three-bedroom, one-bath house in the relatively new West Park section sold for $60,000; by late 1982, with 300 houses flooding the market, the same house listed for $35,000. Harrison Avenue cash-register receipts declined sharply; several liquor stores, a shoe store, and two gas stations closed their doors, and the JC Penney and Skaggs Drug outlets announced plans to pull out.

The state and national media reported Leadville as an economic disaster. According to *The Denver Post*, Leadville was "a classic example of a busted mining camp," a town "that had carried all its eggs in one basket." The *Post's Empire* magazine featured Leadville in an article titled "Hard Times Ahead"; a *New York Times* article headline read "Mining Town Tries to Cope." *Newsweek* reported Leadville's plight in July 1982, in a story titled "Rocky Mountain Low."

> Two miles up in the Colorado Rockies, the town of Leadville was booming a year ago. Attracted by good wages and Leadville's mountain surroundings, thousands of workers had flocked to the area to mine its deposits of molybdenum, a vital ingredient in high-grade steel. In 1981 alone, the Climax Molybdenum Company, a division of AMAX, Inc. . . . fueled a thriving real estate market, retail economy—and twenty bustling saloons. Then the steel market collapsed, and the price of molybdenum dropped. . . . Early this year, Climax laid off half its work force, and in June it idled the remaining 2,600 employees by temporarily closing its two mines. Hundreds of miners have pulled up stakes, and the town is in deep trouble. . . .

Months later, desperately trying to revive its battered economy, Leadville inaugurated "Operation Bootstrap," hiring a development specialist to study its economic predicament and formulate a recovery plan. Ironically, the proposed recovery plan was a haunting echo of the 1962 Denver Research Institute study, which had warned against relying on a single industry and, particularly, on a single mine. The recovery plan recommended developing tourism and further diversifying the local economy with light manufacturing and cottage industries.

Charles Stott became general manager of the Climax Mine in January 1983. Stott, an engineer from the Colorado School of Mines who also held a law degree, began his Climax career in 1972. As general manager, Stott took over a mine that had not produced in six months.

In just over a year, the price of molybdenum had fallen from $8.00 per pound to $3.00—about eighty cents less than Climax Mine production costs. But by August 1983, inventories had dropped a bit and the price recovered to $3.75, not high enough to reopen the mine, but enough to generate a glimmer of hope.

Climax recalled 100 employees on a "two months on, two months off" rotation basis to perform maintenance work. The *Herald Democrat* reported the limited recall in an article that hardly inspired long-term hope.

324

. . . The company said that the benefit of this program is twofold. First, it will help the upkeep of the mine and if business conditions are such as would permit the company to start up operations, they would be ready to do so. Second, it will help employees by reestablishing their eligibility for unemployment insurance compensation benefits, should the company not be able to resume operations for a period of time.

The company also stated that this program is subject to immediate termination in the event it should decide to "mothball" the mine. . . .

But the molybdenum market slowly strengthened into the fall, stirring new rumors that an AMAX decision about reopening the Climax Mine was imminent. AMAX announced its decision in early November—but it wasn't what Leadville and 1,000 out-of-work miners had hoped to hear. AMAX, "for purely economic reasons," would reopen the Henderson Mine, when and if warranted by future economic conditions.

Reactions in Leadville ranged from shock to outrage. Leadville knew that Climax had been the cash cow that built the Henderson Mine; to consider opening Henderson while Climax remained shut down was the ultimate insult. Lake County Commissioner Ken Chlouber, a Climax management hand who, for the time being, still had a job, fired off a letter to William Bilhorn, president of the Climax Molybdenum Division in Golden, expressing public sentiment.

It was with deep regret and even greater disappointment that I learned of the decision to re-open the Henderson Mine prior to the Climax Mine. It is my conviction that the Climax Mine was treated unfairly and judged without consideration for the generation upon generation of Climax miners and their families who are the real backbone of AMAX. These are the people who drilled, blasted, hauled, crushed and milled so that AMAX could grow into the mining great that it is and so that other mines, such as Henderson, could be built.

It is these people that AMAX owes an obligation. And it is to these people that AMAX has seemingly turned its corporate back. These people have nowhere else to turn. The communities that depend on the Climax Mine have little or no alternative employment. The Henderson miners have Denver at their back door. Our back door is the national forest.

I am told that the company's decision is purely economic; a "don't tell me what you did yesterday, what can you do today" attitude. That apparent position makes myth of a much needed corporate morality. And if the Henderson decision is pure dollars today, how can the people of this community believe our mine will reopen before the Henderson

325

Mine is at full capacity? Surely if demand increases it would be a lower cost to increase production at one mine than to open another. It would appear that this is the proverbial "dangling carrot" whose only purpose would be to keep unemployed miners close at hand or to appease public opinion.

But even forgetting, as apparently has happened, what is just, what is moral, and forgetting the houses that sit vacant in Leadville, the grade school that had to close and the families that had to separate to survive, I believe we can compete dollar for dollar with the Henderson Mine. . . . And we'll do it this year, next year, in 10 and 20 years we'll be competitive with anybody. And we'll do it with the same people AMAX grew up with. We'll do it with the people AMAX needed yesterday and the people AMAX will need tomorrow. The same people that need AMAX today!

Chlouber used hard guilt to try to persuade AMAX to reopen the Climax Mine, but Carl Miller, chairman of the Lake County commissioners and a Climax electrician who had already lost his job, emphasized past loyalty and support, along with present willingness to cooperate and do anything it would take to resume limited production. Miller wrote directly to Pierre Gousseland in Greenwich, gently reminding the chief executive officer that, without the Climax Mine, there would have been no Henderson Mine and no AMAX.

. . . the Climax mine is MUCH MORE than a valuable ore body waiting to be mined when market conditions improve. The mine is the "life blood" of Lake County and several neighboring communities. Men and women who invested ten, twenty and thirty years of their lives desperately await the reopening of the Climax mine. Their hopes, dreams and very futures hang in the balance. The local schools and business communities are also experiencing a time of great peril.

The Climax mine AIDED by the Lake County community played a dominant role in developing and shaping AMAX into the mining giant it is today. Over the years the long-term stockholders have received a generous yield on their investments due, in part, to the substantial return the Climax mine has made to the corporate treasury. Local elected officials and the community, as a whole, never hesitated to support and flex our political muscles to defend the company's position on such issues as severance tax, land reclamation, land transfers and a host of other important issues. . . .

Pierre, I am told that adversity, struggle and hardship are not strangers to you. Perhaps, for that reason you can empathize with our situation in Lake County. I remain confident that you will assist us if it is at all possible. We need the mine re-opened immediately. Please help us, and counsel us in ways we can assist you to rapidly restructure, alter or change existing corporate plans in such a way as to allow the Climax mine to resume limited production immediately.

Leadville residents sent numerous letters to AMAX executives discussing, pleading, reasoning, and demanding the reopening of the Climax Mine. Their reasons included corporate morality, economic relief, community responsibility, and the consideration that if AMAX were to "walk away" from Climax and Leadville, its reputation as a poor community citizen could preclude development of major projects elsewhere.

From the AMAX standpoint, market conditions simply did not warrant limited production from both the Climax Mine and the Henderson Mine. And there was no question that the new, modern Henderson Mine, more efficient and blessed with higher grades of ore, could produce molybdenum at less cost. From a purely economic standpoint, the Henderson Mine would be the logical mine to reopen.

In a difficult decision, and one clearly not based purely on economics, AMAX ordered the reopening of the Climax Mine in early 1984. Recalling 584 laid-off employees, Climax organized a comprehensive retraining program at Colorado Mountain College covering everything from benefits to job skills and mine safety. Bumper stickers proclaimed: *Climax Mine Reopens—Hug A Moly Miner!* At the main gate of the mine, a big white sign announced: *WELCOME BACK!* On April 18, 1984, when the spring snow was still deep atop Fremont Pass, 700 Climax employees resumed production in the mine and mill for the first time in seventeen months.

By December 1984, Climax had recovered 16.8 million pounds of molybdenum and daily production steadied at 20,000 tons per day. Molybdenum recovery amounted to only 30 percent of that of 1981, but the more telling statistics were that it had been done in only eight months and with 75 percent fewer employees. The cost to mine and mill one pound of molybdenum had dropped 20 percent to $3.00 per pound, a major cost reduction that reflected two points: the Climax Mine had grown grossly inefficient during the 1970s, but the potential existed to regain competitiveness.

In Leadville, many Climax employees and former employees believed that the 1984 reopening and the greatly improved production efficiency marked the beginning of an inevitable Climax recovery, and that with further market improvement the mine would, in time, again employ a workforce of 1,500 or more.

327

But the full picture of the restructured molybdenum market and the position of molybdenum in a restructured AMAX was just emerging. In Greenwich, Allen Born had replaced Pierre Gousseland as president and chief executive officer of AMAX. Born, a metallurgist and former Climax mill superintendent in the early 1970s, continued the changes Gousseland had already begun. AMAX now focused on current markets rather than minerals, while emphasizing proprietary products and processes rather than the generic research that often benefited its competition and other industries.

Born quickly reversed the broad diversification of the past fifteen years, pulling out of copper, iron ore, phosphate, nickel, and general metal refining, leaving AMAX with core businesses of gold, coal, aluminum, and, least important, molybdenum. During the late 1970s, molybdenum, the heart and soul of AMAX, accounted for 25 percent of booming corporate earnings; but in 1984, molybdenum provided only 7 percent of far-lower corporate earnings.

AMAX even temporarily dropped the familiar term "*Climax* molybdenum" in favor of generic marketing. Analysts believed AMAX preferably would have divested itself entirely of molybdenum, but, considering the weak and unsettled molybdenum market, selling the Climax and Henderson mines was virtually impossible. AMAX, one market analyst noted, was "stuck" with molybdenum.

The new molybdenum market bore little semblance to the market of 1980. In just five years, overall molybdenum consumption declined 25 percent, mainly because steelmakers had replaced molybdenum in standard alloys with vanadium and other alloying metals. Copper mines now supplied most of the market with coproduct and by-product molybdenum.

Both the Climax and Henderson mines had become "swing producers." If production costs could be cut further to assure market competitiveness, they would produce only when warranted by market conditions. Unlike the "old days" when the Climax Mine controlled the market, the market now controlled Climax. In 1985, the Climax Mine produced seventeen million pounds of molybdenum, a mere 8.5 percent of world production.

The problems of operating successfully as a swing producer soon became apparent. Amid market uncertainties, corporate restructuring, personnel cuts and reassignments, early retirements, and questions about exactly what AMAX planned to do with its molybdenum business, the Climax Mine had a succession of general managers, which did little for supervisory continuity. Bob Kendrick returned for a second brief term before his retirement, followed by George Stephen, John Leahy, and Tom Irwin.

Molybdenum prices swung unpredictably between $2.90 per pound and $4.00, then fell again. In 1985, the planned month-long Fourth of July shutdown extended into September, prompting new rumors that Climax would again suspend production. But production resumed at 20,000 tons per day and continued through the winter, the longest sustained production period in three years.

Another round of shutdown rumors started in spring 1986, when molybdenum prices sagged below $3.00 per pound. Climax extended its scheduled Fourth of July shutdown for six weeks and offered more early retirement plans. Only days after the Climax Mine resumed production in September 1986, the *Herald Democrat* told of another layoff.

CLIMAX MAKES CUT OF 300
Only Two Hundred Will Be Left
The axe has fallen so often at Climax in recent years that one would almost think they were chopping wood—but it has fallen again. . . .

Open pit operations halted on September 8, 1986. Mining continued only on the Storke Level at 6,000 tons per day, or 12 percent of mine capacity. This time, the cutbacks had an ominous finality to them. Climax closed the main gate to all but truck traffic, then consolidated its files and offices in the Storke Level dry building.

To cut costs of clearing and maintaining railroad tracks on the mine property, Climax informed the Burlington Northern Railroad that it would use trucks for all incoming and outgoing shipments and would no longer require rail service. The Burlington Northern immediately requested permission from the Interstate Commerce Commission to abandon service on the Leadville-Climax line. With the petition unopposed, the Interstate Commerce Commission granted quick approval. In late fall 1986, trains stopped running at Fremont Pass for the first time in 105 years.

As expected, Climax suspended production again in March 1987, laying off its remaining miners and mill hands. A month later, Climax shut down the heating plant for the first time ever, an act that many old-timers interpreted as the symbolic "turning off of the lights." Total employment at the Climax Mine dropped to just sixty-five men and women.

After the shock of the initial 1982 shutdown and layoffs had subsided, Leadville had pinned its hopes for quick economic recovery on tourism, but learned it was far behind in the competition for regional tourism dollars. Nor was Leadville united in its effort to promote tourism. Tourism jobs tended to be seasonal and generally low-paying, and former mine employees often chose instead to wait for a recall back to $12.00-per-hour Climax jobs.

Many Leadville residents were pensioned Climax retirees who wanted to be able to retire in the Leadville they knew, not a "newfangled tourist trap." Tourism and development proponents became frustrated with the "entrenched mining mentality" they perceived as standing in the way of their renewal plans. For the first time in its long, rich history, Leadville was confronted by an identity crisis: Was it or wasn't it a mining town?

Leadville finally hit rock bottom in its economic bust in 1986-87. The low point coincided with reluctant acceptance of the fact that Climax would never again operate as a big, 1,000-plus-employee mine. Hundreds of miners and their families had moved, many to jobs in the booming Nevada goldfields. In 1980, 2,000 out-of-county residents had commuted to jobs in Lake County; by 1987, 1,700 Lake County residents—half of the entire county workforce—commuted to low-paying resort-industry jobs in Eagle and Summit counties. Many former Climax families that once earned $30,000 per year with one parent working were now lucky to earn half that—with both parents working. Parental control declined and children lost their professional role models. Lake County High School, which once sent 45 percent of its graduating seniors on to four-year colleges, now had one of the highest dropout rates among schools in Colorado's rural counties. Nevertheless, by 1987, Leadville had survived the worst of the bust, not so much by economic transition and renewal, but by adapting to a lower economic level.

After suspension of limited production in March 1987, AMAX ordered General Manager Tom Irwin to implement a "hard shutdown" that might last five to ten years. But simply shutting the mine down solved few if any problems. After shutdowns, start-up costs were very high. The greater concerns were the "holding" costs—costs that didn't "go away," not even during hard shutdowns. Holding costs at Climax accrued from such expenses as security, planning, plant maintenance, insurance, utilities, water quality maintenance, the payroll for the skeleton crew to provide basic administration, and taxes. The latter included very substantial county property taxes on 11,320 acres with buildings, roads, dams, pipelines, conveyors, and other facilities and improvements. Climax originally projected annual shutdown holding costs at $10 million to $13 million, only to learn they were closer to $20 million.

To cut holding costs, Climax embarked on a major downsizing program. Demolition crews removed the big crusher on the 600 Level and tore down many buildings. Climax closed its outfall water treatment plant in favor of a less expensive chemical precipitation-neutralization process, then wrote off the Storke Level, 600 Level, and 900 Level. By 1988, downsizing, together with the sharp drop in production, had reduced Lake County's valuation of the Climax Mine from $82 million to $39 million, thus cutting annual property taxes from $9 million to $5 million.

1985.
Aerial view of the
Climax Mine and
Fremont Pass, showing
Bartlett Mountain,
the Glory Hole
and core, and the
open pit benches
on Ceresco Ridge.

In June 1988, Bob Kilborn took over as general manager to continue the downsizing and cost-cutting programs, which in some ways were more difficult than expansion. Basic production of concentrate from ore was a complex, interrelated process of mining, hauling, crushing, milling, and tailings disposal that achieved maximum overall efficiency only at capacity production. At reduced production levels, high efficiency in one operation could actually lower efficiency in others, and simply reducing tonnage was no guarantee of cutting overall costs. Kilborn reported a prime example of such "lingering" costs in the relationship between production and the cost of tailings pond water management.

> . . . Due to our geographic location (about twelve miles upstream from Dillon Reservoir) we have a major commitment to keeping our discharge effluent within the parameters specified in our permits. Therefore, we designed a process water system to handle both our production requirements and whatever environmental clean water requirements were necessary. When we temporarily ceased production, that system was no longer usable for the purpose for which it was designed—which was production; you can't turn it off and you can't walk away from it; you have to keep it in operation because the driving force behind that water system is now environmental regulation. . . . You might think that you turn off production and let everything else go. It doesn't work that way in a temporary shutdown, and right now to comply with the environmental portion of just that one system, we are pumping and distributing as much water as if we were in full production. Our water pumping costs have not decreased, because we had an environmental process intertwined with our production process. It's more economical—until you shut down your production process.

As a swing producer, Climax encountered many problems. Periodic shutdowns caused the loss of key, experienced employees; start-ups, difficult to anticipate and plan for because of erratic market conditions, required rehiring and retraining and were slow and costly. Furthermore, vital efficiency studies could not be performed during shutdowns or the rough start-up periods that followed. Another problem was deterioration of equipment during long periods of inactivity, particularly in the mill. The longer the mine and mill remained shut down, the greater the chance they would never reopen.

Kilborn believed that limited production might actually be more cost-efficient than a simple shutdown. The mine would operate at a loss that would be partially offset by the value of the concentrate produced. Limited production would also maintain the mill, while permitting efficiency and cost-reduction studies to make the mine more competitive and profitable.

Since the market was unlikely to warrant sustained production, alternative work programs in reclamation and demolition would be necessary to retain a core of experienced, full-time employees. Climax would have to perform a great deal of environmental work sooner or later. And the downsizing program already called for demolition of half the buildings at Climax, including the Max Schott School and the superstructure of the moly oxide plant, to further reduce property valuation and county property taxes.

The Henderson Mine, operating at 75 percent capacity with 460 employees, supplied all the molybdenum AMAX could market. Nevertheless, AMAX surprised everyone by agreeing to resume limited production at Climax in spring 1989, at the rate of 6,000 tons per day, or 12.5 percent of capacity.

Since downsizing had eliminated the Climax Personnel Department, Climax turned the job of interviewing and hiring 100 workers over to the Colorado Job Service. Because employee recall lists had long expired, the Job Service hired solely on the basis of specific job qualifications, mostly drawing upon a pool of former Climax employees. The mine and mill resumed production in May 1989 with 165 employees, the smallest production workforce since the 1920s. Fifty miners pulled ore from the soon-to-be-exhausted Storke Level in the last underground mining that would ever be done on the existing Climax levels. Only forty-five mill hands were enough to mill 6,000 tons of ore per day.

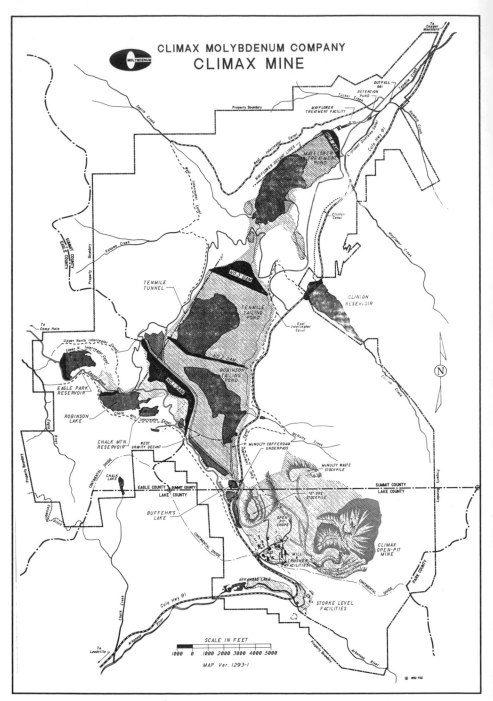

A drawing showing the main features and extent of the Climax Mine property in 1990. —drawing by Frank Zancanella

13
New Directions
The 1990s

Today's challenge is not to create a market, as it was in the early 1920s, but to become competitive with other world sources of molybdenum within a radically restructured market.

Following the molybdenum-market crash in 1981, it remains arguable whether AMAX, the Climax Mine, or Leadville suffered the greatest devastation.

The grand AMAX expansion and diversification plans collapsed, and emergency corporate restructuring in the mid-1980s was unable to stave off disaster. AMAX survived temporarily on coal, gold, and aluminum, but when it lost molybdenum, it lost its corporate heart and soul. By the late 1980s, AMAX, no longer a leader in mineral resource development, had become an overextended, undervalued corporation ripe for a takeover.

Leadville had been economically as well as socially devastated. In 1990, The *Los Angeles Times* listed U.S. counties with the highest population losses during the 1980s. Lake County, Colorado, headed the list at 50 percent.

Climax emerged as a shell of the mine it had once been. During sporadic periods of limited production from September 1982 through 1990, a period of more than eight years, Climax mined and milled just three million tons of ore. In the "old days," Climax would have mined and milled that volume in just three months.

Nevertheless, in 1990, Climax was again in limited production. In April 1989, miners began "cleaning up" the last of the Storke Level ore. With total employment at 160, the mill operated at 6,000 tons per day, its lowest practical production level.

Amid a gloomy long-term market outlook, the U.S. Bureau of Mines predicted 1990 molybdenum demand would decrease 10 percent from the previous year. That report started the first rumors that AMAX would sell the Climax Mine. On January 25, 1990, the *Herald Democrat* reported denials from company spokesmen.

RUMORS OF CLIMAX SALE UNFOUNDED

Recent rumors of the sale of Climax are untrue, according to Pat Wadsworth and Bob Kilborn of Climax.

Business Week magazine recently ran an article which said that AMAX stock is undervalued, making the corporation a potential target for a takeover.

Wadsworth feels that the article was the source of the rumors.

New York AMAX executive Mitch Badler said: "Climax is not for sale. Never has been, never will be."

Perhaps the Climax Mine wasn't for sale, but not because AMAX wouldn't have liked to sell it. Climax had become an albatross around the AMAX corporate neck, but selling the mine was virtually impossible. Prospective buyers were wary of the depressed molybdenum market and of the fact that acquiring the Climax Mine also involved an enormous environmental reclamation liability estimated in excess of $100 million. Nor was it good business sense for AMAX to retain the Henderson Mine as a producer while selling the Climax Mine. A buyer could conceivably reopen Climax and, with a low-cost operation, compete directly with the Henderson Mine.

Climax was also a problem for Lake County. Climax had battled the county before over taxes, and it was about to battle again over the assessed valuation of the Climax Mine. The trial convened on April 16, 1990, and the *Herald Democrat* carried the story.

AMAX PRESENTS OPENING ARGUMENTS IN COUNTY TRIAL

On Monday, the trial of AMAX, Inc., versus the Lake County Board of Equalization got underway. . . .

Climax is suing Lake County over a $30 million dispute in assessed valuation.

The trial will determine the value of the Climax mine during the period from Jan. 1, 1987 through July 1, 1988.

The County and AMAX disagree over the assessed value of the Climax mine during that 18 month period. . . . AMAX, using one method of appraisal, determined that the assessed value of the Climax mine was $10 million. This includes deductions for physical deterioration and economic obsolescence.

The County, on the other hand, assessed the value of Climax at $40 million. The two are $181,000 apart in tax dollars. County Attorney John Dunn termed the trial "the second most important case in the history of Lake County." The first important case was when the court determined that the Climax mine was in Lake County, rather than Summit County.

At stake are the taxes which the Climax mine must pay the County. This includes the tax bills for the years 1989 and 1990.

If AMAX prevails, the County will be forced to abate Climax taxes and refund the excess paid for those two tax years. The decision will influence all taxes which Climax must pay in the future. Tax relief for Climax would impose a heavier burden on the citizens of Lake County.

The burden of proof will be on AMAX, which must convince the court that Lake County's assessed valuation is incorrect.

The County maintains that its appraisal is correct, and disregards AMAX's claim that the Climax mine is economically obsolete. . . .

District Court Judge Richard Hart handed down a decision in November 1990. Basically agreeing with the Climax contention of economic obsolescence, Hart set the assessed value of the Climax Mine during the contested time period at $15 million, higher than the Climax figure of $10 million, but far below Lake County's assessment of $40 million. The court ordered Lake County to repay Climax $844,000, and ordered the Lake County School District to repay $1.3 million.

As Lake County scrambled to make financial ends meet, Climax also asked the district court for reimbursement of costs. The *Herald Democrat*, its headline hinting at Lake County's frustration, reported the court's decision.

MORE MONEY TO BE DISHED OUT TO CLIMAX
Following the resolution of the Climax case in District Court, Climax asked to be reimbursed $110 for costs and $82,000 for expert witnesses. After reviewing the request, District Judge Hart ruled that the county would have to pay $110 for costs, and just $5,000 for expert witness fees, in addition to over $844,000 owed by the county back to the mine.

In October 1990, Bill Hinken replaced Bob Kilborn as general manager of the Climax Mine. Hinken, a metallurgical engineer from the South Dakota School of Mines, began his career at Climax in 1959 and previously served as general manager of the Henderson Mine.

337

Open pit production resumed at 6,000 tons per day in January 1991. When Storke Level miners completed their cleanup work in May, Climax declared the level abandoned. Since 1953, the Storke Level had produced more than 200 million tons of ore. When the Storke joined the Leal, White, Phillipson, and Ceresco levels in abandonment, Climax held a "retirement" luncheon in its honor. Market conditions, however, did not warrant continuation of open pit mining, and Climax suspended operations the same month.

The Climax Mine remained inactive during 1991. Work focused on demolition and downsizing, open pit reclamation, haulage of open pit waste to the tailings dams, consolidation of mill operations, and hydromulching reclamation.

Climax invested $4.4 million in a new mill instrumentation system; consolidation of control rooms, sample rooms, and assay labs in a new building; and replacement of many mill flotation cells. The modernization provided better control of primary grinding and flotation circuits, increased rates of both recovery and concentrate grade, and reduced overall mill power costs.

When Bill Hinken retired at the end of 1991, Robert Dorfler took over as general superintendent. Dorfler was the twenty-fifth individual to fill the mine's top management position, part of a long succession that began in 1917 when Max Schott appointed John H. "Jack" White as the first Climax general superintendent. Through 1983, a period of sixty-seven years, there had been only sixteen general managers. Seven individuals filled the general manager's position in the decade that followed.

Among Dorfler's first duties was ordering yet another layoff, which the *Herald Democrat* reported on January 23, 1992.

CLIMAX LAYOFFS AFFECT 43; 118 WILL REMAIN
Representatives of the Climax Molybdenum Mine announced Thursday that 43 employees would be subject to layoffs at the end of the month. . . .

The layoffs are viewed as "temporary," spokesman Pat Wadsworth said, but the duration of the layoffs depends upon the future demand and price of molybdenum.

Remaining employees will work on continued demolition of unneeded buildings at the mine site, reclamation, and decreasing the size of and modernizing the mill and other projects.

Twenty employees took voluntary, early retirement last month, also a part of reducing the number of employees at the mine.

Climax resumed limited open pit production in April 1992, producing 60,000 tons of ore, just enough for an operational shake-down of the modernized mill facilities. Production halted the following month.

Even with the mine inactive, water rights associated with the 11,320-acre Climax property continued to appreciate in value. In August 1992, Climax sold the Clinton Reservoir, which it had constructed during the mid-1970s tailings-pond expansion and relocation of State Highway 91.

The Clinton Ditch and Reservoir Company, a consortium of recreational interests that included Summit County; the cities of Breckenridge, Dillon, and Silverthorne; Copper Mountain, Inc.; Keystone Resorts, Inc.; and the Winter Park Recreation District, purchased the Clinton Reservoir and immediately adjacent land for nearly $9 million as a source of water for snowmaking.

Climax started another major water project in 1992 at the old moly oxide tailings pond at the head of the Eagle River drainage, where highly acidic tailings had been a problem since 1967. Climax sold future water rights to Vail Associates, Inc., for $3 million, then began removing and chemically neutralizing the acidic tailings to convert the pond into the freshwater Eagle Park Reservoir. Crews began removing the tailings to bedrock by a "hydrology mining" process that converted compacted tailings to a water slurry for piping into a regular tailings pond for chemical neutralization and final disposal.

By early 1993, with molybdenum prices still flat at $3.00 per pound, the outlook for the market, the Climax Mine, and AMAX seemed dismal. The Henderson Mine easily produced all the molybdenum AMAX could sell. Climax had not earned an operating profit in ten years, and many wondered how much further AMAX would go in maintaining the inactive mine and mill.

AMAX had owned the Climax Mine since The American Metal Company merged with the Climax Molybdenum Company in 1958. Over those thirty-six years, Climax Mine earnings had brought enormous profits to AMAX, built the Henderson Mine, and fueled the corporate expansion plans of the 1970s. But after the molybdenum market collapsed, AMAX had focused on its own survival. In the following years, corporate attention shifted from molybdenum toward gold, coal, aluminum, and oil and gas. By 1993, the skeleton crew of remaining Climax employees was losing faith both in AMAX and in the position of molybdenum within the corporate business structure.

Rumors of a merger arose in spring 1993. The prospective partner was Cyprus Minerals Company, a smaller, younger, aggressive mineral resources company headquartered in Englewood, Colorado, with primary interests in copper, coal, natural gas, lithium, and iron ore. Like The American Metal Company forty years earlier, and AMAX in the 1970s, Cyprus Minerals, also a molybdenum producer, was a company seeking expansion.

But molybdenum posed a problem. Combining the molybdenum assets of AMAX and Cyprus Minerals would create the nation's largest molybdenum producer and a possible violation of federal antitrust regulations. The U.S. Department of Justice approved the merger only when Cyprus Minerals sold a primary molybdenum mine and AMAX divested itself of its molybdenum conversion plant in Langeloth, Pennsylvania.

The merger's first immediate effect on the remaining fifty Climax employees came in the mail in late October, two weeks before the merger was even formalized. To comply with federal job-loss notification laws, AMAX sent each of its 20,000 employees a letter stating that their services might no longer be required after December 29. On November 7, *The Denver Post* reported the imminent merger of the two big mining companies.

MERGER OF MINING GIANTS

. . . To many of those AMAX employees in Colorado, the deal forged in May is starting to sound a lot more like a takeover than a merger. Cyprus and its employees, they claim, come out ahead. To wit:

*Cyprus Minerals, a smaller, younger, and less diverse company than AMAX, will be the one to survive the merger.

*The new company will be headquartered in Englewood in the current Cyprus offices and headed by Milt Ward, the current chairman, president and chief executive of Cyprus Minerals.

*AMAX's New York corporate headquarters will be shut down or pared way back. . . .

"Cyprus is going to get rid of a lot of high-priced overhead," said Daniel Roling, a mining analyst with Merrill Lynch Capital Markets in New York.

That high-priced overhead includes not only AMAX's poorly producing subsidiaries and many of its employees, but corporate airplanes and even an Indy race car that AMAX owns.

340

Few AMAX executives are expected to wind up at Cyprus. Some won't be offered new jobs, others may not prefer to leave New York for Denver and some are expected to simply take their money and run, cashing in on lucrative golden parachute clauses in their contracts. . . .

From the minute he was hired little more than a year ago in an effort to turn faltering Cyprus around, Ward has focused on cutting costs and eliminating company functions that aren't absolutely necessary. . . .

"A lot's being gained by having the largest mining firm headquartered in Colorado with someone like Milt Ward at the helm," said one Colorado mining industry observer who did not want to be identified, "but a lot's being lost in Colorado in terms of AMAX jobs, its history in the state and some of the good it's done with local communities and environmental programs."

AMAX's strength started in great part when it acquired the molybdenum business and the Climax Mine in Leadville in 1957. It later created the Henderson Mine and at one point provided nearly all of the world's supply of molybdenum, a steel strengthening mineral.

No one expects any problems with the merger other than a few glitches that come with bringing any two huge organizations together.

Corporate cultures may clash a little at first, observers speculated. AMAX historically has been a company with plenty of high overheads and perks for its executives while Cyprus prefers a lean operation.

The Cyprus culture will prevail, and prevail quickly, analysts said. Ward is not one to tolerate clashes or problems. . . .

Ward's most recent coups were in the international arena: forming a joint venture to develop a gold mine in eastern Siberia, taking over an Australian coal company and submitting a winning bid in a joint venture to mine what's believed to be the world's richest copper deposit in Chile.

AMAX, on the other hand, had not made a lot of recent acquisitions. It's seen as a big, lethargic company surviving on a reputation earned long ago. With its headquarters in New York, AMAX is considered something of a "blue blood" company disassociated from its workers and its operations.

"AMAX lost that grand old history it had, mainly because molybdenum crashed," one mining consultant said. "Like many companies, it gets its grandeur from some ore body, then there's a crash, but they think of themselves still as a leader. They may be big, but they're no longer a leader."

The shareholders of both corporations approved the merger by vote on November 11, 1993. Two days later, AMAX and Cyprus Minerals formally became the Cyprus-AMAX Minerals Company, the largest mining company in the United States. With assets exceeding $5 billion, its primary strengths rested in copper, coal, and gold. The

Climax Mine remained a part of the Climax Molybdenum Company, which in turn became a division of the Cyprus Climax Metals Company, a wholly owned subsidiary of the Cyprus-AMAX Minerals Company.

Many Climax veterans believe the Cyprus-AMAX merger brightened the long-term outlook for the Climax Mine, for the Cyprus-AMAX Minerals Company had a better cash position to maintain the mine in a condition to facilitate reopening if and when warranted by market conditions.

In 1994, the Climax Mine began its seventy-seventh year with twenty-seven employees engaged in five areas of work: treating water and maintaining environmental quality, maintaining the mine and mill, continuing to reduce holding costs, environmental reclamation, and development of water resources.

In one way, the Climax Mine had come full circle, for its predicament in the 1990s is not unlike its predicament seven decades ago. Today's challenge is not to create a market, as it was in the early 1920s, but to become competitive with other world sources of molybdenum within a radically restructured market. And big steps have already been taken in that direction. In the past decade, the insurance- and tax-reducing benefits of downsizing have significantly reduced annual holding costs. Climax has restructured many of its traditional concepts, cut costs, and improved operating efficiency. It still has a world-class ore body that can be exploited by low-cost open pit mining. Much depends, of course, on eventual recovery of the molybdenum market, which may be the final step necessary in a long-term transition to enable a grand old mine to produce again.

Epilogue

Since February 1918, when mules hauled the first production ore from the Leal Tunnel, the Climax Mine has mined and milled some 470 million tons of molybdenite ore. That volume is roughly the amount that would be mined in driving a large-diameter highway tunnel for 600 miles—the straight-line distance between Denver, Colorado, and Las Vegas, Nevada.

From that enormous quantity of ore, the Climax mill has recovered more than two million tons of molybdenite concentrate. Contained in that concentrate were 1.9 billion pounds—946,000 tons—of elemental molybdenum with a cumulative, "year-mined" value well in excess of $4 billion, one of the world's highest single-mine production values.

Behind those world-class tonnage and dollar figures stand more than 60,000 men and women who worked at the Climax Mine over the course of seventy-six years. Some were transient workers who contributed to the high labor turnover rate and whose paychecks bought little more than meals, a few beers, and a grubstake for moving on. But others built lives and families around Climax careers. Their loyalty, dedication, and hard work helped build Climax, and their Climax paychecks bought the material necessities of richer lives, college educations for sons and daughters, investments, and, eventually, retirements. Over those seventy-six years, Climax employees shared a cumulative payroll of more than $1 billion.

Unfortunately, mining has always been a dangerous endeavor, and the Climax story must be measured not only in tons, dollars, and jobs, but in lives as well. Eighty-one Climax men and women lost their lives, mostly in underground accidents.

Mining and milling 470 million tons of ore, half of it before the age of environmental regulation, has greatly impacted the environment. Climax has dismantled an entire mountain, inundated five miles of a mountain valley in tailings, and completely reworked the drainage system of the first eight miles of a mountain river. Yet Climax, working at the headwaters of three mountain rivers in an alpine area of great scenic beauty and ecological sensitivity, has limited its impact solely to the Tenmile drainage. Because of costly water treatment and diversion projects, Climax has minimized pollution of Tenmile Creek and, during the past twenty-five years, substantially upgraded water quality.

While the Environmental Protection Agency has designated many far smaller mines and mining districts as Superfund sites to be cleaned up at public or mandated company expense, Climax has not become a public liability and maintains, at its own expense, high levels of water quality. Climax continues to develop water projects as future sources of fresh water to help assure the growth of regional tourism and recreational industries.

Tens of thousands of travelers each year, both winter skiers and summer tourists, cross Fremont Pass and look upward at Bartlett Mountain, the Glory Hole, and the open pit workings on Ceresco Ridge. At the foot of Bartlett Mountain, Climax is still an impressive sprawl of "earthtone" structures, even though only half have survived the recent downsizing program. Just north of the pass summit, the old Climax Ski Area runs are visible in the timberline pines on the side of Chalk Mountain. Hidden on the forested north slope of Chalk Mountain are two abandoned solar observatory domes, one the dome of the original Harvard College Observatory, which played such a vital role during World War II.

Northbound travelers pass Buffehr's Lake, just west of the highway, where German settler John Buffehr once had a ranch and sold milk and eggs to Denver, South Park & Pacific Railway passengers while the narrow-gauge steam locomotives took on water at Climax Station. The highway signs marking the Lake-Summit County boundary at Buffehr's Lake remind us of the "County Line War" of 1918-19, which reestablished the county line and eventually diverted more than $100 million in property taxes from Summit to Lake County.

One mile farther north, at a point overlooking the upper Tenmile Valley, a stone monument reads in part:

IN THIS VALLEY THE TOWNS OF ROBINSON,
KOKOMO AND RECEN EXISTED. KOKOMO WAS
THE HIGHEST MASONIC LODGE IN THE U.S.A.
1882-1966   ELEVATION 10,618 FEET

Below the monument to the west lies the Robinson Tailings Pond, the first and highest of the post-1936 ponds that now cover the old Tenmile mining camps. A half-mile farther, the highway crosses McNulty Gulch, where Charles Senter sluiced gold and built his cabin in 1879 before climbing high onto Bartlett Mountain to stake his three Gold Reef claims.

The overall impact of Climax extends beyond Fremont Pass and the Tenmile drainage. Although Climax shift changes and paychecks may never again dictate the pace of Leadville life, the Climax Mine still accounts for a big part of the Lake County property tax base. The county population includes more than 300 pensioned retirees and many more former Climax workers.

West Park, the controversial Climax housing development of 1957, remains one of the county's most pleasant residential areas. Many of the reminders of the old Climax town, the flat-roofed duplex units, houses, and three-story apartment buildings that "came down the hill" in the big move of 1961-62, are still occupied. Public events are regularly held in the AMAX Community Room of the Lake County Public Library. Climax also continues to support the mine-drilling contests that are a popular and traditional part of Leadville's "Boom Days" annual summer festival.

AMAX granted $25,000 to the National Mining Hall of Fame & Museum in Leadville in 1989, a critical juncture in the new museum's growth, to help it become a major tourism attraction. The three-dimensional model of block cave mining operations within Bartlett Mountain, viewed by tens of thousands of visitors at the Climax visitor reception center, is now a featured museum exhibit.

Leadville's gradual shift away from a mining economy is symbolized by changes to the Leadville-Climax rail line. A year after the last revenue freight runs in 1986, a Leadville couple acquired the line along with some rolling stock from the Burlington Northern Railroad for the write-off price of $10.00. The old line came to life again in 1988 as the Leadville, Colorado & Southern Railroad Company, which now carries tourists on a scenic rail journey from Leadville to within sight of the Climax Mine.

Among the Climax Mine's greatest contributions to Leadville was its work to establish the Timberline Campus of Colorado Mountain College in 1967. The Timberline Campus has grown into an invaluable educational, economic, and cultural asset to the Lake County area. Timely and innovative associate-degree career programs, notably in the fields of environmental technology and mountain recreational industries, have replaced most mining-related courses of study. Today, the Timberline Campus, which includes facilities in Buena Vista and Salida, is among the top five employers in Lake County and has an annual enrollment of more than 2,000 full-time and part-time students.

In the end, the Climax story returns to where it began—Bartlett Mountain, a mountain caved nearly to its summit and dominated by the gaping Glory Hole. Extensive caving and open pit mining have removed all traces of the old Upper Camp and the Leal and White levels, and have exposed underground workings of the abandoned Phillipson and Storke levels.

Some geologic secrets of Bartlett Mountain, once probed only by diamond drills, are now plainly visible. The hard, silicified, barren core of the Upper Orebody, a remnant of thirty-million-year-old mineralizing events, protrudes from the center of the Glory Hole as a massive shoulder of rock. The shear zone of the Mosquito Fault, which made driving the Phillipson Tunnel in 1930 such a difficult and tragic job, appears as a 100-yard-wide dark streak slashing across the western edge of the Glory Hole and the bench cuts of Ceresco Ridge.

Bartlett Mountain represents the history of the Climax Mine as well as its future. Even after mining 470 million tons of ore, huge amounts of ore still remain in place. Although underground workings and reserves have been written off, open pit reserves are estimated at 137 million tons with an average grade of 0.317 percent molybdenite. Contained within those ore reserves are 400 million pounds of elemental molybdenum worth in excess of a billion dollars.

How much of the open pit reserves will ever be mined, and when, cannot yet be answered. Resumption of mining at Climax depends upon such complex, interrelated variables as economic and political developments, trade and tariff regulations, advances in mining technology, possible disruptions of current molybdenum supply and demand, and the ability of Climax to become competitive in a global market. For a decade, the Climax Mine has remained in the shadow of the Henderson Mine. But at its current rate of production, the Henderson Mine could be exhausted in just fifteen years, shifting production emphasis back to Climax.

Today's environmental ethic is itself a justification for continuing mining at Climax. Before new deposits of molybdenite are opened, and more land is impacted by mining, the prudent alternative would be to complete the job of mining Bartlett Mountain.

Any discussion of the Climax Mine inevitably leads to the topic of environmental reclamation. Full reclamation, or more accurately, the reclamation that will be possible, must necessarily await the day when that last ton of Bartlett Mountain ore is mined. No operation can mine and mill a half-billion tons of ore without permanently altering the topography. But future travelers on State Highway 91 may someday journey through the upper Tenmile Valley without realizing that the flat, vegetated, and possibly developed valley floor is actually compacted, stabilized, capped tailings of ore that was mined and milled in another time.

But little will, or can, be done with Bartlett Mountain. Perhaps fittingly, the Glory Hole will remain as a reminder of one of the richest mineral deposits ever discovered and as a symbol of that great mining adventure called Climax.

347

Sources,
Acknowledgments,
and Thanks

This history of the Climax Mine was compiled from numerous records and publications, and with the assistance of many libraries, agencies, and individuals.

The most valuable and comprehensive sources of operational, developmental, and historical information were the files and records of the Climax Mine, including company correspondence, personnel records, maps, geological and engineering reports and drawings, and the many volumes of monthly operating and activity reports that covered most of the life of the mine. The following company periodicals and publications were very helpful: *Moly Mountain News* (1949-1971); *Moly News* (1962-1971); *Hi Grade* (1962-1986); *A Short History of American Metal Climax, Inc.,* by Seymour S. Bernfeld in collaboration with Harold K. Hochschild, 1962; *AMAX Journal* (1972-1979); *This is Climax Molybdenum* brochure series; *Technical Information of the Climax Property,* 1974 and 1979; and *The AMAX Century,* Arthur J. Wilson, 1987.

The following Climax papers, reports, and presentations were excellent informational sources within their specific time periods and subject areas: "Molybdenite Mining At Climax, Colorado," Dennis F. Haley, 1918; "Mining and Milling Practice on Climax Ore at Climax, Colorado," William Coulter, 1930; "The Relationship of Safety to Efficiency in Mining," James K. Richardson, 1938; "Mining at Climax," Robert Henderson, 1945; "Geology of the Climax Orebody," Fred H. Powell and Herman T. Schassberger, 1953; "Colorado Mineral Assets," 1953, and "Moly Looks Promising," 1954, by Arthur H. Bunker; "Public Relations at Climax: A New Staff Function for the Mining Industry," Gordon Weller and Don Stephens, 1954; "Storke Level at the Climax Molybdenum Company," Edwin Eisenach and Edward Matsen, 1954; "Training Engineers at Climax," Edwin Eisenach, 1954; "Training of Engineers for Management," John Petty, 1954; "Safety at Climax," P. M. Wadsworth, 1959; "The Unforeseen Perils of Downsizing," Bob Kilborn, 1987.

The memoirs of C. Carl Cunningham, transcribed by Thelma Workman in 1981, provided a personal view into the early 1930s at Climax. An excellent and foresightful study of the economic relationship between Climax and Lake County was provided by John S. Gilmore, Industrial Economic Division of the Denver Research Institute, University of Denver, in his 1962 report, "Proposed Economic Development Program for the Leadville-Lake County Regional Planning Commission."

Of the many books useful in researching various aspects of the Climax story, the following were especially helpful: *Gray Gold*, by Otis Archie King (Big Mountain Press, Denver, 1959), for the author's role in the battle for Bartlett Mountain; *Molybdenum and Rhenium: 1777-1978*, by Alexander Sutulov (University of Concepción, Concepción, Chile, 1978), for the metallurgical history of molybdenum; *Ore Deposits of the United States: 1933-1967* (AIME, New York, 1968), "Multiple Intrusion and Mineralization at Climax, Colorado," by Stewart R. Wallace, Neil K. Muncaster, David C. Jonson, W. Bruce MacKenzie, Arthur A. Bookstrom, and Vaughn E. Surface, for the definitive account of the geological and mineralogical origins of Bartlett Mountain; *Leadville: Colorado's Magic City*, by Edward Blair (Pruett Publishing Company, Boulder, 1980), for general historical background of Leadville; my own *Leadville: A Miner's Epic* (Mountain Press Publishing Company, Missoula, 1984), for a general mining history of Leadville and Climax; and *Mining the Summit*, by Stanley Dempsey and James E. Fell (University of Oklahoma Press, Norman, 1986), for the history of the

350

Tenmile Mining District and an account of the Climax land transfers and acquisitions of the late 1960s.

Three government publications were helpful with the general background of United States molybdenum deposits and early operations at Climax: *Molybdenum Deposits of Colorado*, by P. G. Worcester (Colorado Geological Survey Bulletin 14, 1919); *Molybdenum Deposits: A Short Review*, by Frank L. Hess (United States Geological Survey Bulletin 761, 1924); and *The Climax Molybdenum Deposit in Colorado*, by B. S. Butler and J. W. Vanderwilt with Charles Henderson (United States Geological Survey Bulletin 846-C, 1933).

Among many periodicals, the following articles were in-depth sources for their particular time periods and subject areas: "Molybdenum Mining at Climax, Colorado," by Harry Brown and M. W. Hayward, *Engineering and Mining Journal*, December 20, 1918; "Recent Developments in Molybdenum," by L. F. S. Holland, *Mining and Scientific Press*, October 19, 1918; "Molybdenum and Molybdenum Steel," by W. E. Simpson, *Mining and Scientific Press*, December 20, 1919; "Climax: Premier Producer of Molybdenum," by William Coulter, *Engineering and Mining Journal*, August 1935; "Element No. 42," *Fortune,* February 1936; "Hole in a Mountain," "More for Moly?" and "Climax Tax Truce," *Business Week*, December 21, 1940, and March 15 and August 23, 1941; "The Climax Molybdenum Enterprise," special Climax issue of *Mining and Metallurgy*, June 1946; "High Life in the Rockies," by Leigh White, *The Saturday Evening Post*, February 18, 1950; "King of Moly," a two-part article based on interviews with Otis Archie King, by Robert "Red" Fenwick, *Empire* magazine (*The Denver Post*), July 26 and August 2, 1953; "Salute to Climax Molybdenum," special edition of *Empire* magazine (*The Denver Post*), by Robert "Red" Fenwick, May 23, 1954; "Climax Molybdenum Expansion," special issue of *Mining Engineering*, August 1955; "AMAX," special issue of *Engineering/Mining Journal*, September 1972; "Wills Sainte Claire: The Gray Goose and Its Founder," by Maurice D. Hendry, *Car Classics*, June 1978; "The Sheikh of Climax Mountain," *Forbes*, February 4, 1980.

The books that provided a look at the Climax Mine from the perspective of railroading included: *Narrow Gauge in the Rockies*, by Lucius Beebe and Charles Clegg (Howell-North Books, Berkeley, 1958); *The Mineral Belt: Old South Park—Across the Great Divide* (Volume II), by David Digerness (Sundance Books, Silverton, Colorado,

1978); and *C&Sing: Colorado & Southern Narrow Gauge*, by Mallory Hope Ferrell (Pruett Publishing Company, Boulder, 1981).

Two transcribed talks presented at the Timberline Campus (Leadville) of Colorado Mountain College were also helpful: "Railroads to Leadville," by Terry Fitzsimmons, 1968; and "The South Park and High Line," by the late Donald "Mac" MacDonald, 1969.

The most valuable Colorado newspaper sources were the Leadville *Carbonate Chronicle* and *Herald Democrat*, which in their specific publication years provided detailed, continuous coverage of events at Bartlett Mountain from 1911 to the present. The *Summit County Journal* (Breckenridge) provided supplementary coverage during the years of World War I and the "County Line War." Background about the seizure of the alien-owned interest of The American Metal Company during that same time period came from the pages of *The New York Times*.

Materials and assistance were also provided by the Colorado Department of Highways, Denver; General Reference Office, National Archives and Records Administration, Washington, D.C.; Office of the Research Administrator and Historian, U.S. Postal Service, Washington, D.C.; U.S. Board of Geographic Names, U.S. Geological Survey, Reston, Virginia; Geological Names Unit, U.S. Geological Survey, Denver; the offices of the county clerks of Lake and Summit counties, Colorado; the Cloud County Historical Society, Concordia, Kansas; and the Cass County Historical Society, Plattsmouth, Nebraska.

The staffs of the following Colorado libraries and research facilities provided assistance: the Arthur Lakes Library, Colorado School of Mines, Golden; the Leslie Savage Library, Western State College, Gunnison; the Research Library of the Historical Society of Colorado, Denver; the Research Library of the U.S. Geological Survey, Denver; and the Western History Collection, Denver Public Library, Denver.

Thanks to Dave Parry, former director of the Lake County Public Library and Mountain History Collection, Leadville, and to current director Nancy McCain. Thanks also to Sharon Moller, director, and Jean Parry, former technical services librarian, of the Learning Resource Center, Timberline Campus, Colorado Mountain College, Leadville.

The following individuals provided valuable help through interviews, suggestions, or research assistance: Warren Alloway, Harry

Ashby, John Balderessi, Fran Bochatey, Roger Bonewell, Mike Bradley, Tom Cherrier, Ken Chlouber, Laura Christensen, Rick Christmas, John Cirullo, Frank Coolbaugh, Dodd Craig, David Le Count Evans, Tina Flores, Joe Forrester, Bill Frank, Nelson Fugate, Virginia Grayson, John Hamm, Chris Harnish, Pat Harvey, Bill Hinken, Scott Johnson, Bernie Joyce, Bob Kendrick, Dan Larkin, Paul Latchaw, Gerald Luoma, the late Donald "Mac" MacDonald, Marjorie MacLachlan, Charles Marshall, the late Charles Martshinske, Jim McCabe, the late Don Moffett, Ted Mullings, Joe Nachtrieb, Diana Orf, Donald Orth, Frank Pace, Barbara Randall, Ken and Donna Reasoner, the late Ken Reynolds, James Richardson, Dick Rodgers, Ralph Schuster, Don Stephens, Darryl and Bruce Stewart, Margie Cunningham Thorpe, Howard Tritz, Eleanor Wadsworth, Frank Windolph, LeRoy Wingenbach, Ted Wiswell, Jim Witmer, Patti Wood, and Frank Zancanella. My apologies to those who provided assistance but whose names have been inadvertently omitted.

Special thanks must go to several individuals whose help was invaluable: Pat Wadsworth, former community relations director of the Climax Mine, who gave me a key to the files, use of a copy machine, free coffee, and a place to work; Bob Kilborn, former general manager of the Climax Mine, who was most generous with his time and knowledge; Jim Ludwig and Ralph Barnett, both former general managers of the Climax Mine, who volunteered to read the manuscript for accuracy; Christopher Janes, vice president and general manager of Cyprus Climax Metals Company, for assisting with publication of the book; Carl Miller, president and executive director of the National Mining Hall of Fame & Museum, Leadville, for generously providing graphics from Climax archival materials; John Clapper, general superintendent of the Climax Mine, for reviewing the final chapter and providing graphics from company files; and Terry Fitzsimmons, former director of public relations of the Climax Mine, without whose personal interest and efforts this book would not have been written.

Finally, I'd like to thank my wife, Lynda La Rocca, for her encouragement and editorial assistance throughout the researching and writing of the Climax story.

Index

Numbers in **boldface type** indicate
pages with illustrations.

356

No. 4 Shaft, 234-35, **235**, **258**
No. 5 Shaft, 248
"Shot No. 1," 122-24
shutdown of 1918, 70
slusher system, 146-47, 164-65
tailings, 142, 146, 279, 285-86, 290-91,
    300, 309, 332
Training Department, 296
Upper Camp, 46, **47**, 54-55, **69**, **76**,
    88, 104, 106-7, **137**, 195
women in underground, 65, 296
Climax Molybdenum Company, 52-53,
    61, 69, 73-75, 77, 81, 83-85, 87-90,
    92, 94, 96, 107, 116, 118, 122, 124,
    128-29, 132, 144, 149-51, 164-69,
    173, 176-77, 179, 185-87, 192-94,
    199, 201, 202, 208, 217, 233-34, 321,
    323-24, 339
    advertisements, 79-81, **79-80**, **82**,
        119, **141**, 194, **194**, 217, **218**,
        236, 260, **260**, **282**, 283
    "Climax fortune," 128-29
    Detroit Research Laboratory, 126, 179
    established, 52
    Henderson Mine, 280, 283, 285, 288-89,
        295, 313, 325-28, 333, 336-37, 339
    Langeloth conversion plant, 95, 179, 340
    merges with American Metal
        Company, 233-34
    shares, 74, 92, 128-29
    sued by American Metal Company
        shareholders, 165
    Urad Mine, 279-80, 293, 295
Climax Post Office, 51, **222**, 254
    highest in U.S., 198-99
Climax Ski Area, 181, 199, 211, **240**
Climax Station, 6-7, 11, 34, 39, 43, 65
Climax stock (geological), 23
Climax Syndicate, 36-37, 39, 40-43, 47,
    49, 52, 165
Clinton Ditch & Reservoir Company, 339
Cohen, Phillip Abraham, 32
Collins, George, 11
Colorado Iron Works, 86
Colorado Midland Railroad, 50
Colorado Mineral Belt, 21, 23
Colorado Molybdenum Company, 12-13
Colorado Mountain College, 277, 317
Colorado School of Mines, 7, 9, 127, 272
Colorado & Southern Railroad (C&S), 11-12,
    17, 34, **44**, 45, 50, 52-53, 56, 58, 64,
    67, 74, 84, 95-96, **98**, 99-100, 105,

113, 120-21, 143-45, **143**, 148-49,
    172, 190-91, 252, **252**
Colorado, State of:
    Civil Defense Agency, 268
    Department of Health, 270, 301
    Division of Mines, 301
    Employment Bureau, 139
    Job Service, 333
    Labor and Industrial Commission,
        193, 301
    Tax Commission, 166-67
Commercial Bank of Leadville, 323
Congress of Industrial Organizations
    (CIO), 149, 189, 251
Continental Ski Club, 181, 199
Coolbaugh, Frank, 208-9, 224, 274-76
Copper Mountain, Colo., 309, 339
C. Ryan & Son, 196, **196**
Coucher, Urban, **251**
Coulter, George, 124-25, 160-61, 189,
    198, 212, 215
Coulter, William "Bill," 93-94, 100, 103-6,
    103, 109-10, 112-14, 116-17, 119,
    122, 124-28, 131-32, 134, 136, 140-41,
    147, 149, 171, 182-85, 188, 208-9
"County Line War," 63, 72-74
Cunningham, C. Carl, 116-18, 134, 234
Cunningham, Gladys, 117
Cyprus-AMAX Minerals Company, 342
Cyprus Climax Metals Company, 342
Cyprus Minerals Company, 340-41
    merges with AMAX, 341

Defense Materials Procurement Agency,
    201-2
Delay, Dan, 275
Dempsey, Stanley, 286-87
Denig, Brig. Gen. Robert H., 179
Denver, Colo., 3, 6, 12, 31, 34, 37, 43,
    47, 66, 74, 86, 140, 144, 148, 176,
    212-13, 221, 224, 267, 271, 296, 319
Denver No. Two claim, 11, 41, 65, 69
Denver Post, The, 216, 319, 323-24, 340
Denver Research Institute, 257-58, 324
Denver & Rio Grande Railroad (D&RG),
    5-6, 37
Denver & Rio Grande Western Railroad
    (D&RGW), 145, 149
Denver, South Park & Pacific Railway
    (DSP&P), 5-7, 11, **46**, 191
    "High Line," 6, 96
Denver Water Board, 286

358

361

molybdite, 25, 271-73
monazite, 195
Monberg, Luther, 243-44
Morrison, Mary, 199, 222
Moses, Raphael, 32
Mosquito Fault, 21, 24, 105, 107-9, 111-13
Mosquito Pass, 3-4
Mosquito Range, 1-2, 21
Mountain Chief claims, 10-11
Mountain Maid claims, 10-11
Mt. Emmons Project, 313
Moyer, Rusty, **251**
Mullings, Ted, 219-20, 242, 284
    cartoons by, **278**, **284**, **314**

National Aeronautics and Space
    Administration (NASA), 269-70
National Bureau of Standards, 264
National Labor Relations Board, 189,
    256, 301
National Municipal League, 242
National Safety Council, 193
National Science Foundation, 270
Navy, U. S., 177, 185-87
    Office of Naval Research, 270
Nelson, Bill, 263, **263**
New Jersey Zinc Company, 266
Newsweek, 324
New Tunnel. *See* Climax Mine
New York Times, The, 48, 107, 168, 324
Norway, 8, 13-14

Occupational Safety and Health
    Administration (OSHA), 301
Office Professional Employees
    International Union (OPEIU), 319
Oil, Chemical and Atomic Workers
    Union (OCAW) Local 2-24410,
    250, 316-17, 319
Olson, Olaf, 153
"One Hundred Million Dollar Special,"
    50-51, 66
open pit mining. *See* Climax Mine
Organization of Petroleum Exporting
    Countries (OPEC), 294, 313
Oro City, 28

Palmer, A. Mitchell, 47-49, 61
Palo, Walt, 122, 136
Park County, 58, 72-73, 96, 148, 267
Parker, Edward, 109
Parker, Stonewall Jackson, **178**

Park Range, 20-21
Pecos Mine (American Metal Company),
    85, 94
Penrose, Spencer, 50
Petty, John, 151, 225-26
Phillipson, Brainerd F., 75, **76**, 77,
    79-81, 84-85, 87-90, 92-94, 98-99,
    102-3, 106-7, 119, 122, 124, 129,
    135, 221, 304
Phillipson Tunnel. *See* Climax Mine
Pierce, Cy, 167
Pierce, George, 225
Pikes Peak gold rush, 5, 28
Pingrey Mines & Ore Reduction
    Company, 14, 41, 45, 50-51, 60, 64,
    74, 89
Pingrey, Wilson H., 14
Pitkin County, 277
Pooler, Chuck, 151
Port, Ralph, 169
Powell, Bill, 263
Pressman, Lee, 197
Primos Chemical Company, 13-14, 279
Proctor, Jim, 151
Public Service Company of Colorado,
    45, 104, 184, 216
pyrite, 1-2, 23, 195, 202

Real People (ABC-TV), 316
Recen, Colo., 5, 287, 290
recession, economic, of 1980, 311, 315
Red Mountain, 13-14, 279-80, 293
Renault "baby tanks," 38, 77, 80
Renick, Ira, 40, **40**
Resurrection Mining Company, 237
Reynolds, Ken, 221
Richardson, James K., 157
Roberts, Walter O., 186-87
Robinson, Colo., 5, 142, 205, 285
Robinson, G. B., 99
Rocky Mountain National Park, 198
Rocky Mountain News, 319
Romig, W. E. "Tex," 121-22, 132-33, 136,
    139-40, 143-45, 148, 151, 157, 208
Roosevelt, President Franklin D.,
    163-64, 170
Rossi, Mickey, 144-45
Russia, 14, 69
Ryan, Lee, 195

Salazar, Charlene, 297
Sanders, George, **251**

362

San Juan Mountains, 21, 198
Sargent, Dr. George W., 39, 88, 90
Saturday Evening Post, The, 79, 204-6
Sawatch Range, 20
Scheele, Carl Wilhelm, 8
Schemerling, August, 109
Schott, Alice, 222-23
Schott, Max, 31, 34-39, **35**, **36**, 56, 63,
    68, 71, 74-75, 93, 119, 124, 127-29,
    132, 140, 146, 149-52, 159, 163-67,
    169-70, 176, **178**, 179, **180**, 185-86,
    188, 192-93, 222-23
Schuster, Ralph, 307
Scientific American, 79
Seaman, John, 166
Senter, Charles J., 1-5, **2**, 7, 11, 13-15,
    18, 28, 41-42, 46, 49-50, 59, 74
Shafer, Don, 154
Sharp, George, 122
Sherman Silver Purchase Act, 7
Shriver, Warren, 261, 280
Sims, Porter, 302
Slifka, John, 134
Sloan, Art "Doc," 131-32
Smith, Lloyd, 241
Smythe, Chuck, 308
Southern Rocky Mountain Ski
    Association, 181
South Park, 5, 63
South Park Railroad, 149
Soviet Union, 163-64, 193, 201
Spencer, Bill, 151
Standard Oil of California, 295, 320
Starr, Thomas J., 167
State Highway 91, 96, 98, 142, 144-45,
    169, 179, 181, 204, 221-22, 246-47,
    264, 267-68, 285, 289-90, 300, 339
States, Kenneth G., 154
Stephen, George, 329
Stephens, Don, 207, 221, 236-37, 242,
    257, 277
Storke, Arthur, **78**, 90-93, 192-93, 196, 199
Storke Level. *See* Climax Mine
Stott, Charles, 324
Stout, Les, **251**
Studebaker Corporation, 83
Summit County, 2, 7, 13, 49, 53, 56,
    58-60, 62-63, 72-74, 96, 148, 166-67,
    169, 208, 267-68, 277, 287, 339
Summit County Journal, 49-50, 53, 56,
    70-71, 218

Summit County Liberty War Bond
    Committee, 64-65, 296
Summitville, Colo., 198
Sussman, Dr. Otto, 36, 89, 107, 118-19,
    129, 188
Swansen, B. A., 167

Tenmile camps, 5-7, 67, 151, 181, 245
Tenmile Canyon, 5-6, 25, 28, 142,
    285-86, 291
Tenmile Creek, 6, 24-26, 28, 42, 243,
    245, 286, 291, 300
Tenmile Mining District, 13-14, **16**, 186-87
Tenmile Range, 21
Tenmile Valley, 5-6, 45, 51
Theobald, Robert, 242-43
Thomas, Weston G., 234-35, 244
Thompson, Ralph C., 174, 176, 187-88
Thompson, Wayne, 230
Thornton, Governor Dan, 222
Thorpe, James, 119
Thuis, Dennis, **251**
Thurman, Bonnie, 316
Timken Roller Bearing Corporation, 83, 88
tin, 23, 195, 202
Trading with the Enemy Act, 47
Trains, 191
Trevethon, Jack, 280
tungsten, 23, 195, 202, 298

United Alloy Steel Corporation, 83, 88
University Corporation for Atmospheric
    Research (UCAR), 269
Urad Mine. *See* Climax Molybdenum
    Company
U.S. Steel Corporation, 119
Utah Copper Company (Bingham
    Canyon Mine), 10, 50, 193
Utes, 26, 28

Vail, Colo., 309
Vanderbilt, Gloria (Countess Szechenyi),
    48
Verant, Michael, 178
Ver Steeg, Bob, 212-15
Veterans Administration, 240
Vincent, Art, 280
Voice of America, 204

Wadsworth, Eleanor, 197-98, 228-29, 250
Wadsworth, Morgan, 197
Wallace, Henry, 197

363

About the Author

Stephen M. Voynick, a former Climax miner, lives in Leadville, Colorado, and writes regularly for several national magazines. *Climax* is his eighth book and fifth for Mountain Press. His previous works include *The Making of a Hardrock Miner* (Howell-North), *Leadville: A Miner's Epic, Yogo: The Great American Sapphire, Colorado Gold,* and *Colorado Rockhounding.*